Postcolonial Paris

AFRICA AND THE DIASPORA
History, Politics, Culture

SERIES EDITORS

Thomas Spear
Neil Kodesh
Tejumola Olaniyan
Michael G. Schatzberg
James H. Sweet

Postcolonial Paris

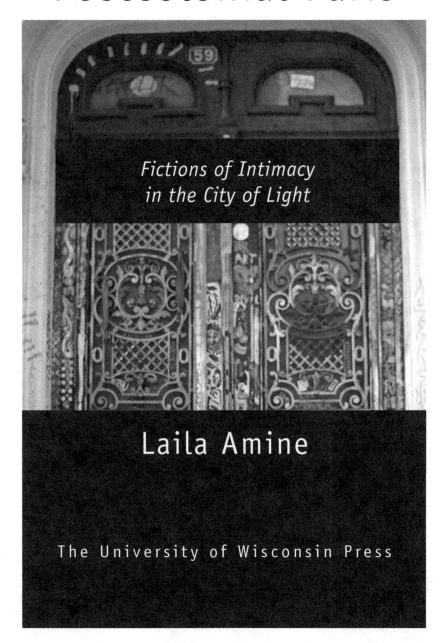

*Fictions of Intimacy
in the City of Light*

Laila Amine

The University of Wisconsin Press

The University of Wisconsin Press
1930 Monroe Street, 3rd Floor
Madison, Wisconsin 53711-2059
uwpress.wisc.edu

3 Henrietta Street, Covent Garden
London WC2E 8LU, United Kingdom
eurospanbookstore.com

Printed in the United States of America

This book may be available in a digital edition.

Library of Congress Cataloging-in-Publication Data

Names: Amine, Laila, author.
Title: Postcolonial Paris: fictions of intimacy in the City of Light /
Laila Amine.
Other titles: Africa and the diaspora.
Description: Madison, Wisconsin: The University of Wisconsin Press, [2018] |
Series: Africa and the diaspora: history, politics, culture | Includes
bibliographical references and index.
Identifiers: LCCN 2017044982 | ISBN 9780299315801 (cloth)
Subjects: LCSH: Paris (France)—In literature. | French literature—France— Paris—
North African authors—History and criticism. | African American authors—
France—Paris. | Postcolonialism in literature.
Classification: LCC PQ150.N67 A46 2018 | DDC 840.9/35844361—dc23
LC record available at https://lccn.loc.gov/2017044982

A ma mère **Najia**,
mon père **Hammad**,
et mon frère **Karim**
A **Michael**

There is no work. No lodging. No help. No fraternity. There are only . . . identity checks and unemployment cards and promises.

Driss Chraïbi, *The Butts*

In Paris, *les misérables* are Algerian. They slept four or five or six to a room, and they slept in shifts, they were treated like dirt, and they scraped such sustenance as they could off the filthy, unyielding Paris stones . . . though they spoke French, and had been, in a sense, produced by France, they were not at home in Paris.

James Baldwin, *No Name in the Street*

Flower city—That's what they call it! Acres of concrete. The smell of piss. Cars, cars and more cars. And dog turds. Row after row of tall, soulless apartment blocks. No joy, no laughter, just heartache and pain. A huge estate, sandwiched between motorways, ringed by factories and by police. The estate's got a tiny playground for the kids, but it's been boarded up. Flower city!

Mehdi Charef, *Tea in the Harem*

Young people ask themselves: Why? Why can't we have access to that? And there's no answer. Raw, brute racism is clear, it's easy to identify. But there's something more subtle and dangerous, a neo-colonialist feeling that still infuses society. . . . It's not about racism, it's about treating people differently.

Faïza Guène, interviewed by *The Guardian*, June 5, 2008

Contents

Illustrations

Acknowledgments

This book would not have been possible without the support of many individuals and institutions. At Indiana University, Matt Guterl has provided encouragement and direction from the very beginning. His scholarship, enthusiasm, and infinite generosity have nurtured my work. I am also indebted to Vivian Halloran for invaluable guidance and continued mentorship. For her big-heartedness and cheerful curiosity, I am grateful. Deb Cohn and Purnima Bose read numerous chapter drafts and provided discerning comments. I am profoundly thankful for their mentorship and support. Trica Keaton has kindly offered support, resources, and time to talk about the key ideas in this book. Her own scholarship on Paris has been foundational for my own approach. Merci infiniment, Trica. Ann Delgado, Karen Dillon, and Tanisha Ford gave me feedback on several chapters and sustaining fellowship. Caroline Fache, who also works on immigration in African Diaspora fiction and cinema, is a wonderful fellow traveler on conference circuits, coeditor, and friend. Our discussions about race in France have led to many insights in this book and beyond. I am also thankful for the suggestions, advice, and encouragement of Akin Adesokam, Valerie Grim, Eileen Julien, Michael Martin, Frederick McElroy, Oana Panaité, Iris Rosa, and Micol Seigel. Much of the joy of my Indiana University years came from sharing my life with friends. Thank you to Danielle Chatman, Jen Heusel, Kellie Hogue, and Byron Thomas for the best years. Long live Memorial Hall! I am grateful too for the friendship of Meg Arenberg, Mario Bahena, Siobhan Carter-David, Paula Cotner, Byron Craig, Paloma Fernández, Lizi Gebballe, Yasmiyn Irizarry, Burcu Karahan, Sandi Latcha, Julianne Mora, Ioana Patuleau, Melissa Quintella, Holly Schreiber, April Smith, Denise and Steve Stuempfle, Byron Thomas, and April Witt. You make me nostalgic for Bloomington.

In 2011–12 I received a postdoctoral fellowship at the University of Illinois at Urbana-Champaign, where I became part of a lively community of postdoctoral fellows. I am thankful to Jessica Bardill, Alex Chávez, Laura Fugikawa, Charama Kwakye, Karen Roybal, Anantha Sudhakar, and Erica Vogel for our workshop sessions, coffee shop writing, and dinners. I could not have imagined a more fun year of writing and camaraderie. Thank you as well to Badia Ahad Legardy, Chris Freeburg, and Adlai Murdoch for our conversations. I owe great thanks to Maxwell Leung and Jeanette Roan for keeping me on track with our virtual accountability group and Jeanette specifically for her incredibly helpful feedback on several parts of my work.

My appreciation goes out to colleagues at the University of North Texas who made suggestions, provided feedback, and read portions of the book. I thank Baird Callicott, Gabriel Cervantes, Nora Gilbert, Walton Muyumba, Dahlia Porter, and Kelly Wisecup for their helpful comments. I am also grateful to Jacqueline Foertsch, Stephanie Hawkins, Irene Klaver, Masood Raja, Javier Rodriguez, Alex Petit, Nicole Smith, Jae-Jae Spoon, Robert Upchurch, Jennifer Jensen Wallach, and Michael Wise for our productive discussions. My undergraduate and graduate students' curiosity for unfamiliar narratives and settings makes it a pleasure to teach comparative literature. I am grateful for their energizing engagement. At the University of North Texas, I found a family away from home in La Colectiva. Thank you, Bertina Combes, Amy Kraehe, Annette Lawrence, Val Martinez, Sandra Mendiola, Mariela Nuñez-Janes, Alicia Re Cruz, Andrea Silva, and Priscilla Ybarra for your mentorship and affection. I am grateful to Prathiba Natesan for our mood-boosting get-together sessions and dinners. You all made Denton the finest place to live.

I have had the opportunity to share several parts of this book with supportive scholars. At a summer workshop, "Avanzamos: El Taller Chicano/a," organized by Priscilla Ybarra and José Aranda at Rice University, my writing was stimulated by joining a community familiar with race and ethnicity scholarship but not with the specifics of the French context. I have fond memories of our exchanges and dinners, especially the one we collectively prepared at José's home. Many thanks to José F. Aranda, Lorena Gauthereau, Brittany Henry, Samuel Coronado, Elena Valdez, Noreen Rivera, Scott Pett, Amanda Branker Ellis, Yolanda Flores Niemann, Melina Vizcíno-Alemán, Lourdes Alberto, John Escobedo, and Priscilla Ybarra. I also thank my generous readers, Sylvie Durmelat, Kim Greenwell, Jarrod Hayes, and Adlai Murdoch for their detailed comments on parts of the manuscript. My friend Stacie McCormick provided priceless and timely feedback during our self-made book completion boot camp. I look forward to continuing working together.

Several institutions funded my research and writing at various stages, including an Indiana University College of Arts and Sciences writing fellowship and the Chancellor's Postdoctoral Research Fellowship at University of Illinois at Urbana-Champaign. At the University of North Texas, I benefited from a Junior Faculty Summer Research Fellowship, two Scholarly and Creative Activity

Awards, and smaller grants to support my archival research. I am grateful to the friendly librarians at the Musée national de l'histoire de l'immigration, the Bibliothèque nationale de France, and the Schomburg Center for Research in Black Culture. Thanks to Craig Allen for lending me his copy of Wright's "Island of Hallucination" and to Bergis Jules for putting us in touch.

An earlier version of chapter 2 appeared as "The Paris Paradox: Color-blindness and Colonialism in African American Expatriate Fiction," *American Literature* 87, no. 4 (2015): 739–68 (copyright 2015 by Duke University Press; all rights reserved, republished by permission of the rights holder; www.dukepress .edu). Parts of chapter 5 were revised from "Double Exposure: The Family Album and Alternate Memories in Leïla Sebbar's *The Seine Was Red*," *Culture, Theory, and Critique* 53, no. 2 (2012): 181–98.

The University of Wisconsin Press has been a pleasure to work with. Since our first contact, Dennis Lloyd has been an amazing editor, and I thank him for his commitment to this book project, along with the series editors for Africa and the Diaspora: History, Politics, Culture. Amber Rose, Sheila McMahon, and Jennifer Conn have been responsive and efficient throughout. I am especially indebted to my readers for their invaluable critiques on the manuscript and for investing their time to make this book better.

I am forever grateful for the friendship of Priscilla Ybarra and Sandra Mendiola. Priscilla has been a wonderful friend from the moment I set foot in Denton. Our many conversations, her insightful feedback, and her contagious enthusiasm have been vital beyond the writing of this book. Sandra has been my sister traveler in this journey, too. Big thanks for your caring support and for reminding me what really matters: Z! Thank you both for making life in Denton happier.

My spouse, Michael, to whom I dedicate this book, has been generous with his time, reading the manuscript in its multiple stages, and unwavering in his cheerleading role. His patience, affection, and great sense of humor continue to sustain me. My family in France, Morocco, and Trinidad followed every twist of my journey, kindly accommodating my schedule and lifting me up with their love. My life is more grounded and joyful because of them.

Postcolonial Paris

Introduction: The Paris Kaleidoscope

Too often, French Muslims and the city fringes they inhabit only enter broad public discussions in moments of spectacular crisis, such as the 2015 terrorist attacks or the 2005 riots. What we know about these presumed outsiders is overdetermined by the mainstream media's singular focus on violent Islamic cultures embodied by belligerent men who commit crimes, repress women and sexual minorities, and promote radical Islam. Bridging the post–World War II era and the war on terror, *Postcolonial Paris* brings together Maghrebi, Franco-Arab, and African American authors who explore everyday life in the Paris periphery and recast it not as a site of primitive cultures but as a site of primitive living conditions. This vantage point reveals the limited reach of *liberté, égalité, fraternité* and expands the narrow scripts of what and who is Paris. Set in specific contexts, these authors respond to the demonization of Arab and Muslim men by rewriting colonial tropes of intimacy (the interracial couple, the harem, the Arab queer) to uncover the long-standing deployment of gender and sexuality in constructing and contesting racial boundaries between Paris and its outskirts, France and Algeria, the West and the rest.

By exploring the ordinary lives of colonial migrants and their French off-spring, this book demonstrates that the postcolonial other is both peripheral to yet intimately entangled with tropes so famously evoked by the City of Light: romance, love, modernity, freedom, and equality. The common association of the capital city with universalist and egalitarian ideas has worked in tandem with the obliteration or vilification of a postcolonial Paris. Its retrieval not only documents the intimate intrusion of race into everyday life in a nation where it does not officially exist; it also imparts long-standing reflections on the meaning of being nonwhite and Muslim in today's Europe.

For a broader global public, the existence of an impoverished multiracial fringe living in the shadows of the City of Light was something largely unknown until the 2015 terrorist attacks. Yet France is home to the largest African and Muslim populations in Western Europe. Islam is the second largest religion in France with more than five million residents of Muslim descent. This population descends primarily from former colonies and has overwhelmingly resided in the urban periphery of the nation's large cities: first in the post–World War II slums and, a generation later, in the depressed multiracial housing projects known as banlieues. While France has all kinds of banlieues, including some affluent ones, in the mainstream media this word describing suburban administrative areas has become pejoratively associated with government-subsidized housing zones with large concentrations of Muslims. These sites are also referred to as *cités*, or in urban policies as "priority zones to urbanize" and "sensitive urban zones."[1] In 2005 this periphery made world news when a riot in Clichy-sous-bois spread like wildfire to more than 300 cities. The riot was sparked by the accidental death of two French youth of color attempting to avoid a police identification check. More recently, on January 7, 2015, two French jihadist brothers of Algerian descent entered the offices of the magazine *Charlie Hebdo* and killed twelve people. In November 2015 Paris was again the site of bloodshed when ISIS terrorists coordinated suicide bombings and attacks, killing 130 people and injuring 368 others.[2] After the *Charlie Hebdo* attack, French Prime Minister Manuel Valls admitted for the first time that "there is in France, a territorial, social, and ethnic apartheid."[3] A few days after the November attacks, French police carried out hundreds of raids in the Parisian banlieues. Suddenly the city's impoverished fringe was thrust into a spotlight of intensified surveillance, hostility, and blame. The exceptional and temporary police measures that constituted the state of emergency were signed into common law on October 30, 2017.

It is precisely in this moment that we need to interrogate past and present understandings of Paris and its seeming outsiders within. Far from intruding into French space only recently or unexpectedly, colonial migrants and their descendants have long been part of the Parisian landscape, and an extensive literary and visual archive attests to their presence. By "postcolonial Paris," I refer to a spatialized imaginary associated with the pauperized outskirts of the French capital where the majority of colonial migrant workers lived since the 1950s and where their children still reside. This urban margin includes the slums of Nanterre, the depressed banlieues, and smaller sections technically within central Paris but generally considered the margins of the city, such as La Goutte d'or and Belleville. Whereas other postcolonial studies cordon off post-coloniality to a specific era and set of authors, filmmakers, and artists, this book relates it to a racialized "imaginative geography" that bridges temporal boundaries and cultural traditions.[4] "Postcolonial" here refers to narratives that probe colonial relations and their legacies in specific metropolitan sites, rather than simply narratives that come after colonialism. These stories intimate an extension of the colony, not in its complex historical facets but in its general exclusion of nonwhites, its grammar of civilization and progress, and its echoes of imperialist paternalistic postures. They include novels, such as *Les boucs* (*The Butts*) by Moroccan author Driss Chraïbi, *The Stone Face* by African American expatriate William Gardner Smith, best-seller *Thé au harem d'archi Ahmed* (*Tea in the Harem*) by Mehdi Charef, and *La Seine était rouge* (*The Seine Was Red*) by Leïla Sebbar; short stories such as James Baldwin's "This Morning, This Evening, So Soon"; films like Ahmed and Zakia Bouchaala's *Origine contrôlée* (*Made in France*); and graffiti art by JR and Princess Hijab.

The banlieue is reframed as a harem, and pockets of the city become exotic sites of sexual tourism or places where youth of Algerian descent commemorate colonial bloodshed. This Paris counterdiscourse to the routine stigmatization of Arabs and Muslims emerges not only in the works of authors from French colonies such as Chraïbi, and their descendants raised or living in Paris like Charef or Bouchaala, but also where it is least expected, in the fiction of select African American authors often thought of as mouthpieces of a color-blind Paris, like James Baldwin.

Generally, these stories that layer the Paris margins across decades do not meet because they belong to different cultural traditions. Maghrebi studies tend to focus on the Maghreb, where race has not been a most salient concern in the scholarship. Literary critics' lack of interest in Maghrebis' Parisian experiences led Crystel Pinçonnat to raise the question: "Maghrebi Paris: An Invisible Literary Capital?" In a 2005 article, she notes that by writing in Paris settings, Maghrebi writers and novelists of immigrant origin "inevitably construct a specific image of the place from which they write: the capital."[5] Examining the French banlieues, Susan Ireland also remarks that "the Maghrebi immigrant novel writes an important chapter of such a history of the spatiality of power as it relates to the urban immigrant population."[6] Similarly contained, *beur* studies routinely start in 1983 with the historic March for Equality and Against Racism or later, as if nothing came before. As influential Francophone Tunisian novelist and essayist Albert Memmi reminds us, the Maghrebi is "not a Russian or Romanian immigrant, a foreigner who has arrived here by accident; he is the

'bastard' of the colonial adventure, a living reproach or permanent disappoint-
ment."[7] Though beur novels and films document racism in overwhelmingly
Parisian settings, critics have not examined how these "new social spaces" alter
our imaginary of the French capital.[8] Least likely in this archive about the Paris
margins is African American expatriate fiction, often understood as love songs
to a racially liberal city. Scholars have pointed out the silence of famous writers
like Richard Wright about French colonization and depicted the relations
between France and such celebrities as "convenient francophilia," a "mutually
beneficial relationship," or a seeming complicity "with the [French] nation-state
at its most racist moment."[9] However, black US expatriate fiction set in the 1960s
casts North African characters who reveal a segregated colonial Paris beyond
the Left Bank cafés. Together, these stories reinscribe colonial legacies in the
metropole, indicating that French colonial history was not contained within far-
away territories, nor did it neatly finish in 1962 with the end of the Algerian war.

By desegregating the study of Paris to reveal the racialized periphery, *Postcolonial Paris* generates a new cultural cartography that challenges several myths
associated with the capital, including the myth of color-blind equality, the myth
of the banlieues as the "badlands of the Republic,"[10] and the myth of the city as
a site of free speech. The myth of a universalist and particularly racially egalitarian Paris, which traverses the African American popular imaginary, portrays
the capital as a space of liberation for populations of African descent. According
to a few scholars, African exilic writing in Paris in the 1980s and 1990s similarly
highlights universalism and individualism.[11] By telling the story of the Parisian
fringe rather than the cosmopolitan center, this book retrieves an alternative
archive. The ex-centered narratives register collective experiences of racial
minorities relegated to the poor sectors of the city and its outskirts, treated as
suspicious "foreigners" no matter the nationality on their identity cards. Where
the myth of race-blindness hides conflict and boundaries, postcolonial Paris
dissects their nature to reveal the invisible bars of the cage confining colonial
migrants and their offspring. It often does so by rewriting the very tropes that
conveyed equality, such as the interracial romance.

The myth of the banlieues, particularly the vast Paris outskirts, deems these
spaces the cultural foil of the republic, namely, lawless zones where misogyny,
homophobia, and Islamism flourish. This myth pervades any representation of
the Parisian outer cities, from films to television talk shows to political speeches.
Stories of postcolonial Paris challenge the sensationalist construction of a primitive other by rewriting primitivism as the existence of a third world within the
first. For example, Charef presents the poverty-stricken Parisian banlieues as a
new harem, in which exoticism is based on difference of class rather than culture. We discover these postwar slums consisting of thousands of shacks with

dirt floors, no running water or electricity, and later their replacement: miles of high-rise concrete buildings that cram hundreds of thousands of working-class families in tiny apartments with no sound proofing. With the decline of manufacturing, which represented the bread and butter of banlieue inhabitants, unemployment soared. Like Charef, many authors of postcolonial Paris consider the resulting poverty and segregation the real obstacles to integration, not cultural difference or Islam. They frame race mainly in relation to structural exclusion, discrimination, and surveillance, rather than desires for cultural or religious recognition. That said, when Maghrebi traditions and Islam surface, they are rarely the threatening matter broadcast in the mainstream media.

The myth of the city as a site of free speech for vulnerable people has been popularized by a diverse array of authors, including African American writers abroad, Iranian women authors in exile, and a few banlieue women and queer subjects. This myth promotes Paris as a site of refuge for minority authors forced into second-class citizenship in their places of origin. In contrast, fiction of the other Paris shows a city rife with various forms of censorship. Chraïbi's Algerian protagonist writes a novel about the terrible plight of his fellowmen in the slums, only to see it rejected by a Parisian editor who condemns his failure to adhere to universalist principles. In the same period, Richard Wright and other black US expatriate novelists explained that although they supported Algerian decolonization, they could not say a word about it because they knew they would be immediately deported to the United States. In the contemporary period, mainstream films that cast nonwhite queer subjects give them two choices: either they are the assimilated subjects who outgrow their family and ethnic milieu or they die by the end of the narrative.[12] As Carrie Tarr claims, there seems to be little room in French cinema for cultural difference that would be valued.[13] The Parisian landscape of memory also silences pluralism through exclusion in Sebbar's *The Seine Was Red*, a novel dedicated to authors, many of whom saw their work confiscated during the Algerian war. In this novel as well as on the city's wall, graffiti appears as a tool to bypass the censors and point to absences: that of veiled Muslim girls in the public sphere, of banlieue youth in fashionable Paris neighborhoods, and memories of the Algerian war. These criminal superimpositions subvert cultural conformity by projecting a more expansive capital.

Spanning 1947, when a new statute allowed for Algerian natives to come to the metropole without a passport, to the 2015 terrorist attacks, this book stages multiple encounters with the other Paris. These face-to-face encounters show the extent to which the city's many landscapes function as a space where racialization belies modernity's narrative of progress in postwar France and today's Europe.

The Other Paris, Then and Now

In 1953, one year before the Algerian war started, the French National Institute for Demographic Studies published the results of a major 1947 survey that measured attitudes toward various national groups, including Algerians. The goal of this study, *The French and the Immigrants* (*Les Français et les immigrés*), was to examine foreigners' adaptation to the French way of life and identify elements that could improve this process.[14] Although Algeria has been part of France since the 1830s, making its natives not immigrants but national subjects, the latter were not permitted to come to the metropole without a passport and a work permit until 1947. That year, a new statute facilitated Algerian migration, resulting in a notable Muslim labor force entering France, the majority of which settled in Paris and its working-class periphery.[15] This population represents the earliest, largest, and most culturally visible nonwhite settlement in Western Europe. Though Muslim natives were mainly Algerian, they were also referred to by more encompassing labels, such as Arab, Maghrebi, French Muslims, and North Africans. The survey noted that the French treated Algerians as culturally different from them based on their physical appearance: their black eyes, black kinky hair (*crêpu*), thick lips, and flat noses.[16] Among the obstacles preventing the integration of these marked subjects in the metropole, the survey underscored the key role of the press in creating a damning image of North African men as excessively virile. Journalists characterized French cities as "small casbahs," where crime and violence were rife, and North Africans as "violent revolutionaries," "bad boys," or "worthless persons, who against all rules of decency and common sense, abandon . . . their wives to come live in France."[17] In the same study, testimonies from Algerian participants addressed the fact that they could only get "the dirtiest and hardest jobs."[18] The bulk of their complaints, however, focused on the media's constant denigration of Arabs and its direct impact on their lives. One respondent stated that "because of the press headlines of Algerians, they think we are all lazy, lying, stealing."[19] The French "ask us if it's true that we live the way the newspaper describes it, if we have several wives, and other myths born out of the journalist's imagination," said another respondent.[20] "They loved us after the war [World War II]," claimed yet another participant, "but now with the campaign orchestrated by the state-controlled media, they see in each Algerian, a vagabond, a thief, a murderer, and they blame us for all sins."[21]

Though Muslim workers from Algeria represented a small proportion of the "foreign" labor force (3.5 percent) from 1912 to 1954, the "Arab problem" aroused the attention of government officials, scholars, journalists, and others.[22] Press clippings or *faits divers* in high-circulation daily newspapers like *Le Monde* and *Le Figaro*, and weekly news magazines like *Paris Match* and *L'Express* would identify criminal perpetrators specifically of Maghrebi, Arab, or North African origin; locate their places of residence; and at times include mugshots of brown faces with black curly hair.

These feared Arabs might have been Kabyle or might have identified themselves through other tribal and local identities, but in their displacement and exile, they became at best "Arabs," at worse *bicots, sidis, norafs,* and *crouillat,* among other demeaning racial epithets.[23] One headline in the Parisian daily *L'Aurore* in November 1948 warned, "In some quarters of Paris, the Arab is King of the night." From 1900 to 1962—that is, before the Algerian war of decolonization—the Parisian press repeatedly stereotyped the Arab as a criminal, a rapist, and a child molester.[24] Capturing the continued sexualization of Arab men in the mainstream media of the 1970s, historian Todd Shepard coins the phrase "l'Arabe-au-sexe-couteau" (the Arab-with-the-sex-knife).[25]

Arab men's alleged deviance was informed by Orientalist clichés about homosexuality, possessiveness, and jealousy vis-à-vis their wives or lovers and an insatiable sexuality. We find echoes of this sexual "perversion" in canonical French novels such as the award-winning 1932 novel *Journey to the End of the Night* by Louis-Ferdinand Céline, in which a café owner is reviled by the bicots, whom he believes are all homosexuals. The waitress of the café disputes this statement, claiming however that "they're pervert . . . Boy, are they perverts!"[26] Over time, these stereotypes about Arab criminality and sexual perversion wove a map of Paris, drawing attention to the supposedly disreputable places where disreputable people live. This media and cultural output may partly explain the opinion poll conducted in the 1947 study, in which Algerians ranked as the most disliked nationalities, joining the Germans they had just fought as part of the French army. *The French and the Immigrants* ultimately provided a rare window onto France's colonial attitudes and how Algerians interpreted their hostile environment. It was unprecedented because although the survey was meant to measure foreigners' adaptation to French way of life, the inclusion of Algerians revealed negative meanings imposed on colonial subjects and the places they inhabit. The survey disrupted portrayals of Franco-Algerian relationship as a harmonious marriage and other fictions of intimacy.[27]

When the French descendants of Maghrebi immigrants came of age in the early 1980s, media discourse portrayed Arabs and Muslims in relation to national security through a series of endangered icons. In 1985 *Le Figaro* printed on its cover a picture of the Marianne bust, symbol of the French republic, in a niqab with the headline "Will we still be French in thirty years?" Another cover in the same journal later featured two Mariannes, one in her revolutionary bonnet, the other veiled in a niqab with the following headline: "Immigration or Invasion?" Joining this Islamization trope are other popular images, such as the Eiffel Tower transformed into a mosque with an aggressive muezzin at its summit, images of collective prayers invading the streets of Paris, and of course privileged signs of so-called radicalism: the long beard and the veil. Scholars have pointed to the media's central role in constructing the Muslim man and woman as the "green peril," the greatest threat to the French republic.[28] Whether these Muslims are French, foreigners, or undocumented migrants, they are presented as dangerous outsiders to France and Western modernity.[29] At the end of the 1990s, half of French people confessed being afraid of Islam.[30] After the *Charlie Hebdo* attacks, a poll taken by *Le Monde* showed that a majority of respondents agreed that Islam is incompatible with French values.[31]

The fact remains, for 1947 as much as for today: racial hierarchy is a distinct reality in France, even though the nation boldly claims immunity from processes of racialization. As a result of the Gallic refusal to acknowledge race, conventional measures to account for it—the census, legal codification—do not exist.[32] The nation's republican ideology posits that all citizens are equal and should be treated as individuals, not as members of a community. To embrace one's particularity in the public sphere (ethnic, sexual, cultural, or religious) is to threaten the nation's indivisibility. Doing so represents a form of *communautarisme*. In the meantime, and under the umbrella of universalism, the public sphere remains the quasi monopoly of the ideal citizen: white, Christian, male, and heterosexual. Unlike and of course against this imposed color-blind officialdom or "racism without races," literary and visual texts by artists of African descent serve as a significant site for examining processes of racialization.[33]

With the settlement of Maghrebi immigrants in the metropole after World War II, new terms designated their children. I employ the terms "Franco-Arab," "beur," "French Muslims," or "French of Maghrebi origin" to refer to this population, depending on the context. For the fiction and films produced in the early 1980s, I use the term "beur" because cultural producers referred to themselves and their protagonists as such. "Beur," reverse slang of the French word "Arabe," appeared as a self-identification taken on by young Parisians who were born or raised in the banlieue.[34] The label enabled this generation to establish differences from their immigrant parents whose appearance they share, and from a society that excluded those like them with Muslim names and Mediterranean physiques. While "beur" created an unofficial racial category that disputed the French tenet of racelessness, this neologism also obfuscated the previous referent "Arab," which carried negative value. Often biographic in nature, early beur fiction focused on pessimistic coming-of-age stories set in the disadvantaged outskirts. Media and politicians had previously employed confusing or problematic labels, such as "second generation," a label tellingly used mainly in reference to Arabs, denying them Frenchness.[35] The media shift to the term "beur," however, led the population it describes to distance themselves from it. In the 1990s and 2000s, novels and films by authors of Maghrebi descent previously labeled beur came to be described under the rubric of banlieue culture.[36] This branding of authors and filmmakers constitutes a form of ghettoization for many of them, whereby they are considered "native informants" about allegedly lawless zones, rather than novelists.[37]

From the mid-1990s forward, the word "Muslim" became the key referent for the same populations previously described as "colonial migrants," "Maghrebi immigrants," and "beur." With the emergence of Muslim associations that coincided with the expulsion of veiled girls from public schools, the focus turned to Muslims. Scholars do not fail to comment on "*musulman*" as a term associated with a slew of others in public discourse: crime, sexual and gender violence, prison, religious fundamentalism, and undocumented migrants.[38] "Muslim" refers to racialized individuals with origins in North and West Africa who may or may not practice Islam. Rather, they are presumed Muslims based on their appearance. Other terminology in use includes *minorités visibles* (visible minorities) and Franco-Arab to distinguish from the *Français de souche* (white French).

With the state's unwillingness to track racial statistics, an increasing number of social scientists writing about postcolonial France have shown the salience of racial inequities, especially in the aftermath of the 2005 riots.[39] North and West African individuals and their descendants face daily discrimination in education, employment, housing, policing, and the criminal justice system. Investigating cases of police brutality, Amnesty International reported "a pattern of de facto impunity" with regard to law enforcement in France. Those with Muslim names are four times more likely to be unemployed, and more than a third of banlieue residents live under the poverty line. Narratives of postcolonial Paris register these plain realities as well as less tractable racial slights that include poor seating and treatment in restaurants and bars, surveillance in stores, or flat-out refusal of service and entrance.

The works under study do not simply lay race like a singular template over the city but map its intricate and intimate intrusions into everyday life. Bridging the mid-twentieth century through today's increasing Islamophobia across Europe, this study reveals the key roles of gender and sexuality in erecting and knocking down racial boundaries between Paris and its outskirts, France and Algeria, and Europe and Africa. From the universalizing metaphors of marriage that described Franco-Algerian relations during colonialism to the particularizing figure of the Arab sexual predator in the Parisian popular press in the 1950s, the trope of the cuckolded Algerian male lover in Maghrebi postwar fiction, or the queer Arab man on screen in the last two decades, the sphere of intimacy molds racial difference into its various shapes.

Among African nationals, Algerians have been French citizens since 1958 and began settling in France long before their nation's independence was gained after a bloody eight-year war. As Todd Shepard asserts, "The Algerian war was the most traumatic case of decolonization in the French Empire," a conflict that involved key political figures from François Mitterrand to Jacques Chirac and Jean-Marie Le Pen and changed France's demographics with the sudden displacement of one million European settlers to the metropole and 91,000 *harkis* or Muslim Algerians who fought on the French side.[40] Crucially, with Algeria's independence emerged new understandings of immigration that continue to frame political debates across Europe.[41] In 2006 five million French were of Algerian extraction. Gallic culture—music to food, literature, and film—reflects this major presence. Yet while numerous studies have explored the varied communities and contestations of a postcolonial London, no comparable work has asked what it would mean to reimagine the equally if not even more iconic city on the other side of the channel.[42] Instead, with the exception of scattered visual texts such as *Le Paris Arabe* and *Le Paris noir*, scholars analyzing literary Paris and the African diaspora have focused almost exclusively on the city's cosmopolitan and universalist character. Drawing on France's most important colonial venture, *Postcolonial Paris* offers a different perspective by unsettling and stretching the current imaginary to include the racialized periphery, those relegated to live in the city's fringe and in-between spaces.

This other Paris comes into our line of sight only briefly during the riots in 2005 and the multiple terrorist attacks of 2015. The spark for the riots, the largest civil disturbance since May 1968, was the death of two French teenagers from the impoverished Paris suburb of Clichy-sous-Bois: seventeen-year-old Zyed Benna, of Tunisian descent, and fifteen-year-old Bouna Traoré, of Mauritanian origin. Both were electrocuted as they sought to avoid a police identification check by taking refuge in an electrical substation. For many, this terrible accident was no accident at all and represented the all-too-familiar and tragic confrontation between police forces and French youth of color that has led to several riots since the 1970s, most notably in Vénissieux in 1981 and Toulouse-Le-Mirail in 1998. From the end of October to the middle of November 2005, suburban youth across three hundred cities responded collectively to the event, angered by the degrading routine of identity checks that principally targets them and often leads to long hours at the police station for individuals not carrying their

French identification card. To curb the riots, the government resorted to a "colonial management of the banlieue crisis" according to activist Mimouna Hadjam, by calling for a state of emergency with curfews and mass arrests of suspects. French authorities previously deployed this extraordinary measure in 1955 to deal with an uprising in Algeria.

On November 14, 2015, President François Hollande declared another state of emergency, which has since been extended five times and made into law in 2017. Expanding a logic of securitization already well under way in the banlieue since the 1990s, the state of emergency violates many measures of the European Court of Human Rights. Following the death of eighty-four people killed by a terrorist truck driver on Nice's seafront on Bastille Day in 2016, the French legislature increased already extensive police power to detain suspects without approval of a judge, seize data from computers and mobile phones, and search homes, luggage, and vehicles without judicial warrant.[43] Beyond police searches in private or public spaces, the measure facilitates the mobilization of the army.[44] Poll after poll shows that the French public is largely in favor of this extension of police power. This is not surprising because these restrictions of fundamental liberties and rights do not affect all French residents equally; they principally target Arabs and Muslims living in the banlieues.[45] Muslims inhabiting low-income areas and housing projects have been the principal subjects of some 400 house arrests and 3,600 warrantless searches leading to virtually no arrests.[46] This French version of the USA PATRIOT Act, now inscribed in the constitution, can be deployed in normal as well as emergency situations. The Ministry of the Interior can put anyone suspected of being a threat under house arrest, a procedure that can involve a request to visit a police station three times a day. Administrative searches are more widespread and generally happen at night, when "heavily armed special forces break open the door to an apartment, hold the residents at gun point, pin adults to the ground, handcuff them, and turn their belongings upside down."[47] When public hysteria gets whipped up around terrorism, the fear is not just about terrorists but about whole communities suspected of fomenting their plans, harboring them, sharing their faith, or failing to embrace French values. Propping up discussions around terrorism are expansive networks of relations and communities and economic and social realities that do not get named explicitly but are instrumental to the policies put in place to curb terrorist activities. This risky institutionalization of everyday Islamophobia and state-condoned racial violence ravage an already frayed national cohesion and foment more resentment.

Against the brief, distant, and partial lens of the media on the Paris periphery, this study travels across the train tracks and highways to offer a sustained examination of the lives of Algerians and their descendants. *Postcolonial Paris* brings forth collective concerns about state violence, social exclusion, and racial discrimination in a society that defines itself as individualist and colorblind.

Fictions of Intimacy

Derived from the Latin *intimus*, meaning "innermost," intimacy has long been theorized as the private domain of the interior. Critics such as Julia Kristeva and Jean Baudrillard have defined this term in dialectical opposition to the social and political domain. But other scholars have noted that, far from turning away from power, the intimate offers another way to study it. Postcolonial scholars have extended the study of the intimate from the domain of the personal and private to social, economic, and power structures that connect and associate us deeply with others. Intimacy has been read as a window onto colonial power, a social and sexual practice managed by the state, and a residue that shows the embeddedness of our neoliberal philosophy and culture with economic exploitation of slaves, colonial subjects, and indentured servants.[48]

Like this scholarship that has emphasized asymmetrical or nonreciprocal relations, *Postcolonial Paris* takes intimacy as its methodological lens to study processes of racialization across various Parisian contexts. I approach intimacy as not just the domain of sexuality but also the domain of connection through proximity, thus covering a wide range of interpersonal relations: same-sex and heterosexual couples, families, friends, and neighbors. As a social notion that emphasizes relationality, intimacy provides a fresh vantage point from which the tensions between assimilation and cultural difference, universalism and particularism can be reexamined. In addition to being a social notion, intimacy also refers to space. The Latin term *intimus* can mean proximal, "nearest . . . a spatial proximity with corporeal resonances."[49] As a spatial notion, intimacy relates to embodied experiences of space, as well as feelings of social and affective closeness or distance. It can help us understand shifts in the social construction of space, thus bringing together separate scholarly conversations about colonial, immigrant, diasporic, and minority cultures.

In her book collection *Haunted by Empire: Geographies of Intimacy in North American History*, Ann Stoler noted that "to study the intimate is not to turn away from structures of dominance but to relocate their conditions of possibility and relations and forces of production."[50] Stoler defends intimacy against charges of depoliticization precisely because rhetorics of intimacy have often worked to conceal structures of dominance, such as colonial and state violence. For example, we are familiar with the imagery of the harem that eroticized the colonial encounter in Algeria in French travel narratives, paintings, and postcards since the 1830s. Depictions of the harem unveiled native women to present Algeria as an intimate sexual adventure for young Frenchmen. The bare-breasted female natives conveyed a space at once morally different from the metropole and inviting of its conquest. Other depictions of imperial domination are couched in metaphors of harmonious marriage and benevolent parents. Similarly, interracial unions convey nationalist consolidation.[51] A microcosm for the empire or the nation, the interracial couple or family thereby symbolizes nonviolent forms of assimilation. These malleable "tender ties" of empire, as historian Sylvia van Kirk has described colonial intimacies, circulated through print and visual culture and masked how rigid colonial violence, or "tense ties" (in Stoler's words) affected the life of Algerian natives, including the calamitous conquest that lead to a decline of the native population by nearly a third.[52]

The literary production that preceded decolonization in Algeria has been largely characterized as assimilationist, consisting of fictions of intimacy between the French and the Algerians that hid pervasive colonial inequities. The few novels penned in the first half of the century by French-educated Algerian native writers, such as Aissa Zehar, Saad Ben Ali, and Djamila Débêche, expressed Algerian protagonists' love for French language and culture. Their fascination with the motherland translated their desire to be recognized as French. As Zahia Smail Salhi notes about this literary period, these writers "trusted France and had great hopes of her 'civilising mission.'"[53] Interestingly, this cultural production corresponds with the birth of Algerian nationalism with L'Étoile Nord-Africaine (the North African Star), founded in Paris in 1926 by Abdelkader Hadj Ali and Messali Hadj, members of the communist party who advocated for the independence of North Africa.

The interwar period also saw the immense popularity of Elissa Rhaïs, a Jewish Algerian woman writer of sentimental novels who passed for an Algerian Muslim. Her novels either "glossed over" the tension between the French and the Arabs or usually resolved them, "creating the illusion of relative harmony."[54] Lucienne Favre, another woman writer in the interwar Algeria who was originally from France, penned realist portraits of the colony from the viewpoint of Muslims with sympathy for their oppression by settlers.[55] Her male protagonist nonetheless mirrored racial stereotypes of uncontrollable anger and libido that offered a cultural explanation for social divisions of power.[56] Where Rhaïs portrayed communities in Algeria who thought intermarriage unthinkable, Favre showed that Muslim women opposed it most, out of faith.[57] Already in these narratives, Oriental sex and violence abounded in titillating ways embraced in the metropole only because it dealt with a more primitive culture.[58]

In the post–World War II period, the interracial romance continues to translate the relationships between Algerian natives and the French in the colony and the metropole. In Mouloud Feraoun's *La terre et le sang* (*Land and*

Blood, 1953), Driss Chraïbi's *Le passé simple* (*The Simple Past*, 1954), Albert Memmi's *Agar* (1955), Mouloud Mammeri's *Le sommeil du juste* (*The Sleep of the Just*, 1955), and Rachid Boudjedra's *La répudiation* (The Repudiation, 1969), the interracial romance relates rather than hides colonial tensions. This fiction shows that the deployment of intimacy does not limit itself to obfuscation. The authors, filmmakers, and visual artists I examine expose intimacy as a fiction through a double process of revealing and rewriting dominant tropes of colonial encounters. They expose the politicization of intimacy as a tool that naturalizes power and masks French hierarchies. They redeploy tropes of intimacy to debunk the mythologies of the French capital and its periphery. From the vantage point of the outskirts and its experiences, they rewrite ideas of the colonial family (Chraïbi), the Parisian interracial romance (Smith, Baldwin), the harem (Charef), the figure of the Arab queer (Bouchaala), and freedom of speech (Sebbar, JR, Princess Hijab) in ways that make racial logics in the metropole legible.

By employing the lens of intimacy rather than diaspora, *Postcolonial Paris* maps a different cultural cartography of the French capital than has been offered thus far. Diaspora has been the dominant framework for reading the cultural production of people of African descent in Paris. Scholars have examined the literary salons of the Nardal sisters, the "success stories" of African American expatriates and exiled African writers since the 1920s. In contrast, this book offers the first cultural study of Paris that focuses entirely on the colonial and postcolonial periphery, uncovering collective experiences of social relegation. Intimacy foregrounds the key role of space in shaping kinship and affinities for populations of African descent in Paris, thereby challenging us to move beyond narratives of origin to consider instead concrete and shared lived realities. It also straddles the porous borders between the private and the public, demonstrating how laws, policies, and political speeches affect the quotidian of Parisians in the outskirts.

The intimate stories of postcolonial Paris disclose that French mainstream cultures do not necessarily point at marked bodies and explicitly ascribe values and behavior; rather, they implicitly construct certain subjects as simply more modern than others. Modernity holds a place of honor in postcolonial studies. It was, after all, held as proof of European superiority, their right to rule other territories.[59] Part of the goal of colonization was to "inscribe the colonized in the space of modernity."[60] Given its historical point of origin in Western Europe, modernity has been thought of as a European project.[61] Paris in particular is lauded as giving birth to the key values of modernity: liberty, universal rights of man, a government by the people for the people, and the triumph of secularism. But what happens to that modernity when precisely those others whom colonial projects were designed to modernize reverse the direction of travel and settle in the metropole? As new African arrivals, and old ones that look like the new ones, settle in Paris, their phenotype conjures up foreign provenances associated with cultures and practices deemed primitive. This African presence, today several generations removed, transforms the meaning of modernity as "[a] European accomplishment to be defended against others who may knock at the gate but whose cultural baggage renders the mastery of modernity unattainable."[62] Attendant to this idea of modernity are a range of assumptions about cultural difference that mark populations perceived as least likely to accept political dissent, gender equality, and sexual difference, or to show tolerance toward beliefs and faiths other than their own. Though these ideas about modernity (or lack thereof) fall into racial categories of white and nonwhite, in Etienne Balibar's words, the "dominant theme is not biological heredity but the insurmountability of cultural difference."[63] Culture, here, operates as "a way of locking individuals and groups a priori into a genealogy, into a determination that is immutable and intangible in origin."[64] For novelist and filmmaker Mehdi Charef, this cultural essentialism churns out false binaries that overshadow more concrete social realities, such as widespread urban poverty that affects immigrants, the minorités visibles, as well as white French.

If "modernity" is a European narrative that hides its darker side, "coloniality," as Walter Mignolo asserts, then narratives of *Postcolonial Paris* work precisely to expose this hidden side.[65] They upend ideas of the primitive associated with Arabo-Islamic cultures, relocating them instead in Paris's poverty-stricken territories—the slums, the housing projects, and ethnic enclaves. In doing so, these plots demand that assimilation be measured not exclusively as the province of foreigners but in relation to social structures, government policies, and media and political discourses that thwart it. Colonial assimilation aimed to make Frenchmen out of Africans by exporting French education and culture, which would spur the colonized out of their supposed inertia. But this education in the colonies reached only a very few.[66] In postcolonial France, the term "assimilation" is used in the context of naturalization and refers to a set of elements to evaluate a candidate's claim for French citizenship, including knowledge of language and participation in society.[67] Similarly, the term "integration" describes a state policy that requires immigrants to shed their customs and values and adopt those of France, particularly individualism and secularism.[68] Government debates on the degree of acculturation of some immigrants have led to restrictive revisions of the French Nationality Code in 1993, which inserted a required "manifestation of desire" to become French for individuals born in France. Much of these debates centered on aspects of Muslim culture that purportedly made integration to society difficult.[69] This law evidenced the slippage of the concept of integration applied not only to immigrants but also to individuals born on French soil.

The idea that Arab men are particularly resistant to assimilating French culture is not new, and evidence of this frequently points to their relationship to women. Proof that the colonized needed to be civilized was often found in the status of the Muslim woman. As historian Julia Clancy-Smith explains, "When faced with questions of Algerian assimilation and rights under the French Republic, the colonial authority pointed to women's subjugation as evidence of all Arabs' fundamental and irreconcilable differences from French men and from French colonial settlers, thus providing a rationalization for the local peoples' continued disenfranchisement."[70] Colonialism is thus recast as chivalry or, as Gayatri Spivak so famously put it, European men "saving brown women from brown men."[71] However, French women, too, such as Aubertine Auclert at the turn of the century and writer Marie Bugéga after World War I, have played a significant role in fusing colonial and feminist agendas, giving birth to what critic Anna Kemp calls "colonial feminism." Today, evidence that French Muslims go against French lifestyles and values is strikingly still found in the status of Muslim girls[72] as well as that of homosexuals.[73] Since the 1990s, French (and European) feminists have renewed their interest in the global oppression of women worldwide, especially in Islamic nations. In the new millennium, lesbian, gay, bisexual, transgender (LGBT) organizations have similarly broadened their concerns to the experiences of sexual minorities in the Middle East and North Africa. During the same time, public discourses about France's non-Christian and nonwhite populations have foregrounded urban zones, where men repeatedly violate the rights of women and sexual minorities.

The discourse on sexual modernity that pitches the city center against its nonmodern Islamized outskirt or the French against the Muslim world found some legitimacy in the rise of life narratives by women and queer writers from Islamic nations and the Paris banlieue.[74] Celebrated narratives that exhort the containment of Islam in the West by Ayan Hirsi Ali and Chahdortt Djavann are translated into dozens of languages and their authors, now celebrities, have been showered with prizes. Equally fêted by a large audience across Europe, Abdellah Taïa, an openly gay Moroccan writer, has penned memoirs that feed the popular view of a homophobic Maghreb. In his own story cowritten with a journalist, *Un homo dans la cité* (*Gay in the Projects*), Brahim Naït-Balk transposes this homophobia to the banlieue. Their works are front runners among a deluge of testimonials crowding bookstores across Europe. Ali Behdad and Juliet Williams call this phenomenon neo-Orientalism to distinguish it from Said's definition of Orientalism. During colonialism, Oriental subjects function as stable objects of representation, but in neo-Orientalism, some are the producers of

Orientalist discourse. They paint the superiority of West over East via a narrative of progress that emphasizes secularism and gender equality. The generous inclusion of these new literary delegates demonstrates how national fashioning involves not only redrawing the lines between modernity and its recalcitrants but also admitting ex-Muslims who can be turned into the ambassadors of a revamped civilizing mission. For many scholars, these "paradigmatic assimilated subjects" do not represent a new phenomenon but echo the selective assimilation of a few subjects in the colonies who relinquished Islam.[75]

Integral to sexual modernity, gay rights have become a new civilizational benchmark deployed in Europe to marshal the abjection of Muslim French or immigrant groups marked as the inassimilable intolerant others. For example, the Netherlands has included a film for asylum seekers and naturalization candidates (outside the European Union and the United States) featuring two men kissing and a topless woman as part of a description of the "norms and values" of Holland. In Germany, the state of Baden Württemberg instituted a similar system aimed at gauging Muslim immigrants' attitudes toward homosexuality in 2006.[76] In France, gay rights layers the question of women's rights. In an open letter to the Minister of Education published in *Le Monde*, journalist Franck Chaumont, who wrote a damning book about homosexuality in the banlieues (*Homo-ghetto*), asserts that Franco-Arab queers live "in neighborhoods where modernity has not yet penetrated."[77] This discourse clearly about Muslims locates threats for each nation's way of life from these specific populations, but without openly naming them.

In mainstream cultural discourse, this sexual binary between the modern and nonmodern is mapped onto the city and its outskirts. The city center is a site where supposedly women and sexual minorities are equal to others. As such, it serves as a refuge for Muslim women and queer subjects inhabiting the virile outskirts, what Chaumont relabeled "the homo-ghetto." Shared by much of mainstream culture, Chaumont's assumptions are that queer individuals who stay in the banlieue are condemned to a life of misery, solitude, and violence.[78] The Arab male youth figure is the cause of this caste system. In the words of cultural critics Nacira Guénif-Souilamas and Éric Macé, he is imagined as "the incivilizable hoodlum" who gives "free range to his macho and ethnic compulsions" and is "the fomenter of a new Islamic ethnic chauvinism in France."[79] He allegedly exists outside a French modernity that is secular, individualist, and republican and that espouses equality between men and women, queer and straight people.[80] The veiled woman, yesterday the symbol of an oppressive religion in Algeria, continues to signify "the essence of Arab misogyny."[81] As the imagined antithesis of progress, she is either a brainwashed victim or the dangerous promoter of Islamic fundamentalism; either way, modernity discourse exiles her to the margins. The virile man and veiled woman are part of larger cast of people that figure in discourses on *insécurité* that is equally spatialized. On one side of the train tracks and highways are republican values, law and order, respect of others, the power of the law, and individualism. On the other side is the reverse image of intolerance, disorder, violence, delinquency, and communautarisme (tribalism). Pierre Tévanian notes these discourses are "at best ineffective, [but] at worst they render numerous citizens vulnerable by sowing hatred, enmity, and suspicion between different social groups, nurturing feelings of danger close to psychosis."[82] In postcolonial Paris, the city is hardly a refuge granting more freedom. Instead, authors of African descent depict it as a site where banlieue and immigrant subjects prostitute themselves to make ends meet or send remittances to their families, where nonwhites are asked for their identification papers, where women wearing niqabs are arrested and fined for breaking the law, and where Algerian peaceful demonstrators were clubbed to death by police in 1961 during "the bloodiest act of state repression in the modern history of western Europe."[83] In short, brown bodies in the city have to account for their presence and themselves. Verbally and physically, they are trapped in a perverse binary: assimilation or its absence.

Drawing on the work of postcolonial feminist scholars, *Postcolonial Paris* examines stories mainly by male authors, focusing likewise on mostly male protagonists. The point is not to reinforce gendered relations of privilege but to demonstrate how racialist and antiracialist politics alike capitalize on masculinity to construct affect. On the one hand, French mainstream media, political platforms, and their literary delegates typify men of color as hyperpatriarchal threats to democracy, particularly gender and same-sex equality. As such, gender and sexual contact represent a privileged site for articulations of a clash of civilization between white and nonwhite populations. On the other hand, stories by authors of African descent who condemn this racist typology equally harness gender and sexual differences to focus on masculinity but focus on its absence rather than its excess. Portrayals of intimacy involving men of color in Paris fuse masculinity and the struggle for racial equality. Responding to common clichés about predatory colonial migrants let loose on the French capital, Maghrebi fiction by Driss Chraïbi, Mouloud Feraoun, and Mouloud Mammeri often features emasculated Algerian men in the metropole: humiliated soldiers, impotent or cuckolded lovers, fathers with no authority, illegitimate sons, and censored writers. Together, these protagonists establish emasculation as a symptom of colonialism and, as a result, virility as the means and goal of decolonization. In subsequent banlieue narratives like Mehdi Charef's, Franco-Arab youth are virile figures who seek to differentiate themselves from docile immigrants and men on welfare. At the heart of each treatment of masculinity, whether aggrieved or dominant, is vulnerability. Its recognition is the key that allows protagonists to identify with others and extend solidarity. We find this vulnerability again with the sexual commodification of nonwhites in the city center, or the sexual frustration and impotence of immigrants in the outskirts.

Though some authors in this study collectively challenge the idea of the Arab as antimodern or non-Western, they demonstrate all too clearly how the struggle for racial equality can fold in patriarchal and heteronormative objectives. The "new ethnicities" produced by migration are homosocial: Chraïbi reappropriate the term "bicot" to describe a population that is no longer Algerian, Smith enlarges the meaning of "brothers" to include Algerians, and Charef produces the "banlieusards" as a new scapegoat of 1980s France. These three authors challenge the French construct of white womanhood as threatened by men of color in the capital, but when women of color appear, they are often victims of patriarchal violence that is barely acknowledged by the authors or their male protagonists. Queer subjects of color likewise reveal the primacy of racial discrimination in the capital, but their specific experiences are short-handed. In the same way that these authors' work calls for an expanded vision of Paris that brings into view nonwhite Parisians and their unique experiences, it is paramount that these racial experiences be critically considered in their intersectionality with gender, sexual orientation, and class. The myopic focus on heterosexual masculinity challenges us to read these narratives as not simply oppositional or heroic but as vehicles of various forms of oppression. Importantly, these stories test us. How can we unlink the struggle for racial equality from the objectives of patriarchy? Put differently, how do we approach the postcolonial critique of Paris without turning a blind eye to its violence and without falling into the hands of long-held racist and Islamophobic discourse? Francophone postcolonial studies and the literature of Paris noir have yet to consider these questions.

The Mythology of Paris

In 2013 Paris became the most popular tourist destination in the world, with more than 32.3 million people visiting the city that year, fourteen times the number of Parisians and about half of France's entire population. To understand why *Postcolonial Paris* may appear to some as an oxymoron, one must first gain a sense of how Paris has historically evoked its nation's ideals of individualism, universality, and equality. Below, I review how this mythology was bolstered by the tourism industry as well as French, British, and US writers.

France's cultural, economic, political, and literary prestige has clustered in Paris. Until the 1980s, its most prominent cultural institutions, universities and schools, major corporate headquarters, and administrative bodies were principally located there. It is no coincidence that the French railway system centers around the capital. Revealingly, the expression "monter à Paris" (to go up to Paris), as Agnès Rocamora notes, is a phrase used whether travelers come from a place geographically south or north of the capital. To go *up* to Paris evokes the capital's superior status in relation to *la province*, a phrase that flattens other cities' differences through a homogeneous and singular designation. La province, Rocamora claims, pejoratively connotes boredom and lack of cultural sophistication. Paris centralism has been not only political, with decisions made there and executed in its provinces, but also literary. The capital is an object of desire and prestige for the flawed protagonists of Honoré de Balzac, Émile Zola, Gustave Flaubert, and Victor Hugo. It is a place where the provincial may climb the social ladder, learn the bourgeois codes, and engage in romantic liaisons. Madame Bovary's awe-struck image of Paris from reading Balzac captures well the role nineteenth-century French novelists have played in strengthening the dichotomy between Paris and its provinces. In paintings by Édouard Manet and Georges Seurat, posters by Henri de Toulouse-Lautrec, songs by Edith Piaf and Mistinguette, photographs by Robert Doisneau, Paris has been the central locus of French cultural discourse and republican identity. As the saying goes, "Paris, c'est la France."

In *Mythologies*, French philosopher Roland Barthes broadly defined myth as "a type of speech." Myths, for Barthes, reflect the ideologies of the ruling class and its media, but present them as if they were natural. In other words, myths help create and naturalize dominant ideologies by giving their object the aura of an essence. The agents, labor, and context of myth production remain invisible. Barthes suggests that for a myth to emerge, its politics must be suppressed. The myth of Paris as the center of the world, the guardian of liberty, freedom, and reason, did not arise naturally following the 1789 revolution, as Pierre Citron notes.[84] Writers produced this idea four decades later in representation of the city as universal. After 1830, Alfred de Vigny saw the city as "the Pivot of France . . . the axis of the world" (Rocamora) and Edmond Texier as "intelligence's eye, the world's brain, the universe in miniature, man's commentary, humanity made city," in brief, "the capital of the whole civilized world."[85] Self-celebrated as the kingless capital, the city came to project revolutionary ideals, such as the rights of man, to be disseminated all over the world. According to Pascale Casanova, these French authors and their successors fashioned the city as a model of universalism by denationalizing its representations.[86] Paris, a "universal" literary capital until at least the 1960s, is to be understood as "a literary genre inaugurated in the late eighteenth century . . . gradually codified . . . over time . . . amount[ing] to a 'recitation'—an immutable leitmotif, obligatory in form and content."[87]

In the 1860s Napoleon III labored to make Paris a symbol of French stature, a stage from which the nation and its power would be displayed to the world. Under his guidance, Baron George-Eugène Haussmann refurbished façades and created large straight boulevards lined with trees and gaslights, which improved sanitation, traffic, and the circulation of goods and gave pedestrians monumental views of Paris's architecture day and night. In less than a quarter of a century, Paris was transformed from an endless maze of small streets to open, brightly lit avenues. This new Paris was good not only for industrialization but also for dissuading dissent, which often took the shape of barricades in narrow twisting streets. Haussmann's redevelopment aimed for "the total control of the city," purging it of "the ills of poverty, disease, moral depravity, and revolutionary sentiments."[88] Famed witnesses such as poet Charles Baudelaire lamented the destruction of the medieval city, whereby entire neighborhoods and ways of life were razed in the name of modern "progress." For the Goncourt brothers, the obliteration of the old city meant that one could no longer feel the world of Balzac. Instead, this uniform Paris, Paul Verlaine sneered, took passersby on long monotonous boulevards. As the long avenues lined by gaslights appeared, so did the cafés that give the city its enlivened character. Public parks, which previously were almost nonexistent, now rolled over entire sections of the capital. But not all residents could afford to partake in *le nouveau* Paris. Haussman spearheaded "the wide-scale destruction of working-class apartment blocks and slum housing."[89] With land value up, the state's redesign drove the working classes, often imagined as the dangerous classes,[90] outside the city limits, to the banlieues. Through this renovation, the government appropriated Paris to stage itself as a modern, ordered, clean, and bourgeois nation.

Haussmann's *grands travaux* was scheduled around and prioritized according to the 1855 and 1867 Paris Universal Expositions, when French writers, even detractors of Paris, could be turned into its ambassadors. On the occasion of the 1867 Exposition Universelle, celebrated novelists like Victor Hugo and George Sand, elsewhere staunch critics of the city, contributed to *Paris Guide*, a collection of essays that appeared in conjunction with the World's Fair. Though in *Les misérables* Hugo offered a damning view of the bourgeois capital, in the preface of the collection he stated, "Paris is the place on earth where one can best hear the flutters of progress' great wings." Sand had expressed her own deep aversion for a place overtaken by wealthy tourists in her 1844 essay "Le diable à Paris" (The Devil in Paris), but now praised it as "no other city in the world where ambulatory daydreaming is more agreeable. . . . In the fine weather of spring and autumn, [the pedestrian] . . . who knows how happy he is [is] a privileged mortal."[91] *Paris Guide* promoted the grandeur of the French capital, making it a destination for affluent visitors.

Under the Second Empire (1852–70), visitors, for the most part British, shaped the way domestic and foreign authors painted Paris in blunt strokes.[92] As the main consumers and producers of Paris tourist guidebooks, the British fashioned the city as an inverted image of London, the "city of business." Restricting themselves to the renovated new *quartiers* that gave an attractive and cohesive image of the city, tourist guides provided "a carefully groomed image," omitting the city's grittier realities.[93] Englishmen would travel to the "city of pleasure" and engage in more permissive behaviors than at home, as captured by Toulouse-Lautrec's painting *The Englishman*, which displays a top-hatted gentleman in intimate conversation with two female companions at the Moulin Rouge. London, it was said, had speed, industry, and commerce and cultivated the virtue of home; Paris, by contrast, was described by Balzac as "a vast workshop of pleasures." The Parisians were an outdoorsy people, who like to expose the "fair sex" in public spaces.[94] In the last decades of the nineteenth century, the idea of Parisian pleasure became central to the city's image.[95] Alfred Delveau's *Les Plaisirs de Paris*, an 1867 practical and illustrated guide, established what became a routinized description of the French way of life as insouciant, full of culinary pleasures and entertainment from horse races and the circus to the music hall. Despite the popularity of these cafés-concerts, many French observers started thinking of Paris as "a machine for manufacturing luxury and entertainment for the privileged."[96]

Among its many visitors, Americans participated actively in producing a Paris myth. Adam Gopnik writes, "For two centuries, Paris has been attached for Americans to an idea of happiness, of good things eaten and new clothes bought and a sentimental education achieved."[97] By documenting "the history of an illusion," Gopnik describes the two poles of this happiness: one bourgeois, whereby the capital is a window onto high civilization; the other bohemian, whereby visitors come to be dazzled by new art, erotic experiences, entertainment, and cheap drinking. Under the veneer of happiness lay latent themes of elusive friendship, loneliness, and a sense of insignificance brought on by the absence of social pressures. In fact, the great sense of freedom Gopnik, Donald Pizer, and Andrea Weiss note about US visitors and their protagonists indicates the fact that no one cares what *they* do. In *Women of the Left Bank*, Shari Benstock explored "what it was like to be a woman in Literary Paris" through her examination of more than twenty women (American, British, and French) between 1900 and 1940; some writers, others book sellers, *salonières*, and publishers.[98] For Weiss, the freedom Americans experienced in Paris in the 1920s and 1930s was highly gendered. While many modernist male authors came for adventure, their female counterparts, including Janet Flanner, Sylvia Beach, Djuna Barnes, and Gertrude Stein, found a "rare promise of freedom . . .: the freedom to work."[99] But this Paris that served as a "literary laboratory . . . [where] American styles get made and proffered"[100] ceased to be an inspiration for American men and women of letters in the post–World War II period.[101]

African American tales about Paris gained most visibility then, especially as James Baldwin and Richard Wright wrote about leaving a nation marred by racial strife. They were not the first African American Francophiles. From entertainers such as Josephine Baker and Ada "Bricktop" Smith, artists such as Henry Ossawa Tanner and Lois Mailou Jones, jazz players Sidney Bechet and John Coltrane, Paris's welcome to black America has been mythologized incrementally across decade since the end of World War I. Tales by returning soldiers and of artists' success appeared again and again in the pages of *The Pittsburg Courier*, the *Chicago Defender*, and other African American newspapers and magazines. In *Notes of a Native Son* (1955), Baldwin asserts that the French capital provides African Americans with the terms by which they can define themselves rather than be defined. Similarly, in an essay rejected for publication by *Ebony* magazine, Wright famously claims that he has "found more freedom in one square block of Paris than there is in the entire United States."[102] Post–World War II Paris noir fiction fashioned a color-blind city that serves as a foil to Jim Crow America.[103] There, Baldwin's unnamed African American protagonist in "This Morning, This Evening, So Soon" can become a man like other men. The city became a sanctuary where US minorities could find refuge from racist persecution and second-class citizenship. Novelists painted this *douce* France through the trope of the interracial romance, a symbol of racial equality on the other side of the Atlantic.[104]

Yet African American exiles were also exasperated by the fetishization of blackness in Paris, from the sights of Josephine Baker dancing topless in a banana skirt to assumptions that every black American person was a jazz musician. During the Algerian war, these exiles witnessed police brutality against Arabs and saw bodies floating in the Seine but also knew they would be deported should they openly express support for colonial subjects. In the domain of the interracial romance, it was rarely the mademoiselles involved with black American men but other European women. Even as these expatriate authors witnessed Paris's contradictions, their postwar tales often used the city as a political tool to denounce US race relations.

The Missing Metropole

The mythology of Paris was especially stubborn for those intimately familiar with it, though they rarely set eyes on the city. Martinique-born psychotherapist and revolutionary Frantz Fanon noted that the West Indians "who were privileged to go to France spoke of Paris, of Paris which meant France. And those who were not privileged to know Paris let themselves be beguiled."[105] Because the colonies often oriented themselves vis-à-vis metropolitan culture, "the black man who had been to the *métropole* is a demigod" for the metropole is the "holy of holies."[106] A West Indian's visit there "creates an aura of magic around him where the words, Paris . . . , the Sorbonne, and Pigalle represent the high points."[107] The fantasy attached to the city speaks to colonized subjects' desire for the metropole and its most widely circulated symbol: the capital.[108] Paris served as a reference point of modernity for the colonies to emulate, from its education and its urbanism to its cultural forms and tastes. In Bernard Dadié's epistolary novel *An African in Paris*, upon learning that he will be visiting the metropole, Tanhoe Bertin exclaims "I have a ticket to Paris . . . yes, Paris! The very same Paris we've so often talked and dreamed about! . . . Even I will be able to see Paris with my own eyes."[109] In the impoverished colony of Algeria, Paris also stood for an aspirational bourgeois life of economic security and leisure, a place where the crushing weight of colonial dispossession could be lifted.

This vision of European capitals as a desired world for the colonized is more readily visible on the other side of the English Channel, where numerous studies have called attention to a postcolonial London. Novels such as George Lamming's *The Emigrants* and Sam Selvon's *Lonely Londoners* have depicted the arrival of the Windrush generation to London, a city of self-realization for some and disillusionment for others. *The Enigma of Arrival*, V. S. Naipaul's autobiography, captured his "tenderness towards London."[110] Another famous Trinidadian, Lord Kitchener, sang a melodious love song to the capital on disembarking at Tilbury.

> London is the place for me
> London this lovely city
> You can go to France or America,
> India, Asia or Australia
> But you must come back to London city
> Well believe me I am speaking broadmindedly
> I am glad to know my Mother Country
> I have been travelling to countries years ago
> But this is the place I wanted to know
> London that is the place for me

In Lord Kitchener's imaginary London *is* Britain, London *is* the Mother Country, and has nothing to envy in other revered locations. Antigua-born novelist Jamaica Kincaid explains Naipaul and Lord Kitchener's sense of wonder for London when she claims that though she had never seen the metropole, "England was . . . our source of reality, our sense of what was meaningful, our sense of what was meaningless."[111] Steeped in British history and culture at school, commonwealth subjects heard of Britain and its celebrated capital their entire childhood, learned to enumerate its kings and queens, draw its map, locate its cities and rivers, and even identify its flora. This is what Naipaul means when he says, "I had come to London as to a place I knew very well."[112] Colonial education and its erasure of natives' history and cultural forms produced powerful desires for London, an omnipresent site for all things British, as well as a perceived springboard for social advancement.

We cannot understand colonized subjects' deep disillusionment with the British or French capital without first understanding its idealization. The dissonance between the dreamed and the postwar city has been documented by commonwealth and Black British novelists. Though Jamaican critic Stuart Hall wanted to live in London, and really, if he could, "right on Eros Statue in Picadilly Circus," most colonial subjects lived in what he called the "metropolitan sticks," rather than the "the center of the hub of the world."[113] In Selvon's *Lonely Londoners* (1959), Moses describes this segregation: "We can't get no place to live, and we only getting the worse jobs it have."[114] For this native of Trinidad, London is a lonely city that "divide[s] up in little worlds, and you stay in the world where you belong to and you don't know anything about what happening in the other ones except what you read in the papers."[115]

Similarly, in the Paris of Algerian writers, there is no glimpse of the city's light or glamour. Stories by Mohammed Dib, Mouloud Feraoun, and Mouloud Mammeri take place in the "metropolitan sticks," where Algerian men share cramped rooms and take turns sleeping in a single bed in eight-hour rotations. The settings consist of decrepit dormitories, cellars, and rooms in rundown sectors like Gennevilliers and La Goutte d'Or or the primitive slums of Nanterre.[116] These habitations generally lack running water and sanitation. Sons and fathers migrate there out of necessity to settle debts and save their families from abject poverty. Some contract tuberculosis, many experience hunger, and all face racist hostility. Chraïbi labels the city "the mirage of Europe," which eats "poor dumb Arabs" "like a tapeworm."[117] In this literary imaginary, Paris often represents a stage of disillusionment in young men's lives. Excluded from the promise of liberté, égalité, fraternité, they take stock of their status as subalterns and return home with a sharpened political consciousness. These depictions of a Paris that politicizes its migrants mirror the lives of many African nationalists and "suggests that there was something inherent in the very process of migration that piqued new ways of seeing the imperial order."[118]

In Mammeri's 1955 novel *The Sleep of the Just*, Areski, a twenty-six-year-old Algerian man who enrolls to fight for France during World War II, exemplifies this new consciousness after a series of humiliations, including being served last at each meal after all the Europeans have received their share. Areski comes to term with twenty-four years of lies by literally setting his French education on fire, gathering in a pile "*The Social Contract, Discourse on Inequality, Castigations*, Jaurès, Auguste Comte . . ." and lighting it up. Once discharged from the army in Paris, he becomes active with the Algerian nationalist movement. In Feraoun's *Land and Blood*, another young Algerian native who fought in the French army explains his vision of Paris: "Over there, yes, we see clearly who we are . . . we are not penned, we are allowed everywhere, for sure. But everywhere we are *Norafs* [North Africans] . . . we are rich and poor, there are gangsters and tramps, but we do not belong to any of those categories . . . we are *Norafs*."[119] Feraoun's use of the racial slur "Noraf" conveys that despite colonial subjects' more flexible circulation in the metropole, neither this spatial movement nor differences of class disrupt the entrenched racial stigma the French assign North Africans.

Unlike London, scholarly engagement with literary accounts of Paris from the viewpoint of colonial subjects and their descendants has been largely invisible. Despite the extensive cultural archive on the capital, there has been little critical interest in this postcolonial Paris.[120] A few exceptions include studies on sub-Saharan African writers by Benetta Jules-Rosette, Odile Cazenave, and Dominic Thomas. Another critic who has noted this absence, Pascale Casanova, attributes this invisibility to the historically low status of Francophone literature in France until recently. She explains that for decades, "Paris never took an interest in writers from its colonial territories; or, more precisely, it long despised and mistreated them as a species of extreme provincials, too similar to be celebrated as exotic foreigners but too remote to be considered worthy of interest."[121] The fraught relationship between Paris and Francophone writers, Casanova explains, is due to the position of Paris as "the very source of the political and/or literary domination under which [Francophone writers] labor."[122] In other words, Paris is the place that denies colonial authors literary status for their failure to fit values of universalism and individualism promoted by French fiction.

This tension between a nationalist French literature and a world literature in French crystallized with the publication of a manifesto titled "For a World Literature" published in *Le Monde* on March 16, 2007. The manifesto, signed by forty-four highly regarded writers, including Tahar Ben Jelloun, Edouard Glissant, Jean-Marie Gustave Le Clézio, Amin Maalouf, and Alain Mabanckou, opened a series of debates about the center and the periphery of literature in French. With most of their origins in France's former colonies, the signatories and their supporters are objecting to the ways the metropolitan literary milieu had categorized different productions based on the location and historical approach of writers. Despite the wealth of world-renowned Francophone writers like Frantz Fanon, Camara Laye, Rachid Boudjedra, Assia Djebar, and Maryse Condé, historian Tyler Stovall asserts that their work remains ignored by the French academic establishment.[123] The Manifesto of the 44, as it is known, demanded the end of the institution of "Francophonie," a term commonly used to refer to Francophone writers outside of France.[124]

Excluded from the Manifesto of the 44, and more generally from France's literary field, authors from the banlieues also published a manifesto the same year.[125] The signatories are members of the writers' collective Qui Fait La France? (Who makes France?) that includes Thomté Ryam, Mohamed Razane, and Faïza Guène. Published in a collection of short stories, this manifesto also decries forms of ghettoization against writers from the banlieue. Members of Qui Fait La France? reposition themselves as "artists," "children of a plural France," "products of mixed identities," authors of "a literature that is *engagée* to fight against inequalities and injustices."[126] In contrast to a dominant French literature, which serves as "an outlet for bourgeois whims," they position themselves as providing a more democratic aesthetics focused on "*le réel*" (the real).[127]

A Belated Postcolonial Turn

Understanding the peculiar place of postcolonialism in France can help explain the absence of a postcolonial Paris. In literature departments in the hexagone, the postcolonial lens has been "stigmatized as an excessively simplistic and politically correct 'Anglo-Saxon' model that has little to contribute to the analysis of francophone contexts."[128] The unpopularity of the postcolonial approach and the notion that it is an Anglo-Saxon import are all the more striking given that key postcolonial authors were, in fact, Francophone novelists and essayists such as Aimé Césaire, Albert Memmi, and Frantz Fanon, or that seminal texts, such as Said's *Orientalism*, drew on French literature. Discussions of Francophone postcolonial studies often open with what Charles Forsdick has called "the uneasy engagement with 'postcolonial' thought and wider questions of postcoloniality evident in French intellectual life."[129] Alec G. Hargreaves and David Murphy explicate this uneasiness as they assert that "Francophone" and "postcolonial" studies have often been understood as "rival or even antagonistic academic fields."[130] As such, work that addresses themes of postcolonialism has generally not been labeled as such, to such an extent that in literary studies "Francophone" and "postcolonialism" have described the same realities. Francophone literature and Francophonie (the study of French language outside the metropole) has entered a dialogue with postcolonial studies mainly in US and British universities.[131] Another factor that helps explain the absence of a postcolonial Paris in French studies is the fact that whereas in the Anglophone world, the postcolonial lens has been established in literary and cultural studies disciplines, in the French context, the postcolonial approach has been driven (often belatedly) by historians, sociologists, and political scientists.[132]

Since 2004, four decades after the emergence of postcolonial studies, several events have accelerated the postcolonial "turn" in French studies. First, the law passed on March 15, 2004, banning ostentatious religious signs in public schools emerged as a reaction to Muslim girls wearing headscarves. On February 23, 2005, the fourth clause of another law urged educators to teach "the positive role of the French presence overseas, especially in North Africa." After teachers' and scholars' opposition, the clause was later abrogated. In response, a movement dubbed *les indigènes de la république* (the republic's natives) was launched by racial minority writers from the banlieue. A highly racialized term, the word "indigènes" underscores colonial legacies still at play in contemporary France. The 2005 riots that exploded in Paris and spread across France forced the nation to further confront the question of race. Following these events and subsequent efforts to understand their causes, several classics of Anglophone postcolonialism by Homi Bhabha, Dipesh Chakrabarty, Partha Chatterjee, Stuart Hall, Gayatri Spivak, and Neil Lazarus were translated into French. French historical and sociological studies were published, too, including Claude Liauzu and Gilles Manceron's *La Colonisation, la loi, et l'histoire* (2006), Marie-Claude Smout's *La situation postcoloniale* (2007), Ahmed Boubeker's *Histoire politique des immigrations (post)coloniales* (2008), and Catherine Coquio's *Retours du colonial?* (2008). The authors of the Association pour la Connaissance de L'Afrique Contemporaine (Association for the Knowledge of Contemporary Africa) produced other significant works: *La Fracture coloniale: La société française au prisme de l'héritage colonial* (2005) and *Cultures post-coloniale, 1961–2006: Traces et mémoires coloniales en France* (2006).

This sudden upsurge of postcolonial interest led historian Emmanuelle Saada in 2014 to register a "feeling of colonial fatigue" in the field of French studies, whereby the postcolonial turn seemed poised to become a victim of its own success. Postcolonial inquiries apparently no longer ask new questions but routinize the examination of the Republic's colonial contradictions, generating, in Saada's words, a feeling of "déjà-lu" (already read).[133] For Saada, the postcolonial "turn" has helped broadcast "the centrality of race in the national narrative and in state practices."[134] What is needed now, according to the author, is more work on local processes, on the political forms of empires, and on the specificities of certain places in larger imperial and postimperial projects.[135] By keeping an eye on specific historical discourses and government policies, *Postcolonial Paris* heeds Saada's warning against the tendency of postcolonial theory to produce generalizations across very different contexts, a critique widely shared by other historians of postcolonialism such as Frederick Cooper and literary critic Ali Behdad.

To rejuvenate a field bogged down by "déja-lu," Forsdick has recently called for a postcolonial studies that would put comparison at its center. He reminds readers that a major figure like Edward Said, central to the emergence of postcolonial studies, was trained in comparative literature. Forsdick urges a commitment to comparative scholarship that would illuminate the "interconnectedness of imperial histories."[136] John McLeod also claimed that the field was shifting toward a better understanding of "different European empires, and their legacies."[137] While *Postcolonial Paris* compares across different languages, cultural traditions, and media, it resists the idea that colonial analysis is relevant only to other colonial contexts. In many ways, this book urges us to see the interconnectedness of struggles against racial oppression that do not fit neatly with our predilection for academic umbrellas: Francophone and Anglophone texts; colonial, immigrant, and minority texts. More than ever, the postcolonial lens transcends colonial comparisons and has been applied to studies as varied as Shakespeare, the Cold War, African American expatriate fiction, and Holocaust literature.[138] This transdisciplinary lens looks beyond the conventional division of knowledge and academic fields to produce new vantage points on stories we thought we already knew.

Disrupting the timeline of most cultural studies of French minorités visibles, which start in 1983 with the historic March for Equal Rights and Against Racism, the first two substantive chapters in *Postcolonial Paris* move further back in time to the context of the Algerian struggle for independence (1954–62). This expanded focus uncovers a broader archive of postcolonial Paris that cuts across literary traditions and decenters the conventional focus on nation. The other three chapters are set against the backdrop of the historical 1983 antiracist march, terrorist bombings in Paris in 1995 and 2015, and the 2005 riots. They center on authors' strategies for writing nonwhite working-class populations into the Paris imaginary, constructing a shared city for the future.

The first chapter, "Colonial Domesticity," analyzes the plotline of interracial liaisons in Francophone Maghrebi novels. In Mouloud Feraoun's *Land and Blood* (1953), Mouloud Mammeri's *The Sleep of the Just* (1955), and Driss Chraïbi's *The Butts* (1955), Paris is the setting for romances between Algerian male migrants and French women. The theme of interracial romance supplies an ideal testing ground for whether Algerian and French people could cohabit and whether colonized subjects could integrate French values. This Paris experiment usually fails, leaving Algerian men disillusioned. Excluded from Parisian modernity, most take stock of their status as subalterns and return home with an enhanced political awareness. I focus on Chraïbi's novel, in which Algerian protagonists, though changed by their experiences of Paris, remain in the capital. Literary critics have generally read this narrative, nominated for the prestigious Prix Goncourt, for its universal themes about immigrants, particularly their acute poverty, the hostility they face from natives, and the nostalgia they feel for their homeland. By retrieving this novel's metropolitan and colonial contexts, my analysis reveals a colonial critique woven through the politics of intimacy. The Parisian popular press portrayed North African men as primitive individuals let loose on the city and its vulnerable white female residents. This differential discourse was at odds with the colonial rhetoric of blissful matrimony and harmonious cohabitation that French politicians and novelists used to describe Franco-Algerian relations. Trading the metaphor of the Franco-Algerian couple that erased social conflict between colonizers and colonized for a couple in the flesh, *The Butts* illuminates colonial inequities in the metropole. Setting the stage for how colonial and anticolonial narratives deploy the rubric of intimacy, this chapter demonstrates that gender and sexual politics work to galvanize or inflate conflict between French and Algerian people.

Chapter 2, "Romance and Brotherhood," examines how African American expatriate tales engaged with the plight of Algerians in Paris in the 1960s, when struggles against racial oppression became global and decolonization battles were linked with the US civil rights movement. Addressing interracial romances against the backdrop of the Algerian independence struggle, the chapter argues that key African American expatriate writers' inclusion of North African characters in their fiction reveals a struggle to reconcile the coexistence of a *color-blind* and a *colonial* Paris. This chapter takes authors often regarded as mouthpieces of a raceless Paris to reveal their overlooked engagement with an Algerian Paris. I map out a six-year literary transformation of Paris in expatriate fiction, in Richard Wright's lesser-known novel *The Long Dream* (1958) and its unpublished sequel, "Island of Hallucination" (1959), in James Baldwin's short story "This Morning, This Evening, So Soon" (1960), and in William Gardner Smith's understudied novel *The Stone Face* (1963). In this literary journey that transits from Wright's and Baldwin's tributes to a racially liberal Paris to Smith's shrewd attack on French colonialism, the interracial romance undergirds both the construction and the interrogation of an egalitarian city. Offering competing figurations of the capital, Baldwin and Smith distinguished Parisian spaces through the languages of romance and brotherhood. Black–white intermixing marks the Left Bank of the River Seine as a site of acceptance where African American men become "men like other men." But this universalist vision does not apply to Algerian enclaves raided by police, north of the city, which remind black American protagonists of the ghettos they left behind. This colonial Paris works as a site of recognition that rallies African Americans and Algerians as "brothers" engaged in a comparable battle for equality. Despite their competition, both figurations rewrite the city and help writers establish masculinity as key for theorizing racial equality.

The third chapter, "The New Harem" transitions to the postcolonial era and continues to examine the spatial politics of intimacy through the Orientalist trope of the harem, but it shifts focus to the offspring of colonial migrants born or raised in Paris's impoverished outskirts. In the numerous studies devoted to beur fiction, discussions of intimacy (if addressed at all) are generally limited to the constraints imposed on young Arab women in France's Muslim immigrant communities. In this chapter, I reassess Mehdi Charef's *Tea in the Harem* (1983), the foundational text of beur fiction and a watershed of youth culture, by attending to its creative deployment of gender and sexuality to describe the Paris banlieue as a new exotic. By referring to an Orientalist icon associated with the colonial era, Charef's title promises us some alluring Franco-Algerian encounters, but the narrative disrupts Orientalist expectations. Instead of the Orient, *Tea in the Harem* unveils another hidden territory: the Parisian banlieue. In this isolated setting, the spectacle is one of poverty, enchantment is drug-induced, and sexual adventures provide a multiracial group of young men with a means for social recognition, a chance to differentiate themselves from immigrants and low-wage workers as well as from city-dwellers. By featuring protagonists who are either voyeurs, performing a role for an audience, or objects of surveillance, Charef uses familiar economies of vision to convey and interrogate relations of power between the city and its suburbs, between France and Algeria. Through a focus on vision, Charef reveals how distance (physical, emotional, social) turns destitution into a spectacle and women into sexual objects to be traded for masculine self-worth. In contrast, proximity gives rise to new territorial identities that compete with national and racial allegiances. Published the same year as the historic March for Equality and Against Racism, Charef's firsthand account of home-making in the Paris margins reframes integration debates. Unlike French republican ideology that stresses the difference between citizens and foreigners, *Tea in the Harem* emphasizes the common experience of social exclusion among working-class Parisians, whether they are immigrant or French, thereby encouraging readers to concentrate on borders within rather than outside the nation.

While in Charef's novel, cross-racial solidarity in the banlieue meshes with homophobia and sexism, chapter 4, "Other Queers," documents a cinematic genre set in Paris's enclaves that features Arab men who are sexual minorities. This string of films ranges from comedy to drama and includes Olivier Ducastel and Jacques Martineau's *Drôle de Félix* (*The Adventures of Félix*, 2000), Liria Bégéja's

Change moi ma vie (*Change My Life*, 2001), Ahmed and Zakia Bouchaala's *Origine
contrôlée* (*Made in France*, 2001), Merzak Allouache's *Chouchou* (2003), Amel Bedjaoui's *Un fils* (A Son, 2003), Jean Pierre Sinapi's *Vivre me tue* (*Life Kills Me*, 2003),
Rémi Lange's *Tarik el hob* (*The Road to Love*, 2003), and Sébastien Lifshitz's *Wild
Side* (2004). Drawing on some of these films, particularly the blockbuster comedy
Made in France, I argue that homosexuality is a significant conceptual linchpin
for thinking about the integration of immigrants and French racial minorities
in France. The figure of the Arab male queer brings into relief a grammar of
descent and consent that stigmatizes specific sectors of Paris and the Maghreb.
Bridging contexts of crime in the urban periphery, Islamic terrorism, and illegalized immigration, I contend that this genre of films does not expand our
idea of Arab masculinity, as the critical consensus holds, but contracts it to a
measure indicative of immigrants and racial minorities' potential to "fit" within
modern liberal democracies. These narratives lay bare continuities and shifts in
the representation of Arab masculinity from the colonial to the postcolonial
era. Although prostitution remains a constant in the portrayals of Arab homosexuality, in the postcolonial metropolitan context, Algerian and Franco-Arab
men are no longer associated with homoeroticism but with homophobia, an
antidemocratic threat posed by Muslim immigrants and male chauvinists in
the banlieue. In these films, I posit that queerness largely encapsulates French
contradictions as it serves to racialize a population while professing racial and
cultural indifference.

The closing chapter, "Embodying the City," expands on the two previous
chapters' attention to the visual by turning to the use of graffiti and street art by
postcolonial novelist Leïla Sebbar and internationally known Paris-based artists
of African descent. It argues that through spray-painting and flyposts, protagonists and artists are politicizing the urban landscape by literally painting a
critique of Paris onto the city itself. Whether they take the shape of written
statements, symbols of Islam, or close-up portraits of banlieue youth, the graffiti
marks a shared desire to rehumanize the abject and the abstract. In Sebbar's
novel *The Seine Was Red* (1999), Amel, a French adolescent of Algerian descent,
accompanied by Omer, a young undocumented Algerian journalist, retraces
the steps Algerian demonstrators took on October 17, 1961. Armed with red
paint, Omer literally indicates sites of colonial bloodshed on the Parisian landscape on the twenty-fifth anniversary of the police massacre. Graffiti artist
Princess Hijab spray-paints black veils and niqabs on advertising posters that
line the Paris subway, clothing models with outlawed clothing in some public
spaces. And *photograffeur* JR flyposts giant images of marginalized youths from the
banlieue on walls of a fashionable neighborhood in the city center. Their creations speak in vibrant visual terms against a certain topophobia, an association

of the urban margins with the abject. Together, these street interventions make racialized subjects central to the capital, in ways that interrogate Paris's exclusionary cultural expressions. Finally, the coda takes us to the 2015 terrorist attacks in Paris and offers a context for understanding the place of French Islam since the 1970s.

Colonial Domesticity

L'Algérie, c'est la France," declared François Mitterrand in 1954 in response to the National Liberation Front's demand for an independent Algeria. L'Algérie Française was not officially a colony of France but part of French territory that consisted of three provinces administered by the Ministry of the Interior. Colonial portrayals of the Franco–Algerian relationship as a free union reflected this status. Algeria was not described as a dependent child, like many other colonies were, but as a partner in a "conjugal life"; Algeria could "divorce" and "evict" France, destroying their mutual "household."[1] So large was this icon of the couple that even today "it is impossible to talk about Franco-Algerian relationships without using passionate language, without conjuring up images of the couple as if they were real persons or characters in a novel."[2] Yet already in 1955, Algerian writer Mouloud Feraoun challenged this symbolic marriage and divorce in his journal: Why do Algerians "declare this divorce in spite of the threats that hang over their heads and of the terrible hardships that they have to endure? . . . The truth is that there was never any marriage. No, the French stayed apart. Contemptuously far away. The French remained strangers."[3] Indeed, the uneven coexistence of one million Europeans and nine million Muslim natives in French Algeria did not resemble a marriage of equals. The reality involved apartheid, land confiscation, massive displacements of native populations, and routinely rigged elections. In the words of historians Julia Clancy-Smith and Frances Gouda, the use of the metaphor sought to "accentuate the necessity and normalcy of colonial rule . . . a consensus— albeit a highly malleable and self-serving one."[4]

The rhetoric of French colonial domesticity has been examined in relation to the colonies, including French Réunion, French Algeria,[5] and Vietnam.

France drew on notions of parentage to normalize the relationship with its colonies.[6] In *Monsters and Revolutionaries*, Vergès coins the phrase "the colonial family romance." Drawing from the Freudian idea of the family romance, "a fiction developed by children about imagined parents," Vergès shows how French colonial powers substituted the motherland for the parents of the colonized.[7] This displacement of parenthood worked to frame all sons as brothers, regardless of their different status as French. This family rhetoric projected the image of republican universalism and provided the colonized with a foundation to indict imperialism by asking France to live up to its principles.[8] In *Domesticating the Empire*, authors decode imageries of paternalism, maternalism, and sexual desire that saturated political rhetoric about the colonies.[9] Jeanne Bowlan and Julia Clancy-Smith, for instance, note that colonial authorities in Algeria intimately linked the threat of intermarriage with the colonized's claim of political rights. This chapter shifts the focus from the colony to the metropole, from European men's interaction with female others to Algerian men's encounters with Parisian women, and from the metaphors of cohabitation to their concrete, in-the-flesh complexity. More than any other Maghrebi text, the modernist novel *The Butts* by Moroccan author Driss Chraïbi looks closely at the ideological meanings circulated by tropes of family and home.

The discourses and rhetoric that accompanied the arrival of Algerian colonial migrants in the French capital after World War II framed Franco-Algerian encounters and cohabitation differently in the metropole. On the heels of their defeat in Vietnam, France sent planes of soldiers into Algeria, and thousands of Algerian Muslims, 80 percent of them men, left for France, and mainly its capital, to search for work. They traded family, friends, and a familiar environment for a place whose language many did not speak and whose mores they did not understand. They hoped to send enough money back to save their family from starvation or debt. Despite some politicians' doubts that Algerians could be "grafted" onto the Gallic population, France's economic expansion hungered indiscriminately for more laboring bodies.[10] By 1975 some Algerian natives who had worked in factories and construction industries in the 1950s had returned to their native region of Kabylia, a key migrant-sending site. Algerian sociologist Abdelmalek Sayad interviewed them about their experiences. One man confided, "I will always remember this image of my arrival in France . . . you knock at a door, it opens on to a little room that smells of a mixture of things, the damp, the closed atmosphere, the sweat of sleeping men. Such sadness! . . . The darkness of the room . . . the darkness in the streets—the darkness of the whole of France, because, in our France, there is nothing but darkness."[11]

The fiction of Maghrebi novelists portrays the collective experience of colonial migrants in a way that echoes Sayad's respondents. Authors depict a Paris marked by segregation and primitive lodging, where Algerians struggle to make ends meet at the margins of the city and its economic prosperity. Their daily lives illuminate a side of the city untouched by modernity. This opening chapter that analyzes the use of tropes of family and home in *The Butts* calls attention to a Janus-faced Paris. By giving a panoramic view of Algerian homeless migrants cut off from modern Paris and a close recounting of the unraveling relationship of a Franco-Algerian couple, Chraïbi debunks the myth of an imperial harmonious family. The narrative provides multiple perspectives on Paris: French and Algerian, from the point of view of an évolué and an illiterate man, collective and individual, public and private, bourgeois and working class. Nominated for the prestigious prix Goncourt, this first francophone Maghrebi novel entirely devoted to the experience of Algerians in Paris after World War II relies on the trope of the interracial romance to demonstrate the incommensurability between the French and North Africans, revealing how single North African men came to be viewed as a threat to the institution of family. By investigating Chraïbi's Paris, this chapter demonstrates how French colonial domesticity operates on essentialist understandings of race and gender.

In the years preceding and throughout the Franco-Algerian war, fiction became a platform to address the effects of colonialism on natives' lives and home a privileged theme to address colonial tensions. Politically conscious Maghrebi authors took up the pen to reveal the "hoboization" (*clochardisation*) of the colonized under French rule and challenge the stultifying Arabo-Islamic traditions.[12] In the early 1950s, a group of Algerian native writers formed the 1952 Generation out of frustration with L'École d'Alger (the Algiers school) constituted by European-Algerian figures such as Albert Camus, Jean Pélégrini, and Emmanuel Roblès. For native writers such as Mouloud Feraoun, Mouloud Mammeri, and Mohammed Dib, the Algiers school represented Algeria as *un orient de pacotille* (a counterfeit Orient) strikingly devoid of natives.[13] Aiming to make natives and their concerns visible, Feraoun called for "authentic messengers" as a new generation of Francophone Algerian novelists arose to describe colonized North African societies from the inside.[14]

Chraïbi also revolted against French colonial habits to wall off and silence Arab natives, to speak for them, or to simply pretend they do not exist. But when it comes to genre, fictional rules, or tone, *The Butts* overturns all the expectations of the 1952 Generation. At a time when some key Algerian male native authors identified authenticity and realism as the defining characteristics of an anticolonial literary arsenal, Chraïbi broke all these tenets. In his short and dense modernist novel, readers strain to reconstitute a timeline or tell apart thoughts from reality. With its bitter tone, violent language, attention to bodily function and dysfunction, and a penchant for the grotesque, Chraïbi's impressionistic narrative aligns more closely with Aimé Césaire's surrealist long poem,

Cahier d'un retour au pays natal (*Notebook of a Return to the Native Land*, 1939) than with the 1952 Generation. Literary critic Maurice Nadeau classifies Chraïbi's experimental writing as part of what he dubbed "L'École de l'Afrique du Nord" (North African School), a set of authors that includes Kateb Yacine, Mohammed Dib, and Albert Memmi, who "were galvanized as social critics with literary styles inspired by past and present American modernists."[15] Their work, as Valérie Orlando shows, is equally influenced by "the form and content (or lack thereof) of the French New Novel—which privileged the fragmented, searching subject, living in a world of chaos where things replaced humans in importance," and presented protagonists "who were conflicted and challenged by an identity vacuum in the wake of World War II and a crumbling colonial empire."[16] Chraïbi drew on these narrative conventions to mount an anticolonial critique, but paradoxically questioned the role of the intellectual native as a mouthpiece for the colonized by juxtaposing a writer paralyzed by his French education with an illiterate man who staunchly supports the North African migrant community.

Further singularizing him from his contemporaries, Chraïbi writes about the abject poverty and exclusion of colonial workers in Paris not out of experience. He was born in 1926 to a well-to-do family in El Jadida, Morocco, and moved to France in 1945 to study chemistry. Upon graduating as an engineer, Chraïbi soon turned to literature and published a first controversial novel, *Le passé simple* (*The Simple Past*, 1954). The narrative recounts a native son's rebellion against his father and what the latter represents: Islamic traditions and the marginalization of women. This damning portrait of Moroccan native society was published at a time when it was demanding independence from France. Less attuned to fine discrimination or ambivalence, nationalists quickly denounced the novel as a betrayal of Moroccans and an alignment with French colonial powers. If that first narrative excoriates Moroccan society from the inside, the second takes up Paris from the outside. To write *The Butts*, Chraïbi moved to the overcrowded neighborhood of Barbès and Nanterre on the outskirts of Paris to live with and interview North African workers, largely Algerians. The setting of *The Butts* takes place mainly in these outer areas of Paris, including districts such as Genevilliers and Villejuif.

Set in the 1950s, the novel describes the end of the Franco-Algerian union between Simone, a young working-class French woman, and Yalann Waldick, an aspiring Algerian writer. The couple's lack of future is encapsulated by the imminent death of their son, Fabrice, from meningitis. The dissolution of their relationship is interlaced with depictions of the goats: anonymous and homeless North African men living in the wastelands surrounding Paris. Told mostly from Waldick's consciousness and periodically dipping into the third-person point of view, *The Butts* charts his unsuccessful attempts to find stable employment. Waldick's efforts to publicize the conditions of his North African compatriots through the publication of his manuscript, also titled *The Butts*, are upset by a French editor by the enigmatic Anglicized name Mac O'Mac, who also seduces Simone. Waldick's impotence—as a writer, as head of the household—are framed in decidedly feminine language and are contrasted with the character of his friend Raus, a hypermasculine stalwart in the North African migrant community.

Contemporaneous reviews of Chraïbi's novel were divided. Some French reviewers took the author to task for "that Arab pitfall of never leaving a detail in peace, never loosing its sight . . . to put on it at least ten i, highlighting it, framing it, that's the school of the loukoum."[17] The novel, notes another reviewer, is constructed much like a Moroccan household: one can never find a straightforward entrance, only angles into which one at times crashes.[18] Yet another review highlights that the narrative's episodes are all joggled like "dates in a bag."[19] Despite its nomination for a prestigious prize, these reviews pinpoint shortcomings of excess, nonlinearity, and disorder allegedly consistent with an Arab nature. They reinforce Pascale Casanova's remark that "Paris never took an interest in writers from its colonial territories; or, more precisely, it long despised and mistreated them as a species of extreme provincials, too similar to be celebrated as exotic foreigners but too remote to be considered worthy of interest."[20] However, many reviewers also praised *The Butts* for its ability to "spit in our face a burning prose like lava, a poetic uproar with findings as glowing as embers."[21] Claude Roy called the novel "a big topic, the life of North African workers in France written by someone who is their brother and has a real talent."[22] For Lucien Guissard, Chraïbi writes "the despair of a world that vegetates on our threshold; he makes heard the voice of the voiceless" with what Jean Prasteau called "a passionate, violent, and hard accent."[23] Among the praise, André Rousseaux specifically urges literary juries to pay attention to this book that stands out with the voice of a man and the anguish of a community.[24]

Decades later, varied reviews and analyses of *The Butts* smother the colonial question. They address instead the author's stylistic idiosyncrasies or his treatment of female characters.[25] Literary dictionaries see in *The Butts* "a novel about emigrants' misery" that chronicles the terrible living conditions of North African workers. Noted are the universal themes of immigration, such as uprootedness, nostalgia, and alienation.[26] Warning scholars against this "generalizing mode of [cultural] analysis" also found in postcolonial studies, Ali Behdad turns to *The Butts* to urge us to take into account the historical and cultural contexts that define the content and reception of "minor literature."[27] This chapter heeds Behdad's call by demonstrating Chraïbi's fictional engagement with historical debates about the assimilability of North African subjects, newspaper descriptions of Arab sectors of Paris as a hotbed of crimes, and government policies aimed at containing this chiefly male population from contact with Parisian women. *The Butts* addresses French society's refusal to recognize the colonized as an equal through running metaphors of emasculation, whereby men appear or are treated like women. Paradoxically, the narrative shows how the French justify their exclusion of Algerians by attributing to them an excess of virility that marks them as inassimilable to French society. Both sides privilege masculinity as the linchpin to access either assimilation or nationalist independence.

A Tale of Two Cities

"Algerians thrown out on the street" decried an article in the left-wing Paris newspaper *L'humanité* on February 2, 1955. Twenty-six residents are blocked access to their hotel rooms by police forces, although they paid their rent on time. The owner invoked the need to do urgent repairs, but it seems obvious, the article states, that this expulsion with no due process was made in the hope of taking back these rooms and renting them out for even more money. Ten years after the end of World War II, Paris was still short on lodgings, and North African workers were the most exposed to this precariousness. Accompanying the article is a picture of these men in baggy, worn clothes dragging a cart on which piled-up boxes threaten to fall. These homeless figures appear like relics from another century, brought as if by mistake into the modern age of the fast car. Like the migrant protagonists of Maghrebi novels, they evoke an old world strikingly at odds with a rapidly modernizing France. The Paris of Algerian fiction by Mohammed Dib, Mouloud Feraoun, and Mouloud Mammeri is a city devoid of modernity's hallmarks (cinema, cars, modern appliances, or glittering urban light). Algerian men sleep in decrepit hotel rooms or slums in the outskirts of Paris. They came to earn some money to feed their families in Algeria. After this sojourn in a hostile environment, many return home. But in *The Butts*, Algerian protagonists, changed by their experiences of Paris, settle down.

Born in a small village of Tizi-Ouzou, Algeria, Yalann Waldick, the main protagonist of *The Butts*, hid in a ship heading to France. He plotted a way to reach the motherland ever since his momentous meeting with a French priest at age ten. The man remonstrated the young shoeshine boy for his lack of desire to better himself. To his query about his future profession in ten years' time, the priest was shocked to hear that Waldick wanted to become a twenty-year-old shoeshine boy: "Just think, my child . . . if you were in France, you would already be learning Latin and Greek, and in ten years you would be a man" (123). Assured that France could provide an entirely different future for a poverty-stricken Algerian boy, Waldick shuts his shoeshine box "as one closes the door to the past" (123). The novel ends on the priest's relief at having saved a soul. This closing that regresses to Waldick's childhood after documenting his trials as an adult in Paris rings with irony as it brings the protagonist right back where he started.

Travel to France transforms Algerian natives instead into men of color. Eight years after this fateful meeting, Waldick, who cannot afford the costs required by travel agencies in Algiers, crosses the Mediterranean nestled in a tar barrel. At the welcome center, the French clerk confirms Waldick's rebirth in France as a racially marked subject when he addresses him as "bicot," a slur based from military slang that literally means "small Arab."[28] The insult powerfully names a colonial and racial boundary. Waldick opens his first door in France, one he had awaited "like a deliverance" onto "a prodigious number of Arabs" (71). Instead of France, he observes his own reification as "forty-eight pairs of Arab eyes stung him like as many swords' points. They stripped him down, picked him apart, and assessed him" (70). Foreshadowing his segregated Parisian life, this room full of men sitting on newspaper on the floor paints a prison-like space that provides no pathway to Paris's modernity.

These colonial migrants came to the metropole to work but instead find themselves locked up. Waldick and his fellow North Africans do not actually arrive in Paris the same way as do immigrants from Europe; they go through a ministry that regulates colonial subjects. The text suggests that this specific backdoor arrival results in a different trajectory for this population, for the ministry resembles a hell-like prison that smells of sulfur rather than an administrative building. By blending various terminologies about penal sentences, construction work, and the police, Chraïbi highlights the coercive and hierarchical nature of French administration. A "boss" uses his index finger like "a bayonet" in Waldick's back, leading him to an "interrogation" room where a "captain" awaits him (71–72). Another man, "the sub-sub-foreman" who takes the little money Waldick has left, has jaws that sound "like the clank of a guillotine" (72–71). Prodded and handed from one man to the other, by the time Waldick reaches the "triple chin European," he only has his shirt, pants, and shoes left. Everything else has been seized (72). This last clerk assigns him the number 302, a designation Waldick protests by announcing his proud tribal lineage: "Do you think a man from Tizi-Ouzou is nothing more than a number?" (73).

By stripping colonial migrants of their identity and treating them like criminals, these procedures also work to establish the close relationship between police surveillance and labor management for colonial subjects. Before the 1947 law that permitted Muslim natives from Algeria to come to France without a passport, they had to obtain a vast array of documentation to travel to the metropole, and work permits were required as part of their application dossiers. Exemplifying the proliferation of modern administrative tracking used on colonial migrants, a short anecdote in *The Butts* describes a wanted Algerian worker, Ahmed ben Hamed, who to avoid arrest "had fasted for a full month, and that had completely changed the structure of his face. He had held the tips of his fingers to a live coal until the digital point was cooked away. Then he changed his name from Ahmed ben Hamed to Hamed ben Ahmed" (103). Ahmed's story brings to light the blurring lines between administrative and police work, his prints having been taken on arrival to the metropole before he committed any crime. Historically, these lines merged on many occasions, including when Albert Sarrault, former minister of the colonies, became Minister of the Interior in charge of colonial migrants and hired retired policemen to help with the construction of a complex system of surveillance.[29] By 1960 about 70,000 individuals, nearly half of the Algerian population living in the Paris region, were being tracked.[30]

If colonial narratives of familial cohabitation bind French and Algerian natives through household metaphors, in *The Butts*, Algerian protagonists who made the journey to the metropole are racially and sexually segregated. The novel's title already announces their exclusion. Reminiscent of *boucs* émissaires (scapegoats), the original French title *Les boucs* denotes the banishment of a population's segment, a sacrificed group who carry away the community's faults and sins. The narrator notes, "No prison, no asylum, not even a Red Cross office would accept them" (21). Relegated to the city's impoverished margins, Algerians live in places like the slums of Nanterre, the basements of Gennevilliers, or a 180-square-foot household in Villejuif. Those who cannot secure lodging live where they can, often out of sight. To find shelter for the night, Waldick behaves "just like an animal, by relying on instinct" (94). While a group of twenty-two men inhabit a "taupinière" (molehole), an abandoned truck in the wasteland of Nanterre, others sleep in old houses about to be pulled down, and in the case of Waldick's friend and compatriot Raus, under his truck at construction sites (27, my translation). Imbued with the presence of their residents, rented lodging such as the basements of Gennevilliers are known as "the North African cellars" (137, my translation). These underground sites that cram sixty people in are under the control of the sleep salesmen who unscrupulously capitalize on the postwar shortage of lodging to exploit vulnerable North African populations, renting them unlivable spaces for exorbitant sums of money. With "no air and no lights," residents could only access these sites by crawling on all fours and once there cannot even stand (94). According to Michael Goebel, even during the interwar period, "the starkest example of close-knit enclaves was that of North Africans . . . no other immigrant group lived in such pitiful

Arab children residing in La Folie, the largest slum in Nanterre (© Monique Hervo, Bibliothèque de documentation internationale contemporaine, MHC)

and vile conditions."[31] Chraïbi's repeated allusions to the bestiary suggest the failure of the metropole to open itself to colonial subjects and guarantee them dignity. While Waldick assumed Paris would make him a man, the city downgrades him and his compatriots to the realm of animals.

This spatial cartography of Paris with its financial, legal, and juridical powers and well-to-do populations concentrated at the center of the city and its colonial labor force located by design at the periphery is reminiscent of Frantz Fanon's depiction of the "compartmentalized world" of the French colonized cities. The European sector is "built to last, all stone and steel. It's a sector of lights and paved roads . . . where the streets are clean and smooth, without a pothole, without a stone . . . a sated, sluggish sector, its belly is permanently full of good things . . . a white folks' sector, a sector of foreigners."[32] In contrast, the colonized's sector is "a disreputable place inhabited by disreputable people. You are born anywhere, anyhow. You die anywhere, from anything. It's a world with no space, people are piled one on top of the other . . . [it is] a sector on its knees. . . . It's a sector of niggers, a sector of towelheads."[33] The portrayal of Paris in *The Butts* uncovers a metropolitan equivalent to the highly segregated realities of French Algeria, which the colonial metaphor of cohabitation obscures.

Paris itself seems to delay Algerian natives' entrance into the republic of opportunities, as these men move through migration, employment, and residential doors leading them back to where they first started, much like the plot's regressive itinerary to Waldick's childhood. Paris is a space of social immobility for Algerians. This immobility is paradoxically made visible through their endless circulation in search of stable housing and employment. They do not live in as much as they pass through the wastelands of Nanterre and the dingy basements of Gennevilliers. They travel through boats, immigration and work agencies, prisons, hospitals, and airports. These transitory sites continually open up onto a colonial Paris, a parallel society in which they are trapped.

With the segregation of Algerian bachelor communities, Chraïbi calls to mind a sort of harem-like Paris, where natives are kept captive. Although he notes the utter poverty and exploitation of these men, he lingers most on the aspect of racial segregation. Kept apart, these men have only one another for company. "They had no wives or any ties to the area: nothing more than a shack made of flimsy black boards and . . . cots that they avoided like the plague. They knew very well that sooner or later every night society forced them back among Arabs, stripped bare in front of one another like a group of castaways on a raft" (92–93). Condensed in this metaphor of the castaways on a raft is the utter isolation brought forth by migration and segregation, as well as the shame of being continually exposed to each other's gaze. French author Claire Etcherelli, in her celebrated novel *Elise ou la vraie vie* (*Elise or the Real Life*) (1966), set in Paris, also relies on an image of water to convey Algerian men's sequestration. Arezki, an Algerian worker at the Renault car factory, explains his living situation: "we argue, we hold grudges, we help each other like men swimming in the same fish tank denied privacy, sleeping side by side, washing in front of each other."[34] In the metropole, these men find themselves forced into undesired intimacies with one another.

The title *The Butts*, or male goats, also calls attention to an animal known for its excessive libido—a symbol of lust that corresponds to depictions of North Africans in the Paris newspapers after World War II (discussed later). The narrative discredits the stereotypes of the oversexed Arab by associating Algerian male migration to the capital with the loss of sexual drive. Upon arrival to Paris, clerks take everything from Waldick, including his "puberty" (72). In *La plus haute des solitudes* (*The Highest of Solitudes*), a 1977 book based on a doctoral thesis in social psychiatry, Moroccan writer Tahar Ben Jelloun studied the close relationship between migration and male impotence. For Ben Jelloun, migration to France dehumanized Maghrebi workers, because the metropole "only wants their labor, the rest, no one cares. . . . Capitalism wants anonymous men (abstract ones), emptied of their desires . . . brutish labor force, with no heart, no testicles, no desire, no family, in sum almost not a man."[35] Chraïbi equally indicts the strict interest in numbers: migration control, serial numbers, and profit margins. There is no room for men of flesh, for their struggles or aspirations. Waldick satirizes that for the 300,000 North Africans in France, "if you count sixty kilos per Arab, you end up with some 20,000 tons of suffering" (46). This disturbing market calculation condemns the exploitation of this population as expendable labor and illuminates the interdependence between the "triple-chinned" clerk and the stripped and undernourished colonized subject.

Debunking the myth of Franco-Algerian domestic bliss further, the narrative shows that the presence of Algerian natives in Paris corresponds to their expropriation from their land on the other side of the Mediterranean. During Waldick's brief encounter with a child peanut vendor in Paris, the latter confides that he sends money to his father, who has "no land anymore, no arm anymore, no faith to keep him going" (64). *The Butts* intimates that such expropriation benefits the French directly. In a previous scene, Waldick visits an editor and sees that his house is full of "oriental vases, Arab furniture, rugs or clusters of dates," like "a warehouse of furniture and pottery" (63, 62). Waldick had at first mistaken the line of Arab men in Mac O'Mac's hallway for furniture movers, since each carried something, but he soon realizes these men were "sons of Arab villages" here to seek the French man's help with their "Gestapo dossiers under their arms, their papers of expropriations" (63, 62). Mac O'Mac, a self-proclaimed missionary, sees his work with these men as charity, but for Waldick he is somebody who clearly profits from their forced displacement. The word "Gestapo" brings to mind yet another sinister era when some Parisians benefited from the expropriation of other marked subjects.

The scene that follows this visit to the editor plays on readers' expectations that Waldick would return to Algeria disillusioned, which he does. But the narrative skips his homecoming and picks up instead with Waldick's return to Paris. Unlike his predecessors, Chraïbi is not interested in the Algerian migrant's return nor in framing Paris as a stage in the protagonist's development. Paris may be "the mirage of the North" in *The Butts*, but it is also a catalyst in the formation of a new collective identity shaped by displacement and racial exclusion (55). Chraïbi reappropriates the slur "Bicot" to equate it with a racialized experience of destitution in the metropole. "Bicot" is part of an array of French insults that refer to North Africans in the novel, including *crouillat* (Arabic for "brother"), *sidi* (Arabic for "my lord"), *Noraf* (short for "Nord-Africains"), and *Ahmed* (a widespread Arabic name). Signaling Algerian difference from the French, Chraïbi puts a special emphasis on "Bicot" by capitalizing the word as if it were a person's name. Used as a noun, "Bicot" signals how the French view

North Africans as inferior or it transforms the neutral meaning of nouns, denoting the abnormal. For instance, a Bicot's stomach can digest anything, including rats (14, 17 in original text). Bicot also marks a threshold between acceptable and primitive behavior.

But Bicot signifies more than a boundary between the normative and the abject. It is a term of recognition. Chraïbi's North African protagonists use it to refer to each other, taking back a term used to belittle them and reinvesting it with new meaning. Like the racially evocative image of Waldick's Mediterranean crossing to France in a tar barrel, North Africans discover they are marked men in Paris. The resignified term "Bicot" not only expresses a new consciousness shaped by disenfranchisement; it layers Fanon's notion of the man of color's split vision with additional intricacy. Whereas the Algerian native may view himself through two frames of reference—a French and native one—the Algerian migrant in Paris develops a third frame of reference that distinguishes him from Algerian natives at home. The Bicots are not like Algerians at home "who still have faith" in France, "poor dumb Arabs" and whom "the mirage of Europe eats like a tapeworm" (75, 77, 60). Bicots are men profoundly disillusioned with the promise of migration (26). Upon arrival, Waldick attempted to affirm his tribal identity as a man from Tizi-Ouzou, but after several years in Paris he claims to be neither Algerian nor French. In the epilogue, this Bicot affiliation is expanded to include Isabelle, a skin-and-bones French woman. As such, this racial designation becomes a symbol of the impoverished margins.

Chraïbi turned to Algerians' living conditions as a means to explore Paris's color line. *The Butts* identifies colonial Paris as a dehumanizing site. Through the depictions of a coercive French administration that closely monitors colonial migrants and inhabitable lodgings, the novel challenges the myth of blissful cohabitation between the French and the Algerians. Driven from their native lands by property confiscation and subsequent famine, they become disillusioned by a migration that alters or stifles their libido and turns them into goats: anonymous and interchangeable. But for all its virulent indictment of Algerian exclusion, this panoramic vision of immigration in the Paris margins gives an impression of detachment, a sort of long view of anonymous men and their inability to secure lodging, employment, or even sympathy. The dearth of fully drawn characters reproduces the idea of these men as identical. As such it facilitates what the narrator decried as "a heavy screen" through which the French see Arabs, a perspective marked by distance, as if "they have flown over them as one flies over a city, high above, comfortably fastened into a seat, their stomach full" (15, 89). Though *The Butts* offers a bird's-eye view of colonial Paris that surveys Arab quarters in Gennevilliers and Nanterre, it also offers a close-up view of a Franco-Algerian couple's dissolution. Looking through both ends of the telescope, the narrative zooms in onto a tiny household of Villejuif. This focus on one Franco-Algerian dwelling provides the novel with an anchoring point, some narrative unity, key characters, and a sustained critique of colonial domesticity that reveals deep French anxieties about racial and cultural borders.

Colonial Mixing

Interracial romances between colonial male subjects and French women in Paris were an unintended consequence of the importation of a colonial male workforce. In Algeria, mixed marriages were "statistically insignificant" and deplored by settlers and administrators,[36] but with the influx of a predominantly male Algerian workforce in the metropolis after World War II, interracial intimacy grew quickly. In 1952 the Ministry of Public Health and Population conducted a survey that estimated 3,500 Algerian-European couples (married and not) resided in France.[37] By 1954 the national institute of demographic studies (L'institut national d'études démographiques, or INED) estimated these couples at 6,000.[38] Even during the Algerian War, when some Algerian nationalists virulently argued against mixed unions, a sign of Western assimilation, and in favor of "patriotic marriages," Franco-Algerian unions were common among nationalist leaders and workers.[39]

Several works by Maghrebi and French authors written in the 1950s and 1960s register French public and state opposition to these *unions mixtes*. Albert Memmi's *Agar* focuses on the marriage of a Jewish-Tunisian student and a French Catholic student who met in Paris and return to Tunis to live. They represent a microcosm of colonial friction. As Memmi explained later, "his hopes then rested on the 'couple,' which still seem to me the most solid happiness of man and perhaps the only real answer to solitude. But I discovered that the couple is not an isolated entity, a forgotten oasis of light in the middle of the world; on the contrary, the whole world is within the couple."[40] Mouloud Feraoun's migration novel set in the 1920s, *Land and Blood* (1953), focuses less on the pervasiveness of colonial tensions that invade the private sphere of the couple. Nonetheless, it draws a pretty damning view of the interracial romance as a destabilizing force of French and Algerian so-called cultural integrity. When he stops sending remittances, protagonist Amer ou Kaci breaks his Algerian family's expectations and turns his mother into a pauper. Through word of mouth, the family hears he fell in love with Marie, a French woman with whom he is "en ménage" in a third-rate hotel in Barbès, Paris (19).[41] But in Paris Amer feels like a "foreigner," therefore the couple decides to leave for Algeria (49). In his Kabylia village, it is Marie's turn to become the foreigner, the *tharoumith* despised by all for her different mores and behavior. She reflects that "she was nowhere at home, neither with the French nor with the Kabyles.

It seems to her that they formed a strange and ridiculous couple, that with her he had lost his Kabyle traits and that she too lost those of the French. As a result they seemed diminished and awkward" (96). Marie is not the only one to regret the partnership; soon after her arrival in Algeria, a French administrator receives the pair with "an ironic politeness that was meant to convey all the indecency of their union" (96). While Marie's married life with Amer ou Kaci deviates from alarmist warnings disseminated by metropolitan feminists about Arab men locking French wives in harems on their return to Algeria, the narrative characterizes it as a life of profound solitude.

In Mouloud Mammeri's *The Sleep of the Just* (1955), romance with Parisian women functions as an opium, a way to disengage and soften the harsh reality of second-class citizenship, or a weapon to wield at one's enemy, to challenge the colonial line. Arezki, a twenty-six-year-old Algerian man educated in French schools in the colony, fought with the French army against Nazi occupation but became disillusioned with the racist treatment of nonwhite soldiers, served last at meals. In Paris, the despairing young man "turned to girls to forget. . . . The girls he courted and knew came from all backgrounds . . . he had them enter through the window. His land lady, though shortsighted and hard of hearing, would shriek as soon as she saw one enter" (175). For all the exhilaration of the proscribed romance, it was with another French woman he met during the war that Arezki developed a deep emotional connection. After his arrest in Algeria for militant activism, Arezki, seeking to anger one of the French guards, slips him one of her intimate letters. It has the desired effect of making the guard livid with anger as he calls its author "insane" (244–45). For Mammeri, the various portrayals of the Franco-Algerian romance serve to dramatize Algerian exclusion.

Claire Etcherelli's *Elise or the Real Life* focuses entirely on an interracial romance that blossomed between Elise, a naïve young French Bordelaise hopeful to start a new life in Paris, and Arezki, a taciturn and older Algerian man whom she meets at work in the dirty and hazardous Renault automobile factory. Through the lens of the romance, Etcherelli uncovers the horrendous living conditions of North African migrant workers in 1958 Paris and their subjection to police raids and disappearances during the Algerian War. Paris appears to the couple as an "immense trapped boulevard where they advanced with pathetic precautions" (183). During a police raid in La Goutte d'or, an Arab neighborhood, the pair is discovered in Arezki's squalid bedroom. The officers humiliate both of them, one noting to his colleague: "You call these women?" (218). Another orders Arezki to strip, placing his gun close to his mouth, then his stomach, while a colleague unzips the man's pants and takes off his briefs, laughing. Once the stripping is over and the police are gone, a deflated Arezki asks Elise to leave (217–18). Female coworkers also mock Elise. They rename her Aïcha, a popular Arabic name, and would clap their hands singing "Allah, Allah!" when she entered the changing room (237–38). The novel ends with Arezki's disappearance during a police raid, leaving Elise with no answer as to whether he is alive or dead, in a detention camp somewhere in the metropole, or in prison in Algeria, whether their separation is temporary or permanent.

In these heterosexual romances, readers witness the hostility with which Franco-Algerian couples are met, especially when they involve Algerian men. While the metaphor of interracial desire served to signify harmonious cohabitation, consensual adventure, and reciprocal affection of France and Algeria, the romances-in-the-flesh mark the unraveling of French integrity and betray a profound rejection of Algerian natives, met with the castrating force of the state and the public. Men from the Orient are here associated with a primitive virility, unregulated and unbridled, that must be contained to maintain social order. These scenarios cast the Algerian man as a threat to white women and the family. He is perceived as the "envious man," who dreams of "sleeping in [the colonizer's] bed, preferably with his wife."[42] While these novels tend to underscore the incommensurable gap between the French and Algerians, *The Butts* delves deeper into ideas of the primitive ascribed to Algerian natives and discloses the French woman's assigned role in maintaining imperial and national borders.

In *The Butts*, colonization and the accelerated importation of Algerian migrant workers to the metropole provide the conditions for the protagonists' initial attraction. Waldick finds in Simone's "human eyes" recognition of himself and by extension of North Africans as equal(s) (46). His first words to Simone are for the 300,000 North Africans living in France and his self-assigned role as a literate man to translate their misery and despair (46). Simone's ability to be moved by their plight signals to Waldick the possibility of an alliance between North African and the French, here in the form of a romance. But four years of common life in a racist environment, punctuated by Waldick's jail sentences or unemployment, and their child's meningitis, have wrecked the household, blocking its horizon with the "rocks and cement of hatred" (17).

The narrative suggests colonialism's transgressing effect on the family, leading to the couple's reversal of normative gender roles. Condemned to the domestic sphere by employers who perceive him as an undesirable foreigner, Waldick lives in Simone's modest home in a lost corner of Villejuif on the periphery of Paris. In turn, because he is economically feminized (forced domestic isolation combined with inactivity), Waldick's skin is "so apathetic that the hair has refused, physiologically, to grow on it for a long, long time" (13). Mirroring his receding virility, Waldick reflects that "he was like that for years. Fearful and cowardly" (41). If Waldick's body turns soft, Simone's body becomes "stiff as a board," her "back straightened and her eyes set," "more and more hardened" (45, 51, 52). For Waldick, Simone's transformation is a result of their fateful meeting, which lured her out of the "straight path of respectability and stability" (49).

At odds with Waldick's loss of virility, French neighbors give in to Orientalist fantasies of North African men driven by an unchecked libido that leads to polygamy, incest, or homosexuality as well as an irrational jealousy that turns to violence toward their lovers. In the metropole, this uncontrolled sexual drive leads to imagined lewd acts. Simone's neighbors know nothing of Waldick, yet they obstinately attempt to convince her to leave him, warning her "one day that North African will kill you, dear" (15). Josepha, the elder neighbor whose name evokes a foreign origin, declares to Simone: "we will save you in spite of yourself from this mad man" (111). For this elderly lady, the howling sounds heard at night can only be attributed to the couple's "obscenities," which Simone accepts only because she must be "going crazy" (163, my translation; 111). Waldick, or "the Arab" as Josepha refers to him, is a primitive whose pathologies (madness, sexual bestiality) threaten the neighborhood's respectability. In this hostile environment, Waldick imagines that Simone could end their relationship simply by going to the neighbors. They would do the rest: "yes my dear do sit down and calm yourself just where is this Arab? We must call the Police right away" (52). In this imagined scene, the script is already written: Arab man, French woman, and the police. It is worth noting here that Simone's voice is absent, just like her testimony about leaving Waldick, as if they were unnecessary. The neighbors' ideas about North African masculinity are not theirs alone; they speak to a broader social construction of this population over time.

While the French called on men from their colonies to come fight for France and work in her factories, few anticipated the sexual ramifications of a principally male colonial workforce. As early as World War I, the general population would protest the fact that "colonial men had access to French women in metropolitan brothels."[43] The army opposed any form of interracial intimacy, whether it involved prostitutes or not because such contact supposedly tainted France's reputation as a civilizing force.[44] Some observers noted that white women's sexual reification for the benefit of colonial men would only tarnish French standing in the colonies, where "European prestige depended on the presence of virtuous and inaccessible white women."[45] As a result, even in the domain of sex work, North Africans were treated differently—either refused entrance to brothels or directed to a separate entrance that led to separate bars and stairways to separate rooms in the "maisons d'abbatage" (slaughterhouses) where the quick exchanges were labeled by an opponent "Taylorized coitus" and "conveyor belt sex."[46] However, Franco-Algerian intimacy was not limited to the domain of sex work. In the 1930s, numerous French feminists such as Marcelle Legrand-Falco, an antiprostitution advocate, and Maria Vérone wrote articles warning French women against romances with North Africans. Legrand-Falco alerted women readers that North African students would "revert to their primitive mentality" on their return to their native land and the poor innocent French women would get "locked up in a harem."[47] Away from French law and order, they would be turned into white slaves, beaten, forced into polygamy, and despised by their husband's relatives. Supporting the same goal of stamping out miscegenation in the metropole, the French state favored Algerian family reunification, while city administrators called for the construction of single-sex dormitories for male migrants.[48]

The French feminist script constructs white women at risk in Algeria. By locating the Franco-Algerian union in Paris, Chraïbi reverses this association of primitivism with colonized men and associates it instead with the metropole. In her home country, neither Simone nor her mixed family are safe. Ultimately, she has to choose between saving herself or joining her partner and son in their existence walled off by French racial hatred.

Author Ben Jelloun remarks that after World War II, no one played a role as significant as the press in constructing North Africans as sexual perpetrators "who can only be satisfied through violence, perversity, and crime."[49] Though Algerians represented only 1 percent (at most) of the Parisian population, their overwhelming presence in the news media made them some of the most feared residents in the city. Historian Neil MacMaster revealed that such representations preceded the Algerian War and that the Paris Prefect of Police contributed to such characterizations, leading to a government inquiry, which found his statements about North African crime unfounded.[50] With the Franco-Algerian war, articles in newspapers such as *L'Humanité* would call into question these stereotypes and underscore police and army violence against Algerians in Paris and Algeria, but these were drowned under the crushing weight of right-wing popular press newspapers such as *L'Aurore*, *Le Parisien*, and *Le Figaro* that drew on sensational crimes to construct a portrait of North African colonial migrants as rapists and molesters on the loose. *Le Figaro* carried the following headline: "Abandoned by his girlfriend, a North African stabs her" (1955). Though France did not legally prohibit unions across colonial lines, the media's reiterated warning against North African men worked to socially regulate interracial contact and withhold sympathy toward this population.

The Butts resorts to the grotesque to challenge this perception of Arab male menace that conflates the Arab and the penis. Depictions of North African

men take phallic shapes associated with weapons. According to Susan Corey's
definition, "the grotesque is an aesthetic form that works through exaggeration,
distortion, contradiction, disorder, and shock to disrupt a sense of normalcy."[51]
In one scene, Raus is described as "hard . . . straight and dry and hungry as his
whip" (29). In others, he carries a knife, or a billy club. The emphasis on these
phallic objects assigned to a man who is already perceived as overly belligerent
signals a surplus of virility. This hypervirility becomes a threat to the institution
of family and its expectations of monogamy. To alleviate the absence of sexual
partners for North African men in the metropole, Raus asks Waldick to let him
swap places with him. He entreats, "even Simone would not know the difference if I took your place in bed some night" (34). Although Waldick rejects this
indecent proposition, a later and strange scene mediated through his drugged
perspective describes Raus with "teeth yellow and sharp," attacking Simone
and who, with two "knife strokes," makes her shorts slide to the ground (60). A
remorseful Raus later confides to Waldick that despite appearances, he did not
"take advantage" of Simone. This confirmed aggression muddies Chraïbi's
condemnation of racial stereotypes about Arab masculinity, but this plotline is
left unresolved.

The narrative instead emphasizes the white woman's complicity with colonial forces. Simone aligns with colonial powers by ultimately redrawing the
strict separation between the races. Before his release from jail, Simone visits
Waldick and hitchhikes her way to editor Mac O'Mac to offer him Waldick's
manuscript and herself. Chraïbi resorts to the farcical alliterative name, which
denotes sexual pleasure: Mac Oh Mac. Simone's affair reestablishes the colonial
and gender conventions her romance with an Algerian had first disrupted.
Waldick imagines Mac O'Mac's words in his "hunting villa": "but my dear, our
mission is to civilize and I can't allow an Arab to barbarize a representative of
the French people" (49). In this scenario, Simone has perverted the social order,
mistaken her role as a French individual by accepting living with a colonial
subject, as if he were an equal. She also crosses gender and bourgeois aspirations
by being the sole provider of her mixed family.

Cheated on, Waldick sees himself as deprived of his family, the French man
having reestablished control over the household. Waldick again imagines Mac
O'Mac's words to Simone: "You don't feed an Arab, even if he is an intellectual, with words of love, concepts of love, of a home and family, with expressions
he has never heard before, words that no one knows in the mountains of Algeria"
(50). The sacredness of family based on values of love and belonging allegedly
clash with understandings of family based on subjugation and coercion supposedly prevalent in Algeria. As the author of a highly regarded novel titled "the
holy family," the content of which is never discussed, Mac O'Mac's seduction

reveals the reifying role he assigns Simone in his bourgeois household, a prized commodity among the rare collection of "strange-looking vases" he caresses as he gives her a tour of his second house (84). A contrite Simone later confesses to Waldick that by the end of the tour she was sitting on Mac O'Mac's laps and saw in his eyes "a mirror in which I could see myself. Except that it was not my real image. In it I saw that Simone who was still a little girl, partial to fairy tales and to epics" (86). There is room for Simone in Mac O'Mac's life, only if she accepts the role of the innocent child, a vulnerable and admiring dependent. In the editor's home, Simone feels as if "[she] had not met an Arab . . . had never gone hungry or been cold or felt misery in [her] soul. [She] had never been belittled. [She] had never gone outside [her] little circle. [She] was that little ten-year-old" (86). She juggles between the limited options of abject poverty or becoming a commodity in Mac O'Mac's household. In the end, she renounces the journey back to girlhood. Chraïbi's metaphor about infancy traces overlaps in nationalist and imperial discourses that depict white women and colonial subjects in need of the guidance, authority, and protection of white men.

The French editor's view of domesticity does not include Waldick, except on an abstract level. After Mac O' Mac drives back Simone, who had spent the night with him, he enters the couple's house, acting indeed as if he were the host, indicating for Waldick to close the door, and to sit in a chair, treating him as if "[he were] no more than a guest in [his] own house" (26). The editor also questions Waldick's writing skills and stresses in particular his failure to adhere to representations of colonial domesticity. He asserts that North Africans and the French are kinfolk: "members of a family are not made to devour one another. Underneath all anger there are usually good intentions, and all hatred is definitely a misunderstanding" (26). This description of colonial relationship unifies the French and Algerians as a family, yet it calls attention to some relatives' cannibalistic impulses. But it is not clear here who consumes whom and who is absorbed. What is clear is that the editor demotes North Africans' anger to a misunderstanding, trivializing their exclusion, and instead promotes French lofty intentions. To maintain the benevolent façade of colonial domesticity, Mac O'Mac paradoxically resorts to threats, warning Waldick that "there's only a fine line between indignation and deportation" (38, my translation). His refusal to publish Waldick's book is thus also figured in terms of national security.

Chraïbi wrote this novel following numerous French debates about the role of colonial migrants and European immigrants in France and the need to balance repopulation and the construction of a modern nation. Which population best qualifies for the so-called racial grafting? For Chraïbi, the arrival of the French in Algeria and the Algerians in France constitute "une mauvaise greffe" (a failed grafting, 53). Though European immigrants may fare better, their integration is not guaranteed. The narrative suggests that the French consider both colonial migrants and European immigrants as poor substitute for the Gallic population. They are revoked from their roles as workers, lovers, or spouse as soon as a French person becomes available. This is the case of Madeleine, Mac O'Mac's wife, who though renamed after a sweet French cake has a thick accent that betrays her Portuguese origin. The first night Mac O'Mac meets and seduces Simone, he announces that "the next morning he would begin divorce proceedings" (85). This unstable position may account for Josepha's desire to construct the line separating Simone from North African subjects in their working-class neighborhood, lest she too be lumped with the *indésirables*.

The dissolution of the couple and household serves as a microcosm for understanding how men of color were perceived as a threat to the French family unit. Preceding the breakup of the romance, a domestic scene takes the form of an interrogation, aligning the private realm with that of the colonial adminis-tration and establishing the absence of a neutral space for colonial interactions. After Simone's affair with the editor, the house is under siege for "four days and four nights" (51). While interrogating Simone, Waldick switches the lights on and off, on and off, until "she smelled of fear" (43). It is worth noting that in an earlier scene the olfactory sense divided the couple along the lines of victims and aggressor, as Simone notes that Waldick "smelled like a savage" (19, my translation). Now his prisoner, she is force fed. In a reversal of power dynamic, the siege ends when the interrogated throws out her persecutor for good. When Waldick attempts to come back to patch things up, he sees Simone armed with a mop and bleach, actively cleaning her house white. Revealingly, cleanliness reappears as a metaphor to discuss the end of the romance and Simone's return to her role of housewife. Waldick realizes that he is "suddenly a stranger: we lived together for a long time, but black soap is a good detergent" (84, my trans-lation). The focus on bleach and whitening "good detergent" evoke the presence of colonial subjects as a form of contamination, the traces of which can be erased as if no interracial intimacy or shared residency ever took place.

Masculinity and Assimilation

Whether Chraïbi addresses the surveillance and segregation of Algerian workers in Paris or the failed romance of Waldick and Simone, he is dramatizing France's refusal to assimilate colonized subjects. A cornerstone of French colonialism was the promise of natives' eventual assimilation into twentieth-century moder-nity. The policy of assimilation aimed to propagate French language, mores, and civilization through education and alleviate poverty. Many French-educated natives were in favor of assimilation, because it provided a slim chance of climbing the social ladder. In theory, natives could submit individual requests for access to the rights of French citizens if they relinquished their personal status as Muslims. In practice, only 6,000 Algerian natives accessed naturalization during the entire colonial period.[52] Paris may have freed colonial migrants from the strict *codes indigènes* and offered them close contact with a politicized French working class, but it also established one of the most sophisticated systems of surveillance to keep track of them and their potential revolutionary organizing. In *The Butts* and other Maghrebi novels, Paris is an extension of the colony, where residents believe the indigènes to be racially inferior and inassimilable to the republic. Waldick and Raus, the assimilated intellectual and the common man, personify the dual failure of the assimilation policy. Assimilation here is the endlessly deferred promise of equality. Rather than being a pathway, for Chraïbi French education is a roadblock to independence. It renders him impotent and lethargic, while illiteracy seemingly protects Raus from an inferiority complex and self-absorption. The novel demonstrates that the two men's assimilation (or lack thereof) to French culture is riddled with anxiety about their masculine and nationalist identities.

Encapsulating the endless postponement of North Africans' assimilation, colonial Paris is characterized by temporal stasis. Waldick is always waiting, whether it is for Simone to come home, for his son to recover, or for his manuscript to be published. By the end of the novel, his potential as a husband, father, and writer is never realized. He remains at an early stage of development, to which North African men seem condemned. Orientalists have described the need to wake up Arabs from their "torpor" and "long sleep," and "goading" them to catch up with European modernity.[53] Assimilation thus refers to two distinct discourses: progress and barbarism. Frantz Fanon's 1960s writings on French colonialism in Algeria help us understand how colonial discourse about progress is embedded with implicit ideas about retardation. Fanon relates that "the final aim of colonization was to convince the indigenous population it would save them from darkness. The result was to hammer into the heads of the indigenous population that if the colonist were to leave they would regress into barbarism, degradation, and bestiality."[54] As a result, for Fanon, colonization relied on the colonized's tacit acknowledgment of his savagery. Colonial forces then ascribed themselves the duty not so much to provide for the colonized but to contain their baseness: "At the level of the unconscious, therefore, colonialism was not seeking to be perceived as a sweet, kindhearted mother who protects her child from a hostile environment but as a mother who constantly prevents her basically perverse child from committing suicide or giving free rein to its malevolent instincts. The colonial mother is protecting the child from itself, from its ego, its physiology, its biology, and its ontological misfortune."[55]

Seemingly doomed, this mother–child relationship denotes the adult's endless burden and the child's inability to escape its degenerate nature. Integral to colonial discourse, assimilation is thus partly constituted by the figure of the primitive and his doomed evolution.

By transporting readers to a colonial Paris, where North African natives struggle to make ends meet, Chraïbi emphasizes a primitive existence that is circumstantial rather than ontological. As one clerk at the welcome center warns Waldick: "There is no work. No lodging. No help. No fraternity. There are only copper tags and forms to fill out unemployment cards and *promises*. Nothing else" (78, emphasis added). His statement that indicates the impossible assimilation of North Africans invokes dire conditions that block their progress. The omniscient narrator, however, tempers this view with damning allegations about Arab passivity. He observes that they "seemed made for waiting. . . . their very substance was a succession of waits. They understood this very well. They had never rebelled, they had no idea of rebellion" (22). This essentialist characterization shifts the blame for North Africans' arrested development partly to them for accepting conditions that degrade them and thus unwittingly maintaining the colonial order.

Unlike Raus and other illiterate compatriots, educated Waldick has a sophisticated understanding of colonial history, but this knowledge translates into self-contempt. The names of the main protagonists seem to evoke their respective relationship to French culture. In Arabic, "Yalann Waldick" is a popular insult that literally means "I curse your parents." Each time Waldick is addressed, his parental lineage is repudiated. While he is more versed in a French cultural lineage, including military history, art, and literature, he feels neither recognized by the French nor financially able to further his education. In a highly symbolic gesture, he has to sell his prized French dictionary to make ends meet. Rejected as an author by Mac O'Mac, Waldick imagines that the editor saw his writing as either an "attempt to impose the Orient in Europe" or as the amateurish labor of "pseudo-intellectual from another continent," who might "handle our language fairly well" but "our history, the efforts of two millennia of Frenchmen, accumulated drop by drop, idea by idea, life by life, and our institutions that have grown one out of the other, all of that is foreign to him. He is not the end product, as we . . . are" (48). Waldick imagines his writing career blocked by an exclusive definition of Frenchness, something one cannot acquire simply through knowledge, but is given "drop by drop" and "life after life" as a birthright. Corroborating this racialized notion of culture, the French consider him and his fellowmen barbarians.

In *The Butts*, we are reminded of the clichéd educated or cultural hybrid, known as the *assimilé* in the metropole (or the *évolué* in the colony), painted in other Maghrebi novels as rejected by both the French and the natives (despite the fact that he or she identifies with both).[56] Prone to a brooding passivity, Waldick tends to intellectualize the experiences of North Africans, but neither Mac O'Mac nor his compatriots value his effort. Though he seeks to represent other North Africans, these migrants "have always considered [him] a stranger, a case apart" (61). Revealingly, Waldick writes in French for a French audience on the plight of North Africans so as to "redeem" their image (46). He believes that as an educated man reading and speaking French, he has a duty to salvage the "image" of North Africans, but they refuse to confide in him, to speak their shame. Chraïbi seems to interrogate his own role as a mouthpiece for colonial subjects and the pen's ability to bring about change, while at the same time lashing at those arrogant French specialists of the North African question. After his editor's double betrayal, Waldick bitterly realizes that his status as colonial subject disqualifies him from speaking altogether. This fictional silencing calls to mind the widespread press censorship throughout France that accompanied the 1955 state of emergency in Algerian provinces.

The novel indirectly returns to the issue of stifled voices through the colonial gaze that filters Waldick's thoughts, undermining his intellectual autonomy. The Fanonian split gaze, that is, the colonized's internalization of the colonizer's gaze, prevents Waldick from accessing his own thoughts and perspective: "He seemed dehumanized speaking in third person, with such lucidity that he wondered if that dehumanization were not more of a splitting of personality" (70). Certainly, what we know of Waldick as Simone's lover, as an aspiring writer, or even as a departed is mediated through Mac O'Mac's alleged vision. In one of the many conversations Waldick imagines occurred between Mac O'Mac and Simone, the editor highlights the most damning facts about Waldick as a sort of parasite who latched onto Simone soon after his exit from jail, depleting all of her savings in exchange for promises. Deciding to end his life after Simone threw him out of the house, Waldick swallows sedatives while imagining Mac O'Mac's one-sentence obituary at his funeral: "a North African named Waldick had existed, had wanted to play Gandhi or Tarzan in Europe, and had ended up swallowing 5 grams of sleeping pills" (56). The imagined tribute marks the *décalage* between his leadership aspiration and the French ridicule of his hopes of becoming an anticolonial leader who would usher in North African liberation. Instead of resistance and anticolonial power, Gandhi is reread as Tarzan, a man out of place, a man who belongs to the jungle, someone who is only a rung above animals.

Put to doubt is the bicultural legitimacy as an assimilé. There is no fusion between the Western and Arab sides, no acknowledgment of hybridity, just like in the colonial mind-set about assimilation that calls for the erasure of one culture for another. Waldick describes the encounter of his Arab and French cultural sides through the language of disease: "For ten years now my brain, my Arab brain thinking in Arabic, has been grinding away at European concepts, in such an absurd way it transforms them into gall and even the brain gets sick from it" (39). The disease may stem from the imperative to deny or repress cultural difference. Unlike his friend, Raus has no interest in French culture or in seeking recognition from the French. His attention and concerns are turned toward Paris's North African community, which he nourishes, at times using brutish force and violence. The contrast between Raus and Waldick verges on an association of masculinity with cultural authenticity that resembles Mac O'Mac's colonial logics about racial purity. In juxtaposing the assimilé's impotence to act and the common man's productive action, the narrative correlates virility with agency.

In a context of decolonization across the Maghreb, Chraïbi privileges Raus as a masculine ideal representing values of forceful action and communal sacrifice. The name "Raus," as Waldick explains, refers to "a simple negation, a simple ejection" (46–47). Literally, "Raus" also means "horse manure," possibly a designation that conveys Raus's depreciated value as a former peasant and colonized subject in industrial France, or it may denote the character's ability to feed his community and enable it to grow. Raus stands out as impervious to his hostile Paris environment. Waldick is struck upon meeting him that "he was the first Arab [he] had seen smile since he left Bône" (96). He comes to envy this man with "four members, 32 teeth, and insides and crane to digest anything, anywhere, any time" (44). When we first meet him, Raus had punched a butcher to steal meat to celebrate Waldick's release from jail. For the French, this uneducated man represents the epitome of the uncivilized, their antithesis. Mac O'Mac calls him a "brute," even before Raus utters a word, and Simone hates him with a passion. But Raus would "smile . . . as if all he just heard and seen had no importance at all" (30). Among North Africans, he is known for his "fierce love" (75, my translation). In contrast to Waldick's lack of agency, Raus provides food and shelter for his compatriots and saves the lives of Waldick and his son. Raus's pragmatism makes him fitter for survival, while his generosity and concerns for his fellow men designate him a leader in the community.

Chraïbi's anticolonial critique is inseparable from male supremacy. While he powerfully interrogates French colonial and bourgeois logic that reify men of color and French women, he reinforces patriarchal logic with his idealization of Raus. The juxtaposition between these two men demonstrates how Waldick's education renders him impotent to act, because his anger turns inward in tortuous self-reflection about his exclusion. For instance, he intellectualizes the presence of a stray famished cat in his home, reflecting that the animal is the mirror image of the colonial subject who has been fed by promises until his bones poke out. As a result of his identification with the animal, Waldick provides it with dried peas and caresses, attention he does not share with his own son. In contrast, Raus "had often kicked" the cat's stomach, violently demarcating the line between man and animal (15). Raus also questions the utility of intellec-tualizing North Africans' experiences. Waldick's interest in French literature and history and Raus's disdain for them mark divergent priorities. In a discus-sion with Waldick, Raus admits that he does not know who Marshal Armand-Jacques Leroy de Saint-Arnaud was, adding: "Go on with your intellectual stuff. I keep my projects on a level I can understand: I want enough to eat to keep alive tomorrow" (38).[57] Implicit in Raus's critique of Waldick's futile knowledge of French society is its lack of relevance for colonized subjects faced with starvation and homelessness.

Chraïbi's portrait of educated Waldick's brims with sexual innuendos, aligning his inaction with homoerotic sexual passivity. In several analogies, he is the receptacle of sexual desire, never the initiator. After the Mac O'Mac visit revealing his intimacy to Simone, Raus consoles Waldick in the backyard, holding his friend's wrist, one hand behind his neck, their faces almost touching. At this moment, Raus feels "as if I have flowed into your skin, like a mollusk into a new shell" (49, my translation). Waldick describes this moment in terms that evoke sexual intercourse. For three hours, he notes, Raus "uninterrupted, hammering like a blacksmith on an anvil, a blacksmith with no eyes, no ears, no guts, animated by the need to hammer—and counting a steady rhythm to his strokes. Three hours. So stubborn in loving me that I finally got to my feet with a gleam of murder in my eyes" (38). His role as receptacle carries ideas of penetrability and violation that the narrative associates with the colonial con-quest and its imposed culture. With the realization that Mac O'Mac seduced his lover, Waldick is reminded of a French army officer's famous statement on conquering Algiers in the early nineteenth century: "We will get inside these Arabs like a knife cutting into butter" (37). By seeking a political explanation for a private affair, Waldick shows the significance of sexual images to translate different kinds of power relationships. White virility is a signifier for political and familial domination that presents itself as both subduing and natural. With this analogy, it is not only Simone who is conquered but Waldick himself who is sexually assaulted by Mac O'Mac. The narrative thus equates Waldick's femini-zation with his status as a powerless assimilé.

Chraïbi restricts this sexual passivity to preadolescence in his novel *The Simple Past* (1954). Set in colonial Morocco, same-sex relations among men occur be-tween passive young boys, who tend to be poor and feminine, and active adults who are richer and masculine. As Richard Serrano explains, a young Driss is ushered into adulthood when he refuses to continue to play the passive role with his French classmate Roche and rejects the advances of Si Kettani, an Islamic leader.[58] In contrast, Waldick's sexual passivity in this backyard scene evokes a regression to childhood.

In its closing, the novel again draws on sexual innuendos that equate the success of French colonialism with Arab passivity. Interestingly, Waldick's new love interest, Isabelle, makes this accusation to jolt Waldick out of his apathy. Isabelle concedes that the French are to blame for chasing Waldick and his compatriots out of their land, but she bluntly asserts, "it is you, North Africans yourselves that I condemn the most. You have always let yourselves be exploited. . . . Long before the French got to you, you were nothing more than bastards that everybody passed from one hand to the other, generation after generation, century after century, like a plot of ground" (116). Isabelle describes North Africans as passive objects that other people trade, not even valuable enough to keep around. She also denotes that these men find pleasure in being exploited and handled by others. This condemnation is spoken by a young French woman who survived the Nazi occupation. In other words, the homoerotic insinuation serves to rally for nationalism in ways that oppose cultural hybridity as a form of weakness. As Arnaldo Cruz-Malavé and Martin F. Manalansan IV note, queer sexualities have often been brandished to dispel anxieties about "authentic national belonging."[59] Isabelle goads Waldick to become the master in his own home, evoking the harmful effect of assimilation.

The reliance on gender to represent Raus's permeability and Waldick's receptivity to French culture and expectations reinforces ideas of cultural hybridity as detrimental, dangerous to allegedly pure cultures. Such logic aligns with the French imperative of assimilation that demands the erasure of foreign cultures. Colonial Paris reveals that being an assimilé does not guarantee colonial subjects access to Western modernity, nor acceptance as equals by the French. At the heart of this novel lies a paradoxical mobilization of gender and sexuality. On the one hand, Chraïbi critiques colonialism and its reliance on traditional norms of race and gender, its production and policing of the lines to separate the French and the Algerians. On the other hand, the story frames the hybrid figure Waldick, who blurs the cultural lines as made impotent by his French education, reinforcing normative roles for men and women that Chraïbi first interrogated in the relationship between Mac O'Mac and Simone.

Whether the narrative broaches the effects of Arab exclusion from lodgings and employment or the psychological effect of colonial devaluation of Arab manhood associated with crime, disease, or deviant sexual proclivities, it organizes exclusion by resorting to the category of sexual difference. Encapsulating the racist hostilities faced by the North African bachelor community in Paris after World War II, *The Butts* illuminates the categories of race and sexuality as mutually constitutive in representations of these men as either "Kings of the Night" or castrated. Colonialism, the narrative suggests, denaturalizes men and women. Waldick's masculinity and sexual drive recedes; Simone's body hardens. Sexual difference is invoked to demonstrate the detrimental effect of colonialism, yet the disruption of gender (and racial) norms chips away at normative and regulatory pillars that also erect the colonial edifice. The interracial couple threatens to blur the colonial line precisely by disrupting these norms. In ultimately privileging Raus as a model of masculinity, a man of action who uses violence to do his bidding, the narrative fails to disrupt the norms that structure the colonial system, or to fully interrogate stereotypical ideas of Arab masculinity.

The segregation and utter poverty of North Africans in Paris was strikingly conveyed in a 1953 oil canvas by André Fougeron, the "foremost socialist realist painter in France" (*The Independent*). Titled *North Africans at the Gates of the City* (*Les Nord-Africains aux portes de la villes*), the painting foregrounds a piece of corrugated iron, a material used as roofing in the slums, to mark a division between Paris and its outsiders, modern and primitive living, the City of Lights and its darker side. The iron piece that divides the painting diagonally also covers the bodies of two swarthy men lying on the floor in close proximity, with only their black furrowed eyebrows, uniform mustaches, and pained facial expressions visible. Wrapped in dark blankets that cover their hair and bodies like the white *haik* covered that of Algerian women, one man's gaze confronts the viewer, while the other's is directed at the sky. Next to them, a makeshift stove balances on two red bricks. On the other side of the corrugated iron lays Paris's glorious skylight with its delineated famous monuments: Sacré Coeur, the Montparnasse tower, and the Arc de Triomphe.

The same year, Fougeron completed another oil canvas, *Atlantic Civilisation*, where these two men reappeared in the left bottom corner, but this time on the other side of the corrugated iron lays not Paris skylight but a collage of scenes of a global nature. These variously sized images include an Asian woman carrying a dead baby, a white woman crying over a coffin, a child shoeshiner, a US soldier taking aim from a shiny blue Rolls Royce, a fat white businessman, a fatherless destitute family living in a tent, a Matisse-like circle of children surrounded by industrial pollution, a prison, an electric chair on a pedestal, colonial propaganda posters celebrating the French parachutists, and pet dogs in coats. Together, these snippet scenes show the human cost of war, colonization, and class exploitation. Overtly political, the painting also demonstrates how indictment of the Algerian war crisscrossed with critiques of other anticolonial battles and Cold War policies. In its epilogue, *The Butts* transcends colonial Paris and broaches second-class citizenship globally, noting among other "sacrificial victims" "the Negro in America" (120).

In the same year as the publication of Chraïbi's novel, the milestone 1955 Bandung conference of Asian and African nations strengthened awareness about the global struggle for liberation. In their anticolonial speeches, dignitaries gave a place of honor to familial and housing tropes. On April 18 President Sukarno of Indonesia opened the conference by labeling the historical moment "a Brotherhood Conference," whereby people of different religions unite against colonialism to become again "masters in our own house," saving our children from a "mortgaged" future.[60] Filipino statesman Carlos P. Romulo deployed similar analogies in his assertion that "we come as members of one great family long separated from each other. In this family reunion we are here to talk of man's estate."[61] In these rhetorical configurations, male colonized subjects revise the hierarchical rhetoric of colonial domesticity by constituting a new family where colonized men are the heads united by the shared goal of national independence and economic autonomy. These two patriarchal units, whether they are organized vertically by colonial hierarchies or horizontally by racial solidarities, either exclude women or instrumentalize them in the struggle between men.

Romance and Brotherhood

Colonial Paris appears not only where we expect it in anticolonial Maghrebi novels but also where we least expect it, in post–World War II African American expatriate tales. In fiction by Richard Wright, James Baldwin, and William Gardner Smith, the literary trope of the romance between black American men and white European women symbolizes African Americans' newly held freedom in Paris after World War II. Many African American expatriates considered the city a refuge from the daily frustrations of second-class citizenship at home and Joseph McCarthy's witch-hunt of the black radical left. The Parisian interracial romance, which juxtaposes the subjugation of black men in the United States with their liberation in Paris, constructs a utopian horizon that emphasizes the equality of black and white men and frames American lynching as an anomaly; Paris is a space where freedom is supposedly achieved and manhood recovered. Even in the rare pessimistic visions of the French capital and interracial romance that permeate Wright's 1959 "Island of Hallucination," the author insists on Paris being a place with "no race prejudice."[1]

Yet African American exiles knew that no one in Paris was color-blind. One only need remember the sight of a semi-nude Josephine Baker in banana skirt gyrating her hips in *la danse sauvage*, or Baldwin's exasperation when asked if he played the trumpet, or olive-skinned Chester Himes's and Richard Gibson's fear of getting caught in anti-Algerian police raids.[2] Even in the domain of romance, it was rarely the mademoiselles who were involved with black US men. Rather, these romances involved Swedish, Norwegian, and American women.[3] But while these expatriates experienced and witnessed Paris's contradictions, their postwar tales often used the city as a political tool to critique Jim Crow

America. Their fashioning of a color-blind Paris, however, seldom survived the Algerian conflict that reverberated through the French capital.

In this chapter, I map out a six-year literary transformation of expatriate Paris from 1957 to 1963 that overlaps with the Algerian War for independence from France (1954–62). In this journey that transits from Parisian utopianism to postcolonial criticism, from Richard Wright's and James Baldwin's love songs to racially liberal Paris to William Gardner Smith's shrewd attack on French colonialism, the trope of interracial romance undergirds both the construction and the questioning of a color-blind Paris. I argue that as these writers included North African characters and decolonization issues in their fiction, they struggled to reconcile the coexistence of a *color-blind* and a *colonial* Paris.[4] It is vital to note that what these authors could tell us about Paris was curtailed by the law of April 3, 1955, declaring a state of emergency in French Algeria and establishing large-scale censorship throughout the nation.[5] Guests of France who witnessed anti-Algerian violence in Paris found themselves silenced by threats of repatriation.

Over the past thirty years, scholars have examined the significance of Paris for African American expatriate writers in the twentieth century. Mae Henderson was the first to fully examine themes of exile in the fiction of Wright, Himes, Baldwin, and Smith.[6] Other studies expanded this scope to identify the role of France in black US fiction since the mid-nineteenth century and the emergence of a black colony in Paris after the Great War.[7] This varied and wide-ranging scholarship known as "Paris noir" converges in its characterization of black expatriation to the French capital as a "success story."[8] Since the mid-1990s, however, an increasing number of scholars (including Stovall) have interrogated the idea of Paris noir as emancipatory. They have pointed out the ubiquity of US state surveillance abroad for left-leaning black American figures such as Wright and Baldwin during the Cold War and demonstrated how this espionage turned Paris and Parisian cafés into sites of betrayal and denunciation.[9]

Overwhelmingly, the critiques of a color-blind Paris noir have centered on African American writers' relationship to Francophone colonial subjects and have described these as fraught with unease, conflict, or worse, complicity with French colonialism. Brent Edwards designates 1920s and 1930s Paris as a space of "uneasy encounters of peoples of African descent with each other" and some of their writing collaborations as "a failure to translate even a basic grammar of blackness."[10] For Bennetta Jules-Rosette, this unease transforms into a bitter conflict over colonialism, a polarizing matter during the First International Congress of Black Writers and Artists at the Sorbonne in 1956. At the center of this conflict is the role that African American celebrities like Josephine Baker and Richard Wright play as mouthpieces of French color-blindness and therefore as accomplices in making French colonialism invisible. Scholars have described the relations between France and these personalities as "convenient francophilia," a "mutually beneficial relationship," a "complicity with the [French] nation-state at its most racist moment," and "a moral myopia with regard to the French attitudes" toward their colonial subjects.[11]

These important critiques have not yet considered how the very writers we have dubbed spokesmen for a racially liberal Paris have also condemned the city and uncovered a colonial Paris. For all the scholarship on Paris noir as a liberation narrative, there have been strikingly few critical examinations of the city in black US expatriate fiction. In this chapter, I demonstrate how Wright, Baldwin, and Smith first fashioned a myth of Parisian color-blindness through the trope of the interracial romance, and then subsequently challenged or tempered this myth in post-1960 fiction that coincided with the increased police repression of Algerians in the capital, including the 1961 Paris police massacre of peaceful demonstrators. In fictionalizing this colonial Paris, Baldwin and Smith draw on masculine identities, and especially homosocial bonding, as a medium to articulate their positions. Offering competing figurations of the city in their narratives, Baldwin and Smith distinguished color-blind and colonial spaces through the languages of romance and brotherhood. The two-faced city is located in the periphery of expatriate fiction, in Wright's lesser-known novel *The Long Dream* (1958) and its 1959 sequel, *Island of Hallucination*, an unpublished roman à clef and his only long work of fiction set in Paris; in James Baldwin's short story "This Morning, This Evening, So Soon" (1960) rather than his celebrated Paris novel, *Giovanni's Room* (1956); and in the understudied author William Gardner Smith's last novel, *The Stone Face* (1963). Examining the significance of lovers and brothers in these works highlights telling differences in how each author grappled with French colonialism and how they echoed and reversed each other's writings to position themselves vis-à-vis the so-called City of Light. Together, their narratives demonstrate how colonial Paris surreptitiously came to displace France and Europe as a model of liberation for African American writers. This moment of black American engagement with colonial subjects challenges ideas of conflict and complicity by bringing into focus another Paris that illuminates identification and recognition between African American expatriates and North Africans galvanized by masculine aspirations and brotherly bonds.

I contend that Wright, Baldwin, and Smith adopted interracial sexuality and homosocial bonding as preeminent modalities for thinking about different kinds of affiliations in Paris. Both tropes of romance and brotherhood navigate a Parisian landscape through a transnational masculine imaginary. The rhetoric of black and white lovers promotes racial equality through the path of integration that assumes equality between black and white men, whereas the rhetoric of brothers indicates the alternative path of revolution that requires awareness of racial domination and commitment to defeat it. Located on the Left Bank of the River Seine, delimited by cosmopolitan cafés and lodging, color-blind Paris is a site of acceptance where African American men gain access to the privileges of patriarchy and become "men like other men." With interracial intimacy, these authors typified black American integration (and masculinity) in the capital and a new racial order that broke away from black and white masculine rivalry. On the other hand, north of the city, colonial Paris reminds protagonists of ghettos in Harlem and south Philadelphia, a periphery that keeps Algerian men segregated, monitored, and subject to police violence. This colonial space works as a site of recognition rallying African Americans and colonial subjects as "brothers" whose manhood and rights have been denied. Brotherhood stands for a politics of solidarity among emasculated subalterns that helped these authors envision a new alliance rooted in cross-racial masculine solidarity. While one reading of Paris invests in universalism, the other challenges it, and I explore how the tension between these two readings informs the fiction of Paris noir.

Color-blind Paris noir is represented through the language of interracial romance, a romance that surprisingly tells us very little about male–female relationships but crystallizes the struggle between white and black men. I use the phrases "interracial romance," "interracial intimacy," and "interracial sex" to describe a vast range of sexual contacts mainly between black American men and white European women that include marriage, brief and prolonged cohabitation, and dating, as well as pimping and prostitution. These terms also reference substantively different fictional treatments of sexual intimacy. Scenes of interracial contact are mainly construed as heteronormative, but Baldwin and Smith imagine these also among men. In evoking white men's rape of black men, they associate political disenfranchisement with emasculation. A medium for political speculation and expression, these men-with-men and men-with-women interracial encounters usefully throw light on the psychosexual dimensions of racial hostility, on men's paradoxical longing for masculine power and for protection against its excess. At the same time, these encounters establish black heterosexual masculinity as an integral part of the liberationist project, a means to measure the progress toward racial equality and an instrument to achieve it. The interracial romance overshadows experiences of black women and queer subjects by considering black men as the most vulnerable subjects in the US racist regime, obscuring the significant patriarchal power they wield infraracially. Even Baldwin, who elsewhere eloquently troubles narrow understandings of masculinity, confides that in his narratives set in Paris, addressing the questions of both race and homosexuality "would have been quite beyond [his] powers."[12] Again and again, his narratives revealingly cast Paris as either a foil to US race relations or to its sexual puritanism. In what is arguably the fullest articulation of African American expatriation to France, Smith's novel interrogates dominant literary treatments of the French capital by shifting the focus from color-blind Paris to colonial Paris, from Paris as a paragon of racial democracy to the Algerian insurgence as a model of liberation and masculine empowerment, from the trope of black-white intimacy that pits France against the United States to the trope of black brown brotherhood that sets French colonialism and American Jim Crow side by side. Together, their stories question the idea of Paris as a space of liberation for the African diaspora.

From Mississippi to Paris

Wright's postwar personal correspondence, public pronouncements, and segments of his novel *The Long Dream* extend the mythical image of Paris and France as a color-blind utopia that iconic figures such as Frederick Douglass and Booker T. Washington had fashioned. In *Black Bourgeoisie*, E. Franklin Frazier also notes that "the Negro press constantly draws upon the reputed experiences of Negroes in Europe."[13] After his 1946 visit, Wright observed that "there is such an absence of race hate that it seems a little unreal. Above all, Paris strikes me as being a truly gentle city, with gentle manners."[14] His personification of the city strategically draws on and condemns his own US experience, sullied by racial hatred and brutality. At times, Wright's distinctions between France and his native country were deemed too damning to appear in the US press. Ben Burns, the white executive editor of *Ebony* magazine, rejected his 1950 article "I Chose Exile," in which he famously claimed, "I've found more freedom in one square block of Paris than there is in the entire United States."[15] But in "Island," Wright, like Smith, indicts Parisian life as hedonist and materialistic, turning African American expatriates into bums, con men, pimps, or informers. Whether viewed through the rose-colored glasses of *The Long Dream* or the deep cynicism of its sequel, Wright's Paris helps black American men reestablish their sense of manhood through the prospect of interracial intimacy. Considering "Island" and *The Long Dream* together uncovers Wright's shifting view of Paris and growing disillusionment with its persisting Cold War politics. Considering these two novels against the context of French censorship during the Algerian war discloses other forms of coercion that affected expatriates' freedom of speech and scratched away at the veneer of a utopian Paris noir.

Mentions of Paris in Wright's 1958 bildungsroman *The Long Dream* are brief but significant. Set in the 1950s, the novel chronicles the loss of innocence of Rex "Fishbelly" Tucker, a middle-class black adolescent, ending with his departure from small-town Clintonville, Mississippi, for Paris. As evoked in the title of the last section, "The Waking Dream," Fishbelly realizes that a life of freedom and equality for black Americans can only be dreamed of within US borders. Whereas in Wright's autobiography, *Black Boy*, freedom is sought in a flight from South to North, in *The Long Dream*, freedom is now associated with Paris, a place "to be at last somewhere at home . . . free from fear and pressure."[16] The adolescent's itinerary from Mississippi to Paris, from *The Long Dream* to "The Waking Dream," illustrates the irony that safety and greater freedom can be gained by giving up the privileges attached to US citizenship for the status of "guest" in Paris.

Set in the United States or Paris, black–white romance in 1950s African American fiction emerged against a backdrop of state executions and lynching in the South, including the Martinsville Seven in Virginia (1949 to 1951), Willie McGee (1951), and Emmett Till in Mississippi (1955). Black boys and men were killed for allegedly raping or flirting with white women. In *The Long Dream*, Wright ties interracial sex to the castration of black men in the US South and shows the mutilated black male body as a site where institutional racism becomes legible. As a racial practice, lynching at once denies claims to masculinity through the castrated phallus and citizenship through the killing of black boys and men without the right to due process. Twelve-year-old Fishbelly is a witness to these literal and figurative dismemberments after his twenty-four-year-old friend and hero Chris Sims is lynched by a white mob for his affair with a white woman. As he examines "the dirty, bloody, tattered human form" in his father's funeral home, Fishbelly discovers instead of Chris's genitalia "a dark, coagulated blot in a gaping hole between the thighs."[17] The mob's barbaric act that robs Chris's body of its male function at once asserts and negates black virility, first interpreting it as a threat and then eliminating it. As Paul Gilroy remarks, this "violence articulates blackness to a distinct mode of lived masculinity."[18] Using Chris's death as a lesson, Fishbelly's father, Tyree, explains that the sphere of interracial romance works as a legal façade for the subjugation of black Americans and a mechanism for managing black bodies, rationalizing violence and murder. He orders his son, "NEVER LOOK AT A WHITE WOMAN! YOU HEAR? . . . She means death!" (64). Tyree's view is confirmed when the corrupt police chief frames Fishbelly for raping a white woman. After two years in prison and a trial in which the purported victim never materializes, Fishbelly flees a lawless town and region to join his friends Zeke and Tony in Paris.

The landscape of intimacy that structures Fishbelly's coming-of-age provides fertile ground to compare Mississippi and Paris. In "gay Paree," black men can consort with white women; for the same action in Clintonville, they are lynched or imprisoned (359). Zeke, a US soldier stationed in Orléans, corresponds with Fishbelly and observes that in Paris, "these blond chicks will go to bed with a guy who's black as the ace of spades and laugh and call it Black Market" (360). Through the lens of interracial sex, Zeke indicates that Paris is a city where even the darkest subjects from Africa, though fetishized and commodified as "black market" objects, are physically safe and socially integrated, in contrast with Mississippi, where their exclusion is policed by law and mob violence (360). For Zeke, the banality of Parisian interracial intimacy is something to write home about because it typifies the greater freedom and power enjoyed by black men on the other side of the Atlantic. In idealizing Paris, Wright condemned the racial nightmare in the United States, but he also erased France's brutality toward its colonial subjects by presenting Franco-African contact as consensual desire.

In Wright's "Island," Fishbelly's story is continued and his long dream of Paris is broken. Readers reunite with Fishbelly on a Paris-bound airliner, right where they had left him at the end of *The Long Dream*. "Island" dismisses the romantic idea of the city Fishbelly had gleaned in the letters of his army friends and expounds on his inability to secure trusted friendships and employment within legal avenues or to liberate himself from US racial thinking. This time Wright's Paris offers no positive alternative for human relationships across the color line and, worse yet, no racial solidarity. As William Maxwell perceptively observes, "every set piece of [the blacks-in-Paris] romance is shaken, from the progressive de-Americanization of the journey to the frank sympathy of the Parisian public, from the emotional rescue of flesh-first interracialism to the fail-safe embrace of black Americans by the anticolonial left."[19] "Island" consists of "tales of defeat" and nightmares involving Fishbelly and other African American expatriates (235). However, in the journey from Mississippi to Paris, the false brother replaces the white woman as the personification of danger or death. In this context, the interracial romance is revealed to be a sinister form of sexuality that serves the politics of power and competition among men. The willowy blondes and the young black Harlemite are mirages, behind which lurk a prostitute, a spy, or a con man. As Fishbelly's initial hopes of equality typified by interracial liaisons are quashed, he seeks a new kind of liberation expressed in sexual domination.

The opening interracial romance sets the tone of disillusionment with Paris and Parisians that permeates the rest of "Island." Using the interracial romance as a promise of black and white brotherhood, two sophisticated Parisian crooks extort from Fishbelly a third of his savings before his plane even lands in Paris. Jacques attempts to gain the young man's trust by railing against America's racist "barbarians" and describes Paris mostly in terms of sexual promise (22). Keenly aware of Jim Crow dynamics, he panders: "At Paris you will conquer all the women. . . . The women will make you the king of the boulevards" (23).

Fishbelly would learn French "in the bed from a girl," he claims (19). Jacques's friendship is soon revealed to be a sham, part of a confidence game, whereby he pretends to help his American friend seduce an "electrically" beautiful white girl, in fact his wife and hustling partner (103).[20] Fishbelly "had, of course, heard of the confidence game, but he had never heard of its being used against black men with sex as the bait, with racial balm as the lure, with sympathy as the come-on" (46). Although the scoundrels targeted Fishbelly as a naïve and wealthy tourist regardless of his race, the swindle debunks the myth of Parisians' sympathy for black Americans.

Sex is again the bait in the next interracial encounter, confirming Fishbelly's inkling that seduction and deception work hand in hand in this city. But this time the deception reveals the absence of racial rather than interracial fraternity. In Pigalle, a segment of Paris reputed for prostitution, Fishbelly meets Charles Oxford Brown, alias "Mechanical," a Detroit-born thirty-four-year-old African American journalist who dispatches him to Anita, an English-speaking sex worker expert at screening newcomers and reporting back their political affiliations. If Tyree had warned his son that white women mean death for black men in *The Long Dream*, now another father figure, African American lawyer Ned Harrison, takes him under his wing and warns him against false brothers. Ned apprises that Paris "is the center of the Cold War," and if he does not "KEEP AWAY FROM" spies like Mechanical, he will get "ground up like mincemeat!" (110, 111, 216). Although the novel includes a student demonstration crushed by the police, fights, and threats of death or deportation, for all that Paris is not dangerous. Rather, it is a space of unbelonging, where treachery prevents friendship and the only things the city has to offer are for sale: "cunt, cognac, and communism" (235, 227). We are far from Fishbelly's original hopes for a "Wonderful Romance" (*The Long Dream*, 380).

In the Paris of "Island," interracial sex remains a signifier of domination but offers the African American interloper a chance to turn the tables. Twice drawn out and duped by the promise of interracial intimacy, a hardened Fishbelly seeks revenge on both Jim Crow America and a deceitful Paris by sexually exploiting women. He seduces white girls from France's richest family to "pay these French men back" and exploits white American GIs' sexual frustration, placing himself at the top of the patriarchal ladder (372). Descriptions of the "meat business" call up images of the flesh trafficker at auction blocks as Fishbelly parades naked white women in front of Dixie men, "noting their physical features" (198, 116). Although it is clear that Wright condemns this brand of masculinity as exploitative and self-serving, other scenes reinforce masculine aggression against those who transgress gender norms, including Mechanical, the "nigger homo informer," and Anita, the sex worker who looks like "a castrated man" (262, 57). These transgressing figures in "Island" help paint Paris as "baffling" or "bewildering" (51, 49).

While the negative perception of the city in Smith's *The Stone Face* challenges the myth of a color-blind Paris, in Wright's "Island" it does not. *The Long Dream* and "Island" strategically operate around national binaries that pit a racist America against a racially liberal Paris. A short passage of his latter novel channels Ned Harrison, who claims, "you can't deprive people of their rights under French law" (276). But this myth of equality in Paris did not exist for colonial subjects.[21] Despite Wright's disillusionment with Paris in this novel, Rebecca Ruquist is right to note that the author still paints France as a country where "indifference to race" enables African American expatriates to "lose their blackness."[22] Paris certainly remains the site where Fishbelly fulfills his principal pursuit of "invisibility" even as he realizes that the city is full of "false faces" (105). Tyler Stovall views Wright's Paris as "a last flowering of the naïve faith in French tolerance," distinct from later African American visitors' depictions of the city. Even so, it is crucial to understand that Wright, unlike these visitors, could not express himself freely.[23]

French hospitality rules and censorship during the Algerian war played a considerable role in silencing guests' engagement with anti-Algerian violence in the capital. Expatriates navigated a treacherous line between supporting the end of racial oppression worldwide and placating France by focusing their energies on the US civil rights and British decolonization movements, rather than the Algerian War, whose ripple effects they witnessed on their doorsteps. Wright, the dean of Negro writers abroad, deliberately omits the presence of Algerians in his depiction of the city and conveniently sets the action of "Island" in 1951, three years before the start of the Algerian revolution. Responding to Ben Burns's remark on his silence regarding France's racial problem, Wright confided to him, "you can say or write just about anything you want over here, but don't get started on France's colonies. Whoop, the police will be on your neck and out you go in forty-eight hours. There's no explanation—just out you go!"[24] Wright was already anxious about the US State Department's control over his passport applications and renewals, fearing possible confiscations. With the Algerian War, he knew he could either keep silent about French colonialism or pack his suitcase and land before the House of Un-American Activities Committee.[25]

Throwing light on Wright's anxiety of deportation, a messy 1957 scandal known as the Gibson Affair illustrates black American expatriates' eagerness to condemn French colonialism and their inevitable reluctance to do so publicly. Black American cartoonist Ollie Harrington recalls "an Algerian [at the café Tournon], who . . . was always trying to get Dick [Richard Wright] or myself to write articles in favor of the Algerian revolution. I don't know what kind of idiots he thought we were. . . . And we obviously always refused to do that. . . . We were sympathetic to the Algerians, but we couldn't mention it."[26] Despite his caution, Harrington had a close call in October 1957 after letters critiquing the Algerian War and signed in his name were sent to the editors of *Life* magazine and the London *Observer* without his knowledge. He discovered that fellow expatriate Richard Gibson, with the alleged support of William Gardner Smith, had forged the correspondence, putting him at risk for deportation.[27] In an article published in 2008, Gibson in fact names Smith as the main instigator: "Bill came up with the idea of a letter-writing ring in which we would write American and British newspapers and magazines denouncing French colonial rule in Algeria. Each of the letters would be signed in someone else's name so that, if need be, the real person could go to the French police to protest legitimately about the forgery and misuse of their name in support of the Algerian cause."[28] The Gibson Affair illustrates expatriates' eagerness to condemn French colonialism and their inevitable reluctance to do so publicly. Of course, not every name carries the same weight. Harrington was well known, and Wright's prominence made him an even likelier target of forgery or misquotations in the press, as well as a target of surveillance by the US State Department and the French Sûreté Nationale. Though many black US expatriates left the United States for greener pastures, they found that in France, too, their freedom of speech was regulated.

While Algerians are absent from "Island," we can detect Wright's dissatisfaction with the slow progress of decolonization too often hijacked by troubling ideologies. For instance, British colonial subjects, such as Nigerian Saturday and Trinidadian Lister Bookman, are foot soldiers in the international communist witch-hunt, indifferent to the decolonization question (295). On the other hand, Ali, a French colonial subject from Morocco, trumpets the independence of his country in a monologue that blends anti-Semitism, misogyny, and extreme violence. "Island" also dismisses the support against colonial rule from communist activists eager to launch a new *mission civilisatrice* by bringing another gospel to African workers. This pessimistic vision speaks to Wright's staunch belief that greater commitment, organized action, and autonomy by colonized subjects were needed if African nations were to become independent. But the colonial subtext contained at the periphery of "Island" does not intersect with Fishbelly's principal pursuit of "invisibility," which he fulfills even as he realizes that Paris is full of "false faces" (105).

Although there is no trace of Algeria in "Island," Wright, who strove to move to London, chose to set the final installment of the Fishbelly trilogy in Algeria. In two letters sent to his editor, Paul Reynolds, at Doubleday in March

1959, he locates his main character's "moral, social and political awakening" in Algeria and later black Africa where "millions of men are liberating themselves."[29] After his African stay, Fishbelly would come back transformed to the United States, paralleling in sorts the journey made by Simeon Brown in *The Stone Face*. In both scenarios, the Algerian space (in Algiers and in Paris) transforms African American characters into morally responsible men of action. Unlike Fishbelly's resolve to stay in Paris at the end of "Island," the blueprint of this final novel imagines a commitment to return to black America, just like the main protagonists of Baldwin's "This Morning" and Smith's *The Stone Face* voluntarily do, signaling in the end a discontent with exile and with a city tarnished by anti-Algerian violence.

Still, Wright's legacy is conflicted. Though he remained dedicated to African decolonization as his continued friendship and correspondence with Trinidadian pan-Africanist George Padmore, Ghanaian president Kwame Nkrumah, and Senegalese teacher Alioune Diop indicate, the Algerian War engendered "a new inventory of problems concerning his role as a political activist."[30] The repression of Algerian workers at Wright's doorstep clashed with the assertion made in "Island" that "you can't deprive people of their rights under French law" (276). According to biographer Hazel Rowley, Wright was staunchly in favor of an independent Algeria. Yet in 1959, he praised French colonial assimilation in a public pronouncement:

> The Algerian war is a war which had nothing to do with the racial problem. . . . [French nationalism is] now being employed to forcibly convert Muslims, who are religious fanatics, to Western civilization. . . . My feelings in such circumstances are ambiguous. Frenchmen tell the Muslims at the point of their submachine guns 'You are French.' We, American Negroes, might wish to be forced in a similar way to consider ourselves as American.[31]

In deciphering the Algerian conflict through the prism of US racial integration, Wright simultaneously conflated the struggle of a racial minority group for full citizenship with that of a majority group for state sovereignty, silenced the issue of racial supremacy, rationalized the use of French military force, and expressed reservations about the legitimacy of Algerian decolonization. Ultimately, the inability of this otherwise prominent anticolonial activist to speak about one of the most brutal wars of decolonization and his insistence on depicting Paris as a color-blind if alienating society provided his critics with ammunition to discredit him. Increasingly weary of Wright's influence in the French press, Ben Burns, the editor of *Ebony* who refused the publication of Wright's article about his exile, drew attention to his hypocritical silence about racism in France.[32]

Shortly before his untimely death, Wright worked on getting support and funding for a new book, a report on Francophone Africa articulated in the same vein as the one he did for Ghana in *Black Power*, but the project did not materialize.[33]

The Paris Paradox

A critique of Wright's color-blind Paris came from his fellow expatriate and former friend James Baldwin, whose anxiety about his influence drove him to position himself outside Wright's long shadow.[34] In his article titled "Alas, Poor Richard," published in March 1961, four months after his death, Baldwin claims that Africans and Algerians in Paris distrusted and resented Wright for caring "more about his safety and comfort than . . . about the black condition."[35] Yet Wright's silence about Paris's Algerians was the norm rather than an exception in the black colony. Baldwin and Smith often expressed their views on the Franco-Algerian conflict mainly after it ended and censorship dissolved; on the rare occasions when they condemned French colonialism during the war, they did so quietly. For example, the Arab protagonist in Baldwin's short story "This Morning, This Evening, So Soon" is from independent Tunisia, rather than colonized Algeria. What differentiated Wright from his confreres was his influence as a prominent anticolonial advocate who could have potentially made a difference by taking a stance, though at great cost to himself and his family. In "Alas, Poor Richard," Baldwin concurs that "if one-tenth of the suffering which obtained (and obtains) among Africans and Algerians in Paris had been occurring in Chicago, one could not help feeling that Richard would have raised the roof. . . . But . . . Richard did not know much about the present dimensions and complexity of the Negro problem here, and, profoundly, did not want to know."[36]

Although he also came to Paris in 1948 to escape racism, Baldwin distinguished himself from Wright and claimed that he did not harbor any romantic ideas of the city.[37] Corroborating this view, his 1950 essay, "Encounter on the Seine," condemns French fetishism of blackness and pitying attitudes that "all Negroes arrive from America, trumpet-laden and twinkle-toed, bearing scars so unutterably painful that the glories of the French Republic may not suffice to heal them."[38] Landing in Paris at age twenty-four with only forty dollars in his pocket, Baldwin lived for a while in the most destitute quarters among Algerian workers. Cash-strapped, he even looked for work as a singer in an "Arab nightclub."[39] In November 1949 he was arrested for receiving stolen hotel sheets, an incident that unexpectedly resulted in five weeks of prison and bureaucratic hell that persuaded a despairing Baldwin that Paris was just as wretched as home.[40]

Baldwin's fictional Paris, however, is more "a waking dream" than an "island of hallucination," for it frees his protagonists, even if briefly, from rigid social expectations regarding cross-racial or same-sex desire. Interestingly, when Paris serves as a foil to a racialist United States, Baldwin offers a heterosexual narrative that highlights the equality of black and white men through the symbolic interracial romance. However, in *Giovanni's Room* (1956) and *Another Country* (1962), narratives that posit Paris as a site of sexual liberation for American homosexual and bisexual characters, these men and their lovers are white, even if the impoverished younger beaus are sometimes metaphorized as "black" (Giovanni and Yves). Together, these narratives illustrate Baldwin's instrumental use of Paris to critique America's racial and sexual barriers.

In "This Morning, This Evening, So Soon," a short story published in the *Atlantic Monthly* in September 1960, Baldwin uses black–white intimacy to juxtapose a racist America and color-blind Paris, just like Wright's Fishbelly novels. By featuring threatening or violent agents of the US state (customs officers and policemen), "This Morning" uncovers how the state coercively produces and polices interracial contact. The bulk of the narrative weighs the narrator's emancipation and recovered sense of manhood in Paris against racial traumas experienced in the United States. Yet unlike Wright's fiction, "This Morning" introduces a North African character whose presence disrupts the binary of French liberation and US oppression by hinting at the existence of a different Paris for colonized subjects. The short story registers a careful opposition to the Algerian War, conveying the narrator's sympathy for not only Algerian workers and peddlers "scattered—or corralled—the Lord knows where" but also for a French young male acquaintance who came back from Algeria half blind.[41] The two story lines raise some significant questions: how can color-blind Paris and colonial Paris coexist? How does the Algerian subtext mesh with the kinds of meanings that the interracial romance brought forth about equality and masculinity?

Evoking his own integrationist hopes, Baldwin's depiction of a Parisian mixed family deviates from Wright's depiction of a sexual "black market" or Smith's portrayal of white fetishistic longings for black bodies. The story is set two days before the Alabama-born narrator, a singer and actor who remains unnamed, is to leave Paris, where he has lived for the past twelve years; met his Swedish wife, Harriet; and achieved celebrity status. Deeply ambivalent about this homecoming, he fears that American race dynamics will instill in his son the same kind of "pity" and "contempt" he felt toward his own father and turn his wife into "the lowest of untouchables" for marrying a black man.[42] The narrative borrows its title, "This Morning, This Evening, So Soon," from the chorus of the traditional folk song "Tell Old Bill," about the lynching of a man who would not "leave them downtown gals alone." This title keeps lynching as a looming threat for the narrator. His memories of a previous trip confirm white Southerners' hostility toward black Americans returning from Europe with "foreign ideas" that do not mesh with Jim Crow proscriptions.[43] However, in the course of his last night in Paris, as he interacts with Jean-Luc Vidal, the French director who made him famous; a group of African American students touring Europe; and Boona, a Tunisian acquaintance, the narrator grows more resolved to leave a city marred by colonial tensions.

Baldwin's short story, like Wright's Fishbelly novels, mainly approaches the interracial romance in its national specificity so as to illuminate states' role in shaping and reproducing social relations, in extending or withholding equal recognition to its citizens. The narrator reflects how unlikely his marriage to Harriet would have been had he not moved to Paris more than a decade ago: "If Harriet had been born in America, it would have taken her a long time, perhaps forever, to look on me as *a man like other men*; if I had met her in America, I would never have been able to look on her as a woman like all other women. . . . We would never have been able to love each other. And Paul would never have been born" (149–50, emphasis added). The French and US locations determine his family's possibility of existence as each state fashions affect, sanctions, or outlaws the union. In a flashback the narrator remembers how, on a previous brief journey back home to attend his mother's funeral, he realized that Harriet's cablegram message in his pocket—"Be good, be quick, I'm waiting"—was now the equivalent of "some atomic secret, in *code* . . . they'd kill me if they ever found out what it meant" (163, 175). Evidence of interracial affection, the note displaces the narrator's grief for the loss of his mother with fear for his own life.

"This Morning" translates the exclusion of black US citizens through experiences of emasculation. In retelling a traumatic incident that happened to his sister Louisa in small-town Alabama, the narrator evokes what it means for him to be a black man in America. Driving out on a date with other couples, Louisa's party is stopped by white policemen who think they see a white woman in the company of black men. Against the car's bright headlights, the officers strip and probe the fairest woman, pretending they are submitting her to a racial test, while the young black men watch, unable to stop the attack. In recounting this harrowing story of black female degradation, the narrator excludes Louisa's girlfriend as a victim and focuses instead on the psychological effects of this act on the black men, as if they were the real target of white sexual violence and this woman a mere substitute. The narrator appropriates her public humiliation to register black male impotence: "You know, I know what that boy felt, I've felt it. They want you to feel that you are not a man, maybe that's the only way they can feel like men. . . . That's what it's like in America, for me, anyway"

(175). This rerouted attack against black men evokes a sexual invasion by white men, who replace them as love partners and, as a result, experience a renewed sense of virility. Here and in another more explicit scene in Smith's novel discussed later, whiteness signifies a brutal monopoly on masculinity expressed through heterosexual and homosexual desire.

Both color-blind Paris and the nightmarish United States are partly defined through the quality of masculine interrelationships. From the death threat haunting a mourning narrator's consciousness to the impotence of Louisa's friends, these scenes of black–white intimacy embed the image of an aggrieved black masculinity and weave a larger picture of a disenfranchised population. Critic Marlon Ross elucidates the intersection between race, gender, and sexuality in his contention that "Jim Crow is as much a regime of sexual classification as it is a form of racial imposition . . . with race functioning as . . . a contested gender line of demarcation bifurcating the category 'man' into superior versus inferior males and, on the other hand, gender as a racially contested line of demarcation dividing the category of 'race' into manly versus unmanly groups of men."[44] While denied black manhood conveys US racial logics and African American subjects' struggle for equality and self-respect, it also frames that struggle in traditional patriarchal terms. By considering only the black male body as the most vulnerable site of violence denied protection by the law, this short story models how black patriarchy circulates through ellipses. The sordid sexual assault of Louisa's friend does not lead to any attempt to connect experiences of racist oppression across gender lines and, in fact, emasculation overshadows claims of black female victimhood. What Jim Crow America prevents but Paris enables is black men's ability to choose their lover or wife, to protect their family and have their relationships protected by law. On a Paris bridge with Harriet, the narrator claims, "For the first time in my life I felt that no force jeopardized my right, my power, to possess and to protect a woman" (158). Paris seems to offer a vision redolent of liberation through virile rebirth and conquest. Importantly, the myth of manly rebirth in Paris also obscures the considerable power black men held intraracially.

The interracial romance not only fashions a color-blind Paris noir, it also channels the difference in French perceptions of North African and black American men. Paris is a city where "not even the dirty, rat-faced girls who live, apparently, in cafés are willing to go with an Arab" (184). The absence of Franco-Arab romance discloses colonial subjects' poor social status and exclusion.

Whereas colonialism rules out Franco-Arab romance in "This Morning," the politics of liberation in Africa and the United States gesture toward the possible alliance not only of two protagonists (Boona, a North African former prize fighter, and Ada, a young African American female tourist) but also of two synchronous struggles for freedom. Whereas the black American and white European couple establish Paris as a model democracy, the Boona–Ada coupling provides a new configuration of heterosexual interracial intimacy rooted in identification and solidarity among racial minorities. In meeting Ada and her friend Ruth, Boona sees potential for romance precisely because "the girls are not French and not white" (184). Unmindful of the French racist imaginary that tacitly excludes brown men from the realm of romance, the two black American tourists would not disqualify him as a potential suitor. Boona is quickly won over by Ada's wish to go to Africa and her questions about decolonization, and soon the pair spends the evening talking and dancing, ignoring the rest of the party around them. This budding suit is reminiscent of Du Bois's novelistic attempt to represent transnational subaltern solidarity with an interracial romance between a black American man and an Indian princess brought together by their desire to organize "all the Darker Races in the World."[45] But in "This Morning," the reality of the colonized's indigence interrupts the black and brown courtship, redraws national affiliations, and complicates transracial solidarity. Boona's alleged theft of Ada's money not only cuts the romance short and ends the night on the town; it leads the narrator to conclude that colonial subjects have been "beaten . . . too hard" for interracial friendship or romance to flourish (189). Unlike the African American narrator who has been able to escape his fate by leaving the United States for a new location with different racial dynamics, Boona and the larger North African community fail to escape theirs. "Most of them had no money. They lived three or four together in rooms with a single skylight, a single hard cot, or in buildings that seemed abandoned, with cardboards in the windows, with erratic plumbing in a wet, cobblestoned yard, in dark, dead-end alleys, and on the outer, chilling heights of Paris" (156). Yet the narrator nuances this social determinism in confessing that he does not know anything about Boona's life or Boona himself (187).

"This Morning" establishes the African American protagonist's feeling of brotherhood with North African subjects only to expound on his disconnect with them by emphasizing their different relation to Paris. The narrator explains,

> I once thought of the North Africans as my *brothers* and that is why I went to their cafés. . . . Their rage, the only note in all their music which I could not fail to recognize, to which I responded, yet had the effect of setting us more than ever at a division. They were perfectly prepared to drive all Frenchmen into the sea, and to level the city of Paris. But I could not hate the French, because they left me alone. . . . I love Paris, I will always love it, it is the city, which saved my life. It saved my life by allowing me to find out who I am. (157, emphasis added)

The narrator's brotherly association with North Africans stems from a recognition of shared racial exclusion. He had seen both the French flag and his own "used to dignify the vilest purposes," but in Paris he cannot feel toward the French the same way colonial subjects do (140). His ambivalence toward North Africans brings into relief African American expatriates' multilayered and complex allegiances, their appreciation of living with dignity in Paris, and at the same time, their awareness that the colonized are denied such a life. This ambivalence tempers the pan-Africanist and internationalist aspirations that melded anticolonialism and the civil rights movement into the same global struggle for democracy. It highlights the kinds of "décalage" or dissonances that Brent Edwards notes as constitutive of the African diaspora.[46]

In addressing the paradox of black American liberation and colonial subjugation in Paris, Baldwin troubles the idea of a color-blind city and illuminates a colonial and racial distinction within the category of "French" (Algerians were nominally French citizens since 1958) that was absent in Wright's Parisian account. He also demonstrates that the experiences of denied manhood and second-class citizenship serve as sites of recognition that bring together expatriates and colonial migrants, even as their different experiences of Paris push them apart. In the end, "This Morning" circumvents transnational alliances and returns to a nationalist project invoked in the narrator's admiration for a group of politicized African American students that facilitates his reentry to the United States. This story nonetheless provides a younger generation of African American writers that includes Smith with the key metaphors of romance and brotherhood to discuss Paris noir.

The Price of Recognition

Nothing distinguishes Smith more starkly from his fellow expatriates than the correlation he makes between African decolonization and the civil rights movement. Published one year after the Algerian War ended, when censorship no longer held a stranglehold on expatriates' freedom of speech, The Stone Face employs colonial Paris and the Algerian decolonization battle as a model for the African American struggle for equal rights. Seven years before the publication of The Stone Face, Wright had railed bitterly against Francophone anticolonial writers such as Aimé Césaire and Léopold Sédar Senghor for flattening African American experiences under the rubric of colonialism. Although a major goal of the 1956 First Congress of Black Writers and Artists in Paris was to illuminate commonalities across different African diasporic cultures, Malagasy poet and playwright Jacques Rabemananjara admitted, "there were conflicts, even very bitter conflicts, because what preoccupied us at that time was our colonization. And the Americans did not understand that, because they said they were *not* colonized."[47] In his coverage of the conference for *Encounter* magazine, Baldwin expressed his own doubt about the relevance of debates on a "mysterious continent" for black America.[48] By 1960, nonetheless, these feelings of alienation gave way to new understandings of racial domination as a global phenomenon.[49] Writing the novel in the wake of the 1961 police massacre of Algerian demonstrators in Paris, Smith was preoccupied with the state's violence against its own citizens, whether they were demanding national independence or the right to go to the same schools and universities. Drawing an analogy between these two struggles risks erasing their complexity, but Smith nonetheless anticipates the power of the Algerian revolution for an entire generation of African American writers and critics to come, including Harold Cruse, J. H. O'Dell, David Llorens, Hoyt W. Fuller, and Jake Lamar.

Arriving in Paris in 1951, Philadelphia native William Gardner Smith (1921–74) was considered something of a genius in the black colony, having published two novels before the age of twenty-three. Born in a south Philadelphia ghetto, Smith was already writing reports for the *Pittsburg Courier* at age sixteen and in a US garrison in Germany at age eighteen, an experience that inspired his first novel, *Last of the Conquerors* (1948), and launched his writing career.[50] Yet none of his following novels received the attention of the first, which came out to rave reviews in both mainstream and African American newspapers.[51] Paris offered Smith a measure of racial freedom and a political refuge. A member of the Philadelphia Executive Committee of the National Association for the Advancement of Colored People with Trotskyist sympathies, Smith had a file at the FBI oddly longer than Wright's.[52]

Within the black colony, the Philadelphia native was best suited to write about Algerians in Paris. Smith's fluency in French distinguished him from his peers and won him a job as a desk editor for the prestigious Agence France Presse in 1954, the year the Algerian War started. The work consisted in translating French stories into English, many of which addressed the unfolding bloody Algerian crisis. *The Stone Face* showcases Smith's exhaustive grasp of the conflict, including an intricate knowledge of police surveillance and repression in the Arab enclaves of Paris. Mixing fiction and reportage, the novel is partly a historical document: it chronicles the 1961 massacre and borrows from the testimony of Djamila Boupacha about her rape and torture at the hands of French parachutists.[53] Throughout, Smith reads the Algerian War mainly in relation to civil rights.[54]

The Stone Face, Smith's last novel, charts the political awakening in Paris of thirty-year-old black American journalist and painter Simeon Brown and unfolds against a dense backdrop of Algerian anticolonial resistance and US civil rights activism. When Simeon crosses the Atlantic in spring 1960, he becomes a

"white man," freed of the US racial dynamic and its threat of harm (48). Referring to the embodiment of this threat, the title *The Stone Face* is precisely what
Simeon has seen repeatedly expressed in the faces of his white aggressors in
Philadelphia, a hatred he attempts to re-create from memory in a painting. His
friendship with Algerians in the French capital not only rekindles these memories
of racist violence in his birthplace; it also reveals to Simeon Parisians' double
standard toward racialized subjects, pricking his conscience and informing his
decision to return home. The politics of race intersect with interracial relationships as Simeon has to choose between the hedonistic lifestyle of his fellow expatriates and the anticolonial struggle fought by the Algerians. These competing
choices are embodied by a lopsided interracial romance with Maria, an ambi-
tious Polish exile and Holocaust survivor, and a passionate friendship with
Ahmed, a self-sacrificing Algerian student. In bringing together Paris's exile
milieu and its colonial underbelly, Smith denounces expatriates' escape from
racism and indifference toward Algerian suffering, calling for a global commitment and solidarity among victims of racial oppression.

Though the *New York Times Book Review* called the book "a solid achieve-
ment" and counted W. G. Smith "among the most worthy young writers,
Negro or white," this 1963 novel (whose publication coincided with the March
on Washington) had been more or less forgotten.[55] But in the past twelve years
or so, critics such as Paul Gilroy, Eric Sundquist, and Michael Rothberg have
turned to Smith's *The Last of the Conquerors* and to a lesser extent *The Stone Face*
to illuminate a number of concepts: nonracialogical justice, African American
deployment of the Holocaust as a interpretative framework for understanding
antiblack racism, and collective memory as negotiated, cross-referenced, and
borrowed.[56] Yet only a couple of critics have noted the centrality of the Algerian
War in Smith's novel and tied it to the idea that some expatriates became disillusioned with Paris.

For Smith, colonial Paris is a linchpin for rethinking African Americans'
vision of France and Europe in view of African anticolonial battles. Like Baldwin, Smith frames colonial Paris in a decidedly masculine language of brotherhood. Yet unlike Baldwin's and Wright's works, *The Stone Face* constructs a model
of black masculinity by redrawing the relationship between Paris and mixed
couples. Whether they include or ignore colonial subjects, Baldwin and Wright
portray Paris as a city that nurtures black American men's artistic or profes-
sional potential. Instead of signifying racial equality and masculine empowerment, the interracial romance in *The Stone Face* becomes an illusory integration
that must be sacrificed for these goals to be realized. Smith replaces romance
with brotherhood by introducing Algerian protagonists and their experiences
of the city, in turn instituting Algerian manhood as a model of communal
commitment and sacrifice for African Americans.

Becoming a "brother" is different from becoming "a man like other men." The ubiquity of black–white romance in Paris symbolized a universal manhood that suggested a (gendered) shared humanity. In contrast, "brotherhood," as Smith defines it, demands that with the consciousness of racist oppression across borders comes the moral responsibility of the witness. Brotherhood synthesizes seemingly different feelings: the hurt of institutionalized exclusion, sympathy and solidarity with those who share similar circumstances and interests, and pride in affirming a manhood that has been subdued. As such, brotherhood signals a transnational pledge of loyalty; it represents a successful homosociality based on mutual recognition that counterbalances failed relations between black and white men in the United States. As the principal measure of freedom and the rallying point for the subalterns, manhood is both a means and an end.

If Wright and Baldwin present black men's supposed unmanliness as a product of Jim Crow that epitomizes victimhood and raises consciousness about racial oppression, Smith uses unmanliness to zoom in on what he views as the roots of the US race problem: the failure of black–white homosociality. Baldwin had disrupted the white Southern imaginary that perceived black men as sexual predators by associating sexual violence with white policemen. Similarly, in Wright's *The Long Dream*, a white police officer arrests Fishbelly in a white neighborhood and threatens to cut off his genitals with "a shining knife-blade tip" until the latter faints and brings the squad to their knees with laughter (118). These recurring scenes of white police brutality evoke a legal white monopoly on claims of patriarchy, one that violently polices and crushes any competition. In an early scene of *The Stone Face*, Simeon reminisces on his police arrest in a white neighborhood in Philadelphia. Like Wright's Fishbelly, he is suspected of being on the prowl for white women and is brought to the back room of a police station, where one white male officer pounds Simeon's groin until he faints. When he regains consciousness he is naked and tied down to the floor. Two officers armed with "lengths of rubber hose" beat him as their colleagues watch them having their "fun" (36). One of the officers responds to Simeon's "stifled cry" by "talking softly, soothingly, in whispered joy" (37). The officer's declaration to Simeon, "we are married from now on, you and me," blurs the line between a lover's promise to remain united and an abuser's threat of more violence to come (37). This marriage metaphor pits man against man in a zero-sum game of status and privilege. The policeman's homoerotic sadism that codes Simeon as feminine not only replaces the trope of the black male rapist; it speaks to white men's failure to recognize black masculinity. Simeon reacts to his emasculation by purchasing a gun to kill the officer, a phallic symbol that reasserts his virile attributes, a means and a sign of power that can counteract a "perverse" homosociality.

If the law and its personification emasculate black men, the narrative suggests that only by transgressing the law can they assert their manhood, at great
risk. For journalist Benson, another "refugee" from black America, the interracial romance typifies the relationship between white rule and black manhood
(11). Benson explains that he feels guilty after intercourse with a white woman
and would never consider marrying her, but marriage to a black woman
"would be like accepting segregation. . . . [He] would be staying 'in [his] place.'
Well dammit, no! . . . It's only when [he] break[s] the rules that a Negro man
calls himself a man" (152). Through interracial sex, Benson challenges America's
established order, subverting antimiscegenation laws that legislate his right to
choose his lover or wife and deny his equality with white men. As such, the white
woman offers a metaphorical site for a displaced struggle between white and
black men over the production and extension of patriarchal power. But if this
kind of illegal intercourse can disrupt racial hierarchies in the United States,
what does it accomplish in Paris, where this romance is neither illicit nor
uncommon?

For Baldwin's narrator, interracial intimacy in Paris signals that he has
become "a man like other men." Smith is not so optimistic. On the contrary (as
Wright also suggested with his reference to interracial sex as a "black market"),
white European women read Simeon and other black expatriates as different
from white men, invoking racist ideas of insatiable sexuality. Swedes Ingrid and
Marika let their African American dates know that they came to Paris in search
of licentiousness and exoticism, leaving behind Stockholm, "the dullest place in
the world," a city where men are "too blond" and "not interested in girls" (31).
Here, as in the United States, subjects of African descent possess accentuated
libidos. While black American expatriates note that unlike American men,
French men are not sexually repressed or insecure, still, African American men
are not recognized as equals in Paris but as exotic sexual commodities.

Even the romance between Simeon and Maria, while it transcends the pursuit of exoticism, imposes limitations on his behavior and action. Holocaust
survivor Maria and Simeon both came to Paris to escape a past marked by racial
violence, and their romance is founded on mutual recognition. But Maria's love
for Simeon is contingent on his renunciation of politics and, in time, he sur-
renders. The couple's literal near-blindness evokes a scarred childhood and a
reticence to revisit it or think about ongoing forms of racial subjugation around
them. But while Maria is able to keep her racial traumas at bay, Simeon's are
rekindled through his encounter with Algerians. As his interest in decolonization
and civil rights activism erodes his romance with Maria, it strengthens his
friendship with Ahmed and uncovers a colonial Paris.

For Smith, manhood and brotherhood are couched not in universalist
terms but in the shared racial particularity of the African American and Algerian

experiences. *The Stone Face* is a heart-to-heart with Baldwin; it borrows from his short story a scene of a night out at a club with a North African friend and the skirt-chasing film director Jean-Luc Vidal, as well as the motifs of blindness and nightmares. Surprisingly, the scholarship does not address this intertextuality, even when critics write about these two texts together.[57] Both authors describe colonial Paris as a site of recognition between African Americans and North Africans, a site similar to black America with its dynamics of racial segregation and public stigma. While Baldwin's narrator's contact with North Africans does not explicitly alter his view of Paris and what it signifies for his interracial family, Simeon's friendship with Algerians quickly interrupts his first impression of a color-blind Paris and poses a challenge to his romance with Maria.

Smith's novel rewrites the club scene so as to reverse Baldwin's description of black and brown disassociation. In both texts, two separate and unequal worlds of Paris come into contact: cosmopolitans and colonial migrant workers. In Baldwin's narrative, Boona's alleged act of theft bespeaks the different social status of African Americans and Arabs in Paris and crystallizes the impossibility of a meaningful bond between himself and the narrator. In Smith's club scene, the humiliation of the protagonist's Arab friends—Ahmed, Hossein, and Ben Youssef—does not stem from their own actions but from the "stares, whispers and laughs" of French club patrons (93). Simeon becomes conscious that his friendship with the Algerian "pariahs" risks him his acceptance by the French (93). He notes that "for a frightening second, [he] had rejected *identification* with them! . . . Sitting here with the Algerians he was a nigger again to the eyes that stared" (93–94). Whereas Baldwin's protagonist is thankful to French society for leaving him alone and thereby feels at odds with Algerians' ire, Smith reads disidentification with these subjects as a form of complicity with French racism. Both authors associate solidarity with Algerians with rejection by the French, but Smith focuses on the risk rather than the dilemma of identification and ultimately urges fellow expatriates to take it on, to turn their Parisian refuge into yet another racial battlefield.

Between Baldwin's cosmopolitan Paris and Smith's colonial Paris, the rhetoric of aggrieved masculinity yields to articulations of an aggressive manhood. Wright, Baldwin, and Smith all refer to the violence of decolonization, but only the latter depicts it as ultimately necessary and justified. Whereas a humiliated Boona exits Baldwin's narrative, Ben Youssef insists on his rightful presence and orders the woman who had insulted him to dance with him. This defiant proposal of Franco-Algerian intimacy disputes the status difference between French and Algerian men the woman had emphasized in her snide remark that "really, they let just *anybody* in the Château these days, it seems" (96). The raison d'être of Ben Youssef's demand is to manufacture Algerian masculinity, otherwise colonial Paris has no room for the prospect of interracial romance. Unlike

Baldwin's Boona, who is always looking for a girl, Simeon notices that although "you could not walk down a street on the Left Bank without running across mixed couples . . . he had never seen an Algerian with a Frenchwoman" (78). *The Stone Face* encourages us to interpret the absence of Franco-Algerian couples as Algerians' refusal to be distracted from the principal pursuit of independence. Ahmed explains that the interracial romance is "an opium dream" that misleads African American expatriates into believing that they have achieved freedom, a metaphor analogous to Wright's portrayal of black–white intimacy in "Island" (161). However, another buried reference to the interracial romance conveys the poor reputation of Algerian men in France. They have to do without women, Ahmed explains, though "sometimes, on payday, they go to a prostitute, if she'll have them. Most Frenchwomen won't go out with Algerians" (89). In fact, the only white and brown romance included in *The Stone Face* ends at a police station. Simeon had rescued a young female Dutch tourist from an aggressive Algerian man, only to learn that the woman in question was his girlfriend and had stolen his month's pay, which provides his large family in Algeria with basic necessities.[58]

Besides the evening at the château, other encounters between Algerians and Simeon also intimate that brotherhood requires more than the simple recognition of Paris's color line; it necessitates crossing it. During one of his first days in Paris, Hossein, an Algerian worker and National Liberation Front (FLN) activist, hails Simeon as a "white man," invites him to have coffee, and confronts him about his newly found freedom. Hossein explains that he, too, became "white" by crossing the Atlantic. Recounting the new status his nationality afforded him in America, he describes how he rejected that cachet: "I saw how they treated people like you there, black people. . . . And guess what—in the States, they considered me and people like me white! But I wasn't fooled, I went to the black neighborhoods anyway" (49). By crossing his host society's color line when he was in the United States, Hossein gave up the advantage that a new place with different racial dynamics bestowed on him. Having sacrificed his whiteness in America out of solidarity with black men, Hossein asks that Simeon do the same in Paris. As Michael Rothberg notes, Hossein's interpellation of Simeon as a "white man" is a moment that "implicates" African Americans in French colonial politics as "complicit beneficiaries."[59] What Hossein demands from Simeon is moral responsibility and solidarity with other victims of racial injustice. In Baldwin's short story, Boona's identification with the African American narrator, whom he calls "my brother," requires no reciprocity. In contrast as Simeon grows closer to the Algerians, he is "tested" during the club scene, and in time his solidarity with the "pariahs" gains him the trust Hossein had denied him at first (93).

Bolstered by his friendship with the Algerians, Simeon's widened perspective on Paris leads him to redefine what and who is a "brother," a fraternal bond the French state attempts to stifle. As he travels outside Paris's invisible borders, Simeon maps out a brown metropolis that reminds him of "slum tenements in Harlem or Philadelphia," another nation within the nation (81). He observes, "the further north the bus moved, the more drab became the buildings . . . the streets narrower and noisier. . . . Men out of work, with nothing to do and no place to go, stood in sullen, futile groups on street corners" (75). Smith underscores the pressure the French state exercises on maintaining these borders. When Algerians like Ahmed walk in other sections of the city, police officers ask them for their identification papers and arrest those whose name has already been recorded, labeling them troublemakers. The French state also requires its guests to stay out of colonial affairs. As long as they do not trespass on colonial politics, Paris integrates black Americans, grants them social mobility, and provides them the prospect of inclusive romance. However, when the police find Simeon in Hossein's bedroom, they accuse him of working for the FLN and warn him that he "could be expelled from the country at the slightest suspicion" (83). The officer advises Simeon to leave the Algerian enclave and return to the "nice cafés over there on the Left Bank" (83). As Simeon ventures outside the urban and political boundaries described by the officer, his guest status is jeopardized, and he is eventually treated like an Algerian: arrested and beaten by the police (82, 174). This police repression is precisely what black expatriates have sought to escape. For Simeon, the subjugation of Algerians in Paris speaks of the global scale of racial domination, for in France, too, you find "the ghetto, the cops, the contempt—the same thing" (91).

Corresponding to their social and geographical containment, it is also centrally the space they occupy in the French imaginary that confines Algerians. These literal and imaginary geographies are entangled, of course. Simeon discerns the difference of language used to address him versus the Algerians. Simeon has become "a new man" in Paris, no longer demeaned by epithets such as "boy," for the French address him as "Monsieur" (5). They do not, however, call Algerians "Monsieur"; instead they refer to them in the familiar form of the pronoun "tu" or call them slurs such as "bicot, melon, raton, nor'af" (49–50). When French protagonists refer to Algerians or Arabs, they are not describing any one individual but an imagined homogeneous group. Raoul, a French student, explains to Simeon: "The French don't like the Arabs, but it's not racism. The Arabs don't like us either. We're different. . . . They're a closed people. You can't really get to know them. They scowl when you laugh; you never know what they're thinking. And if you turn your back, they're liable to stick a knife in it. . . . It's different. I assure you it's not racism"

(54). Informed by a colonial imaginary of the colonized world as opaque, Raoul's vision of the Arab is compounded by the war, hence his focus on the Algerian male revolutionary. Similarly, when Simeon witnesses a policeman who "cursed and slapped an Algerian in the face," the officer justified himself: "You don't understand. You don't know how they are, les Arabes. Always stealing, fighting, cutting people, killing. They're a plague; you're a foreigner, you wouldn't know. A night in jail is letting them off easy" (46). In contrast to these scripted perspectives about Arabs that in turn serve to warrant colonial violence, Simeon's friendship with Algerians introduces him to a diverse group including Ahmed, the sensitive and idealist student; Hossein, the revolutionary who is committed to political violence; and Djamila and Latifa, who are widowed activists.

While Wright and Baldwin deal principally with a cosmopolitan Paris, Smith turns to colonial Paris as a site of masculine and moral transformation. Simeon's transformation in the last section of the novel, "The Brother," corresponds not only with Ahmed and other Algerian men's modeling individual sacrifice for advancing the cause of a community but also with the inclusion of young women and girls. In an early segment of the text, Simeon recalls "the chase," a purported game in which black girls from his neighborhood would steal the boys' ball and run toward the city's wastelands, where the boys would finally catch and rape them (17–20). Paradoxically, when the narrative again mentions black and brown women (and girls), it is to suggest that these subjects need protection from Simeon, unlike his white lover. The *Paris Herald Times* picture of a black American schoolgirl threatened by "howling mobs" somewhere in Dixie is a blight on Simeon's peaceful Parisian life with Maria. The courage and determination he reads in the girl's face and posture makes him feel "disgusted with himself" (124). Portrayals of Algerian women, particularly the gruesome torture and rape of young Latifa by French parachutists, serve a similar function—they activate men's indignation against racist violence. When Simeon witnesses a French policeman attacking an Algerian woman holding a baby during the October 17, 1961, protest march, he can no longer remain an observer and strikes the officer, "sw[inging] his fist into that hated face, with all of his strength" (174). Bookending the novel, children and women of color are subordinated into "propaganda tools of patriarchy" in a dynamic wherein men are either brutes or saviors.[60] With colonial Paris, Smith promotes transnational solidarity in the struggle for equal rights but limits the role of men and women within it.

That Wright, Baldwin, and Smith all deployed the interracial romance to fashion their vision of Paris speaks not only to the dialogic nature of their expatriate fiction but also to a shared imperative to transform US race dynamics. As the quintessential metaphor for the inclusion of black Americans in France, the interracial romance intertwined concerns about the equal recognition of citizens and masculine sovereign subjects. It becomes the vehicle through which Wright expresses his disillusionment with Paris and Parisians in "Island." Mobilized as part of social protest, cross-racial desire organized questions of recognition and epitomized the nation through the heterosexual couple while reaffirming the patriarchal order and obscuring cross-gender consciousness and solidarity. Baldwin fashioned Paris as the privileged site of black–white intimacy, endowing the city with notions of racial equality and recovered manhood and indicting America's discrimination against its black citizens. Even when it includes its Algerian minority, Paris is seemingly a means to imagine alternative social arrangements at home, a vantage point from which to interrogate and transform US race politics. Yet the colonial subplot unearths unusual zones of contact and other possibilities of affiliations for black US expatriates. After the end of the Algerian war, these take front stage in *The Stone Face* as Algerian protagonists cease to be a flickering presence in the background. Smith challenged the analogy of interracial romance as a trope of equal recognition and placed it in tension with an alternative route to reclaiming masculine dignity. *The Stone Face* underscores the significance of male friendship with Algerians that transforms Simeon from a fugitive of US racial politics to a determined international "freedom fighter," and replaces the interracial romance as conceived by his predecessors. Smith championed a global consciousness about racial domination that mapped out new sites of state repression and gave full expression to the preeminence of cross-racial brotherhood.

The New Harem

Despite the promise of oriental exoticism in its title, Mehdi Charef's best-selling 1983 novel *Thé au harem d'archi Ahmed* (*Tea in the Harem*) barely travels beyond Paris. It opens in the city's outskirts, in a urine-soaked basement of government-subsidized housing, where eighteen-year-old Majid fails to repair his motorcycle. The narrative then journeys in and out of its overcrowded apartments, ventures a few times to the central city, and ends on Majid's arrest in a stolen car in the panoramic ocean view of Deauville. The bookends and what comes in between speak to the spatial confinement of a generation born to Maghrebi immigrants and raised in France. By referring to the harem, an Orientalist icon associated with the colonial era, to describe a Parisian location, Charef's title calls on ideas of spatial sequestration and traces temporal and spatial links with French Algeria. The opening basement scene when Majid looks up his friend Farid encapsulates some key ideas about this new harem. Also of Maghrebi origin, Farid is a shrunken nineteen-year-old drug addict who lives underground since his family threw him out. In the damp and gloomy cement room, Farid's makeshift bed consists of orange boxes and "an old suit-case as his pillow—brown mock-leather, with its corner all dented" (8). The old suitcase suggests that Farid inherited his forebears' suitcase and perhaps their association with foreign land, as well as their segregation at the periphery of the city. Instead of travel to the Orient and titillating Franco-Algerian encounters in the forbidden harem, the narrative unveils another territory hidden from France's view: the impoverished multiracial banlieue. In this isolated setting, the spectacle is one of poverty, enchantment is drug-induced, and sexual adventures provide young men with a means for social recognition, a chance to differentiate themselves from docile immigrants and low-wage workers as well as wealthy city-dwellers.

We find the harem as a central figure of analysis in the scholarship of Orientalism and colonialism in North Africa, Turkey, and India. It chiefly marks an imperial site of difference for the West and a targeted site for domestication and progress.[1] As a key colonial trope, the harem or seraglio, that is, the private female quarters in a Muslim household, served as a shorthand for a wide range of ideas about the Orient: gender sequestration, sexual proclivity, and tyrannical regimes. As Jarrod Hayes notes, "the Harem, the sequestering of women have come to stand for not only the oppression of women within these societies these practices are seen to represent, but also with the universal oppression of women."[2] A century before the publication of *Tea*, Orientalist authors such as Pierre Loti shared their impressions of *depaysement* or estrangement in encountering North African landscapes and harems; others like Magali Boisnard shared their immersion in indigenous cultures. In Algeria, the exotic "was associated with the Mediterranean beauty of the land and the eroticism of Orientalism" and in particular with ideas of the Arab as "an essentially sexual being."[3] Portrayals of the harem called on female lovers languid with desire, awaiting attention. This site allows the "absolute limitlessness of pleasure," "voluptuous sexual fantasies in which men have their way with vulnerable women who are happy to satisfy their needs," or homosexual contacts among "Oriental" men, evidence of "Eastern" cultures' depravity.[4]

Charef reappropriates this polysemic colonial metaphor in a metropolitan context and space to divulge a refiguration of the exotic. His is a different harem, a hidden society separated from the city by train tracks and highways to which the general reader has no access. Located in the Paris outskirts, the harem invokes a site that is segregated and surveilled, fantasized by the mainstream as antithetical to the rest of the city, a window onto modernity's nonmember, and a locus against which French society defines itself. As Charef's narrator ushers readers into this landscape, he plays on and disrupts Orientalist expectations. By documenting these cultural tensions in 1980s Paris, *Tea* fits neatly the characteristics of the postcolonial novel. As Graham Huggan notes, in postcolonial contexts, "exoticism is effectively repoliticized, redeployed both to unsettle metropolitan expectations of cultural otherness and to effect a grounded critique of differential relations of power."[5] However, Charef's parody of exoticism goes beyond challenging the fashioning of cultural and racial differences. His critique unveils the distance-building process inherent in the spectacle, whether it casts racial minority, female, or poor subjects. As such, the author expands on an icon about imperial dominance, by examining capitalist and patriarchal oppressive forces. Like other postcolonial authors, he offers a staging of marginality by dramatizing his generation's subordinate position in relation to the mainstream and for its benefits.[6] But when he reveals structures of power, he decries postcolonial subjects' complicity with capitalist cultures. These men may be surplus cheap labor parked close to former factories outside the city, but they also treat other subjects as commodities.

Transitioning to the postcolonial era, this chapter examines the politics of intimacy through the Orientalist trope of the harem, in particular, the framing of difference as a spectacle. During the colonial era, the harem became a weapon in the discursive arsenal that sought to justify imperial conquest as benevolent and a force for civilization. The term conjured up native women as quasi-enslaved subjects with no rights to claim and no protection from the law. From Mary Wollstonecraft to Simone de Beauvoir, Western feminist figures summoned the harem to rally their nation's consciousness about gender inequality by comparing their female citizens to the seraglio woman of primitive societies. In the numerous studies devoted to *beur* fiction, discussions of intimacy are generally limited (if addressed at all) to the conservative strictures young Franco-Arab women raised in France have often experienced in Muslim immigrant communities. In the 1990s, authors such as Ferrudja Kessas, Nini Soraya, and Sakinna Boukhedenna have called attention to their struggle for recognition in French society and at home, where relatives suppress their individual and sexual freedom. In contrast, Charef's *Tea*, the foundational text of beur fiction and a watershed of youth culture, deploys intimacy conceptually to disrupt portrayals of the Paris periphery as exotic. Charef questions the lens and register of the exotic, while at the same time using its exteriorizing process to denote the relationship between the affluent city and its depressed outskirts as a spectacle. The "ex" in *exotic* refers to a location "outside" or "exterior" to the familiar and normal. It highlights an experience of alterity. Similarly, Guy Debord says of the spectacle that it is the reign of vision and vision is exteriority. "Separation," he adds, "is the alpha and omega of the spectacle."[7] For postcolonial authors in Europe, this exteriority or separation is complicated. On the one hand, they are immersed in European culture. On the other hand, they are often perceived as foreigners. The exotic discourse they hold about their communities of origin is unique in that they are both subjects and objects of the discourse.[8] In an interview, Charef explains, "I was always under the impression that they looked at us from afar. I wanted to tell the people from the outside, the French: 'we aren't beasts, we too are after something, we want a life.'"[9] Elsewhere he notes that mainstream media describe inhabitants of the Parisian banlieues as "savages . . . living an empty existence."[10] Eager to undermine this primitive vision, Charef wanted *Tea* to "implicate" the reader. By featuring protagonists who are either voyeurs, performing a role for an audience, or objects of surveillance, Charef's novel uses the notion of the spectacle to convey and interrogate relations of power between the city and its outskirts, France and Algeria. With this focus, he addresses the question of distance—physical, affective, and social—that turns destitution into a show and women into sexual objects to be traded in exchange for masculine self-worth. Here, youth from the squalid sectors are not simply the devalued and poor objects of the gaze; they look at other vulnerable subjects as objects for their gratification.

Tea straddles the generation of immigrant families who transitioned from the slums to social housing in the 1970s and the generation of their children born or raised in these concrete jungles. Urban renovation programs of the 1950s and 1960s had pushed foreign workers out of city centers and toward the slums in the urban periphery. By the late 1960s, more than 75,000 lived in these "cardboard cities." The poorest white French workers had already gained access to the banlieues, new concrete blocks that were being mass-produced starting in the late 1950s.[11] At first, these modern lodgings with electricity, running water, and private bathrooms were a huge improvement over the slums, but soon the mainly French residents housed there suffered unprecedented levels of mental illnesses and divorces.[12] In these areas poorly connected to public transport or railways, the majority had commutes to work approximating two hours, only to return to habitations with no soundproofing and neighborhoods bereft of trees, cafés, small shops, or markets. Fifteen percent of families lived in flats that were too small for them.[13] By 1963, the soaring juvenile delinquency was attributed to the habitat and captured in films such as *Terrains vagues* (Wastelands, 1959).[14] In the early 1970s, the cheaply made Parisian *grands ensembles* were deteriorating quickly, the economic crisis having funneled out funds that could have otherwise been used for repairs or improvements. At this point, the state pressured the mayors and owners of public housing to include immigrants and other excluded populations, such as the elderly and the economically disadvantaged, in their estates. The dilapidated areas were to accommodate immigrant families transitioning from the slums and single male workers from other transitory lodgings across the region. After owners vehemently resisted the inclusion of these allegedly insolvent populations, a quota of 15 percent was set. The owners installed immigrant families in the most run-down buildings at the edges of these housing areas and in apartments that were too small for them.[15] These conditions, in addition to diminished employment, high levels of school dropout, and police brutality turned the banlieues into significant sites of riots as early as 1971 in Vaux-en-Velin, culminating in the historic nationwide riots in November 2005.

Through the timely and symbolic friendship of two adolescents, Algeria-born Majid and French Patrick, *Tea* responds to stigmatizing political discourses against immigrants. In the shadow of the 1973 oil crash that led to France's deindustrialization, the crisis of social housing and unemployment became synonymous with the crisis of immigration. In a 1976 interview on television, Prime Minister Jacques Chirac proclaimed, "A country in which there are 900,000 unemployed, but there are more than two million immigrants, is not a country in which the employment problem is unsolvable."[16] Chirac relayed a widely shared view of the newly elected Valéry Giscard D'Estaing's government. One of its first measures consisted in hardening the Marcellin-Fontenet circulars that restricted immigrant residency, by suspending immigration and immigrant family reunification altogether. In addition to these extreme measures, the government ordered massive raids in select neighborhoods and immediate deportation of undocumented foreigners, legalized controls of identity for foreign-looking individuals, and ordered the detention of undocumented persons in prisons. From 1978 to 1981, between 5,000 and 8,000 youths, for the large part Maghrebis, were expelled annually to their countries of birth for small offenses for which they had already served time.[17] Among this major anti-immigration policy blitz, the *aide au retour* (assistance in return), was the only program that was voluntary and consisted in providing financial assistance to foreigners willing to return permanently to their country of origin. These anti-immigrant policies went hand in hand with anti-Arab sentiment. In the press, on television, in local election results, or graffiti on walls, Maghrebi immigrants and their children everywhere got the message that they were not wanted, that *La France [est] aux Français* (France is for the French).

Worse yet, the 1983 publication of *Tea* corresponded to a "new rash of racist attacks all over France."[18] In July 1983 Toufik Ouanes, a nine-year-old boy, was shot dead by an inhabitant of a Parisian banlieue for making noise; in November 1983 Habib Grimzi, a twenty-six-year-old Algerian tourist, was pushed from the window of a running train by three French men, while other passengers looked on.[19] For Charef, 1983 marked the integration of the beur generation, though it was symbolized by another murder. Integration, he notes, started when a fourteen-year-old Arab boy in Nanterre (suburban area of Paris) was walking in his neighborhood and a white man shot him: "The French shot because he knew that the child was integrated, that he would die here. As long as we were only passing through, we didn't get shot. People said: 'they come, they work and go back to Algeria.' Then it dawned upon them, and us too, that we were going to stay."[20] With slogans like "j'y suis, j'y reste" (I'm here, I'll stay here), 1983 was also the year the beurs marched their way into French consciousness. La marche pour l'égalité et contre le racisme (the march for equality and against racism) relabeled by the media La marche des beurs (the Beurs' march), sought to mobilize different political parties against police brutality and racist violence and improve public opinion about banlieue youth. A few days before the march, the press received the following statement from organizers: "To have curly hair is to be a sitting duck for trigger happy gangsters: in the Parisian banlieue, racist crimes are rife, and for the amateurs of 22 long rifles it's open hunting season . . . to those we say: you can reload, we are coming, the hunting season is closed."[21] Organized by an association in the outskirts of Lyons presided over by twenty-year-old Toumi Djaïdja, who survived a police shooting, and advised by pastor Christian Delorme, this unprecedented antiracist march started in complete indifference. A small group of marchers gathered in Marseilles, then the recent site of yet another racist murder, on October 15, 1983, and were received in Paris on December 3 by a crowd of more than 100,000 people. President François Mitterrand invited the core group of organizers to meet with him. The march yielded a ten-year residence card for immigrants and the less concrete yet significant claim to France by the so-called second generation.[22]

Government research agencies sponsored a number of sociological studies of the particular "problems" of integration of North African immigrant youth.[23] At the same time the presence of French-Arabs was examined as an urban problem, beur associations and cultural productions received generous funding.[24] Informed by this historical context and in contrast to mainstream stigmatization of foreigners, Charef's novel illuminates powerful cross-racial solidarities in Paris's urban margins. "Hey! Paris! Hold on tight, here come the *banlieusards*," announces Majid during one of his ventures into the central city, thus proclaiming that inhabitants of the outskirts are a new force to be reckoned with in the city, and more broadly in 1980s France (172). Majid's warning to Paris not only encapsulates the political tensions between dominant and peripheral spaces in a nation crushed by an economic recession but also participates in a constructed and imagined space in which the underprivileged seek avenues of power and recognition. Majid's Paris is divided between a center that boasts abundant capital, main sites of consumerism, decision-making power, and the nation's bourgeois culture and a periphery that concentrates France's multiracial working-class populations and welfare dependents. *Tea* draws attention to that class frontier, thus encouraging readers to focus on borders within rather than outside the nation. However, the banlieue in *Tea* is not a uniform space. In portraying its daily nature, Charef presents two conceptualizations of community. One is based on bloodlines, the other on solidarity that is shaped by spatial and social intimacy. One is embodied by a generation of older, white working-class men who see the arrival of immigrants and their children in their housing projects as the cause of infrastructural deterioration and thefts, the other by a multiracial group of young men who frequently rebel against their parents' cultural or moral dictates. By comparing the predicament of the multi-racial youth to that of Algerian immigrants a decade ago and colonial migrants (before 1962), the novel encourages readers to perceive the margins of Paris as a colony and foreign land. By calling attention to a new harem, Charef debunks the myth of French integration. He rewrites the republic's distinction between citizens and foreigners by encouraging readers to see foreigners (and colonial subjects) as part of the working class, rather than cultural anomalies, rendering these subjects more readily legible.

Few scholars have examined the significance of space in *Tea*. Critiques generally fall in four broad categories of focus, including hybridity and integration.[25] These two foci often demonstrate beur integration by showing protagonists' rejection of their immigrant parents' culture, perceived as a set of alienating dictates and customs. The third set of critiques has mobilized the novel as an illustration of postmodern concepts such as Homi Bhabha's "mimicry" or "third space."[26] Finally, a fourth set uses beur literature, including Charef's novel, as a mirror of a social context.[27] With the exception of Michel Laronde and Hélène Jaccomard, critics of beur fiction have largely dismissed the role of space and place in shaping identities.[28] For example, Charles Bonn claims that in *Tea*, "there is here no place of identification."[29] Similarly, Alec Hargreaves asserts that beur writers wage a struggle of "identity rather than territory."[30] Critics insist not only that place and identity remain separate in beur fiction but also that we find therein "a refusal to belong to any particular group [French or Maghrebi]."[31] Unburdened by place and group identity, beur fiction, according to Abdelkader Djeghoul, "cannot be located in the continuation of a previous literary tradition, be it French or Maghrebian literature in French."[32] Turning to the sociological concept of heteronomy, Glenn W. Fetzer notes that *Tea* characterizes beurs as having "a total lack of identity. This group consists of those who see themselves as belonging neither to France nor to the country of origin."[33]

These critics, however, limit understandings of identity (or lack thereof) and belonging to the nation-state. Rather than being nonexistent or unlocatable, collective identity and a sense of belonging in *Tea* do not necessarily align with national borders. Similarly, the portrayal of immigrants' offspring who are assimilated to French culture does not necessarily mean that the novel promotes the idea of integration as critics suggest. *Tea* certainly questions the economic and social integration of the French and immigrant working classes. This first-hand account of homemaking in the Paris depressed suburbs arguably provides the fullest articulation of a territorialized identity that transcends national and racial allegiances. In a provocative statement, its author simultaneously professes his membership to the Parisian margins and his estrangement from the nations

Still shot of a Paris banlieue (JR, "28 Millimeters, Portrait of a Generation")

of France and Algeria: "My real country, I realize today, is actually the Parisian banlieue."[34] A place marked by poverty, low-wage working families, unemployment, and crime, the outskirts of the city is also clearly a place of powerful belonging, intimate bonds, and a vantage point that can interrogate whom we think of as French in 1980s France. This exotic Paris reveals Charef's identification with the preceding generation of Algerian immigrants, not just absolute difference, a common motif in beur studies.

Domestic Exoticism

Beur writer Mehdi Charef was born in 1952 to an impoverished family in a rural tribe of Maghnia in colonial Algeria. The family joined Charef's father in a slum of Nanterre outside Paris in 1963, where the latter had worked at menial jobs for more than a decade.[35] Charef grew up in the multiracial slums and the banlieue, spent a short time in jail, and worked in a factory as a machinist until his big break with *Tea*.[36] Written in the slang of the Paris outskirts, the novel represents this world from the inside. It was published by the prestigious Mercure de France and positively reviewed by French writers and critics alike; Charef was invited to *Apostrophes*, a select TV program devoted to literature.[37] A reviewer compared *Tea* to the best of Chester Himes in the ways it "attacks our conscience."[38] Another notes that "it is the true voice of those who never speak" (*L'Express*); "This unadorned voice goes straight to the heart" (*Le Monde*). Writing for *Le Figaro Magazine*, François Le Nourissier notes that *Tea* is "wrenched out of suffocation and life's injustices. . . . We discover a hidden society growing in the fringes of ours. . . . Rare are the books able to tell us about that world."[39] Similarly, Mohamed Nemmiche praises *Tea* because "Charef describes this universe as an insider. With sincerity and no complacency, he tells us about his life and that of his friends at the edge of Paris, in Nanterre."[40] Jules Roy does not fail to point out Charef's authentic writing as well, positioning *Tea* in a tradition of anticolonialism and black consciousness, dubbing the author and his characters the "wretched of the earth."[41] Two common themes emerge from these favorable reviews. One points to *Tea*'s revelatory nature and Charef's position as an insider able to unveil a world to which the mainstream reader is not privy. The other praises the tone of the work, free of self-pity, *misérabilisme*, and self-censorship. As a reviewer remarks about *Tea*, it is all at once "terrible, awful, disgusting, bewitching, wonderful!"[42]

Like Charef, *Tea*'s omniscient narrator is a banlieue insider and our ironic tour guide into this Paris underworld. The novel calls on images of travel and primitive cultures to describe Majid and his Algerian family's arrival to the slums of Nanterre. Located on rue de la Folie, Majid's new home is part of "the largest and cruelest of any of the Paris suburban slums, real Brazilian favelas, except for the sun and the frenzied music" (115, my translation). As his mother, Malika, looks at her abode among an endless horizon of shacks with "thick smoke from people's stoves," it seems that she has traveled not only in space but also back in time (98). Deprived of running water, electricity, and paved roads, her Parisian dwelling consists of dirt floors and board walls covered by scraps of corrugated iron—a definite downgrade from the family's home in Algeria. In the winter, slum residents have to build a fire around the only public water pump to thaw it out. The narrator notes, "To get it to run, you have to heat it up, say a prayer, and wait for a miracle. You might as well call in a witch doctor or do a rain dance round it, for all the good it does" (99). Prayers, witch doctors, and rain dances all ironically allude to so-called primitive cultures, and particularly to lives that depend on the goodwill of nature and gods. Charef's satirical remark denounces the fact that slum dwellers await miracles just to survive. If Orientalist travel narratives have portrayed oriental cultures through the trope of the primitive, here *Tea* attributes the imagery of the primitive to elementary living, a result of national and local governments who have discarded these residents to the wastelands of the city where they also unload "rotting garbage" and "wrecked cars" (98). This trash site disrupts the idea of metropolitan modernity by illuminating its uneven distribution.

This Parisian "harem" is paradoxically unknown and exposed to view. Upon gazing on the labyrinth of wooden shacks amid refuse, a shameful Malika bursts into tears, realizing that her family is to be part of this spectacle of disposables. In Algeria, though the family was hungry, "you [could] always hide an empty stomach, but a hovel is there for all to see. Whatever happened to dignity" (96). With migration, the family's destitution is out there for anyone to see, their economic deprivation a defining placard around their neck, like the scarlet A on Hester Prynne's chest. The cartography of the urban periphery, with the banlieues and then modern apartments surrounding the slums, exacerbates residents' sense that their poverty is bared, as if it were a spectacle. The accidental fires caused by defective gas stoves, which families use to keep warm, provide "a weekly event" that "lasted for hours" (98). When twelve-year-old Majid needs to make a fire to collect water at the frozen pump, he does not want to be part of yet another visually striking performance. He self-consciously worries that he may be "an entertaining spectacle for the residents of the tower-blocks" (100). Majid is embarrassed that "there's probably one of [his] classmates up there somewhere, watching him . . . well fed, freshly bathed and warmly dressed in clean pajamas and slippers. He doesn't like to look up; he turns back to the fire" (100). In this panopticon relationship in which Majid can be observed without knowing, he refuses to be a source of entertainment for a privileged audience. The term "spectacle" denotes these potential viewers' voyage into the slums from the safety and comfort afforded by distance and detachment from the realities of destitution.

Class differences constantly displace cultural differences in *Tea*'s depiction of Algerian migration to the metropole. Transplanted at age twelve from Algeria to Nanterre, Majid is "surprised by the Arab children—They all spoke French! They spent their time—the Arab kids, with the Portuguese and the French—playing among the wrecked cars" (98). With displacement, the young boy is exposed to cross-cultural contacts that were not possible in racially segregated Algeria. His mother arrives at the Paris train station wearing a haik and is greeted by her husband in a fez. Although they come from diverse racial backgrounds, the children of the slums don't have much to differentiate them from one another. Their cultural differences matter little to them, and apparently to their classmates and teachers at school, who think of them as different because of the mud on their shoes, a marker of their makeshift lodgings.

With the relocation of immigrant families from "the bareboards of the shanty town" to the surrounding "concrete," the young continue to transcend cultural origins, but the older generation of French white residents does not share their class and cross-racial solidarity (100). Majid's group of friends comes from a vast array of origins: West Indian, Algerian, Tunisian, and Franco-Algerian mixed unions. The main friendships that structure the novel are those of French and Algerian people across several generations. Malika is friends with Josette, or "Chosette" as she calls her, a divorced French woman on the estate, who is for her "one of the family," and Josette's son, Stéphane, who is like "one of her own" (54). Similarly, Majid and Pat are two adolescents who put their friendship above everything else. They often meet outside the thin-walled tower blocks with their neighborhood friends, "Bengston, the West Indian; James, born in France of Algerian parents; Jean-Marc thrown out by his dad and now sleeping rough in a basement of one of the flats; Bibiche, another first generation Franco-Algerian, . . . ; and Anita, the only girl in the gang, who's . . . left school, no job; the daughter of an Algerian father and a French mother" (21–22). This rowdy group of friends gets together on the stairs outside their flats or in basements to escape crowded apartments where they share bedrooms with several siblings. Older white male residents in the banlieue perceive this multiracial gang and their immigrant families as invaders who make too much noise, commit crimes, and generally deteriorate their neighborhood. These older male neighbors fling racist slurs at Majid, such as "bougnoule" and "dirty bicot," while others police their daughters to make sure they will have no chance to have "an Arab boyfriend" (24, 19).[43] With these men's racist attitudes, the narrative foregrounds that the matrix of old and young is where cross-racial fellowship fractures in the Paris housing projects.

Through this fracture, Charef presents different conceptualizations of community. Embodied by a generation of older white working-class men, one idea of community is based on bloodlines and reinforces the republican ideology of integration that stresses the difference between citizens and foreigners. In contrast, the other idea of community represented by the multiracial youth is based on solidarity founded on spatial proximity and experiences of social exclusion. Majid and his friends consider national boundaries irrelevant to their daily life. For them, integration is a sham, a "rotten carrot" they will not be running after (48). In juxtaposing these two visions of community, *Tea* also illustrates how immigration discourses in the 1970s have shifted from a focus on living conditions and the work of immigrants to the cohabitation difficulties with the French population and the question of integration.[44]

To frame this generational conflict between older and younger people in the banlieue, the novel drops the rhetoric on exoticism and draws on French colonial violence in Algeria. From an apartment window, one neighbor shot his rifle toward Majid's gang. A month later, another neighbor hurled an empty wine bottle at them. The novel qualifies older neighbors' brutality toward younger residents as a "ratonade," a racially connoted word that describes "punitive expedition or brutality exercised by Europeans against North Africans."[45]

However, this new "militia" consists of "a group of tenants—often parents who are infuriated by all sorts of thefts, the noise, stolen or burned-out cars, and who have decided to play the cop themselves" (145, my translation). They "go on the ratonade" armed with "blinding gas, . . . billy clubs and iron bars" (121). The banlieue's vigilante group is driven by their "hatred of the youth" and "a fear that they worked up among themselves and which the media fed" (121). Unlike its historical referent, this repressive violence targets not only youth of North African origin, such as Majid, Miloud, and Farid, but also French West Indians like Bengston and French whites like Pat, Delphine, and Thierry. All are caught in this "war to the death . . . between parent and the young people" (21). Although "ratonade" calls up racial violence, Charef dampens the racist motivation for these attacks by focusing on generational conflict.

The use of the term "ratonade" is paradoxical. On the one hand, it denotes temporal continuity by employing a term associated with the Algerian decolonization struggle. On the other hand, there is no attempt on Charef's part to link these attacks to the context of anti-Arab violence in France since the mid-1970s. In a climate of total impunity (which continues today), former policemen and soldiers shot and killed hundreds of young Arab men across France. Critic Fausto Giudice coined the term "arabicide" to describe this phenomenon.[46] Though the French state remained unconcerned and the public took little notice of this violence, the Algerian government temporarily suspended immigration to France, condemning the French government's reluctance to protect its Arab population.[47] Outraged by this blind violence and even more by the indifference surrounding it, novelists Tahar Ben Jelloun and Nacer Kettane recorded the names of hundreds of victims between the ages of nine and thirty and the circumstances of their death in their book essays, respectively titled *French Hospitality: Racism and Maghrebi Immigration* (1984) and *Right to Reply to French Democracy* (1986). Kettane's first novel, *Le sourire de Brahim* (Brahim's Smile, 1985), reads this anti-Arab violence in the metropole as a direct legacy of the Algerian War. Recounting the murder of a young Arab man, Kettane's narrator explains,

> this was not the first racist murder in the region. It was always the same thing. The shooter was often an old policeman or retired military. . . . Incited by a nostalgia for the trigger, they would indulge in a shooting from time to time, preferably on a brown target with curly hair. For them emotions never ran as high as when they could destroy or shoot these bicots; they then earned the praise of their entourage . . . , nostalgics of the ratonades, they thought themselves heroes. (132, my translation)

This passage refers to white men's continued impunity for exerting violence against Arab men from the Algerian War to the contemporary postcolonial

metropolitan context. Cohabitating with Arab and other populations, these
nostalgic men long for bygone spatial divisions between Arab and white populations. Patricia Lorcin's notion of "colonial nostalgia," former colonizers' loss
of sociocultural standing, can help account for these violent men's motivations.
In contrast, Charef's main focus is not the racial quandary faced by the beurs
in the early 1980s but the common struggles and feelings of unity among young
banlieusards. By reappropriating and reformulating the ratonade as a generational war between older and younger working-class residents, *Tea* evokes a
new scapegoated group designated as the origin of social unrest in 1980s
France: banlieue youth. The term "ratonade" helps frame these youth as victims
of brutality by juxtaposing them with Algerian migrants, a group the media
and public opinion had also vilified, most vehemently during the Algerian War,
and who continues to be, poll after poll, one of the most disliked minority group
in France.[48]

In *Tea*, the ratonade is part of a larger climate of fear that engulfs everyone
regardless of origins. Young people are allegedly "thugs, wankers, . . . burners
of cars," they are "taking drugs, thieving, raping old women and so on" (18). As
a result, security firms and locksmiths flourish. Older residents trot their evil-
looking dogs as if "they were loaded guns" (21). The narrator explains: "This
estate runs on fear. It's the local currency or exchange" (18). Translating how
things operate in the banlieues to outsiders, Charef's narrator denotes that
fears and fantasies of danger are not the monopoly of city residents.

The novel is significant for the ways it portrays a "spatial imaginary" of
the outskirts as at once racially diverse and yet imagined as foreign. Spatial
proximity with Arab immigrant populations contributes to a loss of sociocultural
standing for French inhabitants who are nevertheless the majority group in the
banlieue.[49] This space becomes imbued with a Maghrebi presence. Police raids
of public spaces in Majid's neighborhood, such as Maggy's bar, are a "familiar
routine" (116). Customers have to produce identification papers and those
without them "got the treatment" (116). Officers would take whatever papers
they had and go outside to radio the station and check whether they are on a
"wanted list" or "had a record" (116). Majid's white friend Pat refuses to produce
his papers, exclaiming to the officer: "I'm French. This is my country. What do
you take me for, an Arab?" (117). Pat's refusal to prove his nationality reinforces
the idea that one can tell who is who. He reasserts that identification check is
for racially "marked" residents, not for him. Interestingly, Pat's presence in a
bar frequented by customers of Maghrebi origin erases his Frenchness and
whiteness, rendering him suspicious. In this place, he too could be Arab and
therefore foreign, undocumented, or wanted. Such police incursions that treat
all residents (especially the youth) like foreigners in turn render the latter

equally distrustful of French authorities, be they police, teachers, or government officials. Majid's West Indian friend, Bengston, complains that the recently closed government-subsidized youth center in their neighborhood consisted of "just cops in disguise . . . their programme came right from the cop-shop. . . . They set up clubs like this so they can keep an eye on us" (24). This "us" consists of a racially diverse group of youth, mostly male, who feel constantly under surveillance by neighbors and authorities.

As with the term "ratonade," colonialism again serves as a primer in *Tea*'s discussion of education in the impoverished mass housing developments. The narrator calls on colonial tensions in French Algeria to describe dynamics of poverty affecting banlieue students. The beur generation at one point had an 80 percent school failure rate.[50] Regimented by the state, schools' role is to integrate individuals from diverse cultural and social backgrounds into French society.[51] In resorting to a well-known phrase by Algerian writer Mouloud Feraoun, "the-son-of-the-poor-who-stood-no-chance," Charef establish continuities between colonial subjects and the experiences of a postcolonial generation in the Parisian margins. The designation in Feraoun's autobiographical novel *The Son of the Poor* (1954) refers to a young and poor Kabyle's unlikely success in a French colonial school in Algeria. In *Tea*, the phrase denotes the tracking of a racially diverse and economically deprived student population with equally small prospects. Pat and Majid attend technical college, or "the university of son-of-the-poor-who-stood-no-chance" (51, my translation). In the remedial classes for wholly or partially illiterate children are all of the neighborhood kids: "gypsies, immigrants, the children of alcoholics and prostitutes and a variety of mental cases" (83). By tracking and isolating "all the future jail birds" from the better-off population, the French education system defines these kids' future. Growing up in a neighborhood sandwiched between prisons and factories, Algerian-born Balou, a former student in the remedial class, turns into a criminal, a pimp, "as if it was all laid down in advance, as if it was the only path he could have taken, as if he'd become what he was supposed to become" (74). Balou's trajectory represents a certain geographical determinism, the logical endpoint for a student from a deprived habitation zone. His story, glimpsed through different segments, interrogates the idea of French public education as a means of integration for all students.

In less explicit language, the narrative may be referring to the colonial past in its depiction of the banlieue students as animals. Anticolonial intellectuals such as Aimé Césaire, Frantz Fanon, and Albert Memmi claimed that French racist references to the colonized as animals worked to justify colonial exploitation of the natives.[52] Fanon, in particular, notes that "when the colonist speaks of the colonized he uses zoological terms. Allusion is made to the slithery

movements of the yellow race, the odors from the 'native' quarters, to the
hordes, the stink, the swarming, the seething, and the gesticulations. In his
endeavors at description and finding the right word, the colonist refers constantly
to the bestiary. . . . all this is part of the colonial vocabulary."[53] For Majid, Pat,
and Balou, school vocational training, especially remedial classes, creates stigmatizing experiences.[54] They are the "laughingstock of the school," having
landed in the "nuts' classroom" (100, 101). Other students point to them while
making monkey noises. Mr. Raffin, their teacher, is a "wildcat tamer" who uses
blackboard erasers and rulers as weapons against these "beasts" and "mules"
who can only understand the language of force (103). The animalization of
these characters conveys the contempt associated with working-class students
and the justification of violence.

Conveyed by the titular harem, the reinscription of colonial dynamics in
the metropole is not limited to postcolonial subjects but to other impoverished
populations, including the white working class. Kids from Majid's neighborhood are stuck in the remedial classes for years, until they get kicked out and
are left to their own devices. After three years in this class, Majid and Pat find
themselves sitting on the steps outside their apartment buildings, like "two
foreigners." Like foreigners "who have just landed in a new country," the narrator notes, they are faced with narrow choices: either they "adapt to a lifestyle,
demands, and temperament of others in order to survive" or "reject the system
and have society turn against them" (59, my translation). The two adolescents
having no faith in their society's promise of reward, reject the normative avenues
of success. They engage instead in petty crimes (59). By labeling these youth as
"foreigners," *Tea* reframes French republican ideology by highlighting often
unacknowledged divisions of class instead of nationality.

Charef's new harem is a heteroclite assemblage of images associated with
the colonial era: primitivism, colonial violence, animalization, and foreignness.
But in *Tea* these references call attention to class-specific experiences of space.
Together, they help interrogate the concept of integration by metaphorically
constructing the banlieue as a colony within the metropole. Instead of seductive
stories that unveil women and more broadly Arabs' sensual nature for the pleasure of a French audience, *Tea* focuses on class rather than cultural differences.
In this new harem, exposed subjects experience shame and loss of dignity.

Gender, Sexuality, and the Generation Gap

In *Tea*, while social and economic exclusion provides a generational bridge
between Algerian immigrants and their male offspring in the Paris periphery,
cultural differences mark a generational gap. The narrative articulates this gap,
in the same way it positions young men in the outskirts vis-à-vis low-wage

workers or city folks, that is, by drawing on differences of gender and sexuality. Gender and sexuality indeed serve as principal tools to construct both generational conflict and young men's identities in the depressed outer cities. This fashioning of banlieue youth in relation to these various groups reveals the declining relevance of family and racial bonds in the construction of their identity. If earlier juxtapositions of these youths with the generation of Algerian migrants often depicted them as victims, other segments intimate that the victims can also be victimizers.

Tahar Ben Jelloun, who interviewed and wrote extensively about the first generation of Maghrebi low-wage workers in Paris, dubbed this group "the generation of silence." Indeed, there are few firsthand narratives of their experiences in France. Mostly illiterate, poor, they came to work and send remittances to their family. A few sociologists interviewed workers and published their testimonies, such as Abdelmalek Sayad and Maurice Catani.[55] Mainly, what we know of this first generation transpires through film and literature produced since the late 1970s by their offspring, like the moving documentary *Mémoires d'immigrés* (*Immigrant Memories*) by Yasmina Benguigui, in which Maghrebi immigrants open up about their experiences in France and the pain brought by the "ghorba," or nostalgia. Though beur fiction seeks to give their own generation visibility, it also speaks for their immigrant parents, who have occupied low-income, dangerous, and backbreaking jobs. For Akli Tadjer, Algerian immigrants are construction workers who are "under-proletarians condemned to cheap bargaining"; for Nacer Kettane, factory workers whose lungs have been eaten by iron; for Azouz Begag, cement workers with burned fingers.[56] Sometimes they become invalids after work accidents where they fall from cranes or roofs, such as Majid's father in *Tea* or Malika's father in *Beur Story*.[57]

If what we know of this generation is mostly mediated by their children's agenda, how are Algerian fathers represented? What is their relationship to their sons raised in France? In Charef's classic novel, this agenda can seem paradoxical. *Tea* is committed to presenting nonthreatening assimilated immigrants who traded the fez for a Basque beret and stopped sacrificing animals in their bathtubs. At the same time, the text presents familial battles where sons dethrone Algerian fathers and where sexual power and authority intimately intertwine.

Even before this highly autobiographical novel opens, the dedication "for my mother Mebarka who can't read" marks the difference between Charef's generation and that of his immigrant parents. Born in Algeria, Majid came to France at age twelve, but now he barely understands Arabic, dresses like a rebel in leather jacket and cowboy boots, and listens to punk rock. His mother can seldom understand what he says when he speaks slang. As the eldest son and the only child of the family born in Algeria, he is badgered by Malika to do his military service in Algeria so that he can learn Arabic and know about his country; this would "make a man of [him]" (13). Without this, he'll have "no country, no root, no nothing. [he]'ll be finished" (13). To this narrative of uprooting and rupture, which would stall Majid's manhood, the latter offers an alternative. He reflects that "for a long time he's been neither French nor Arab. He's the son of immigrants, lost in-between two cultures, two histories, two languages, and two colours of skin. He's neither black nor white. He has to invent his own roots [and affiliations], create his own reference points" (13). While Majid also acknowledges his dislocation, he does not favor a return to roots or a claim to Frenchness; instead he will create a past and his "own reference points." This emphasis on identity as created or as Stuart Hall claims, "always constituted within, not outside, representation" indicates writers' ability to create "new ethnicities."[58]

Tea explains the cultural gap between Majid and his parents in gendered terms that cast male immigrants as feminine and docile. His father was a roofer until a work accident rendered him "a child, one more" whom Malika "washes . . . dresses . . . shaves" (41, 35). As if to reinforce that his accident made him lose his identity, he remains nameless throughout the story, referred to only as "the little man" or the "old little man" (41). Before his fall from a rooftop, he "loved his kids . . . spoiled them like a mother" (35). In contrast, Malika is "a solidly built Algerian woman" (11). She is the single provider for a family of six, cleaning schools in the morning and offices in the evenings (17). When drunk French neighbor Mr. Levesque beats his wife, she "bursts into the next-door flat like a ten-ton truck . . . completely fearless" and rescues the family (14, 15). Next to his wife, Majid's father "looks tiny" (112). Like in Chraïbi's *The Butts*, the reversal of gender norms serves to highlight the emasculation of the Algerian father in a context of migration. In contrast to the femininity and fragility assigned with his Algerian father, Majid is described as "more solidly built . . . he could pick his father up with one hand" (35). This role reversal signals the difference of this generation raised in urban Paris that took on the characteristic of the concrete environment they inhabit: "they're dry and cold and hard, and to all appearances indestructible" (51).

In the juxtaposition of docile father and rebellious son transpires a certain rejection of a generation of vulnerable immigrant workers. Unlike his fearless wife and tough son, Majid's father is characterized as obedient. "He sits there and doesn't budge" or "he'd just go with the first person to whistle to him" (113). Whereas Majid's father accepted low-wage work, Majid rejects it. After months of unemployment, Majid finally gets a trial at a record factory in a precarious workshop where "piling up cardboard boxes . . . shut out the daylight . . . and all these kids working *with bowed heads*, without talking, no communication" (169, emphasis added). A few hours in, when Pat is fired because he is too slow, Majid quits. Unlike these tamed workers, Majid "walks like an animal looking for a way out of his cage. . . . He has the air of a whole gang of hoodlums all rolled into one" (33). With no stable work, Majid lives off his mother's work and gets pocket money from pimping a French sex worker, seducing and then mugging homosexuals in the city, or stealing wallets in the metro. The money he steals in the city is also spent there on food, drinks, and sex workers. Majid and Pat's rebellion is tied to absent patriarchs. After all, "they don't even have a father to give them a good thrashing" (49). Regardless of origins, there are few fathers in *Tea*. Those who have not abandoned their families lured by younger "sirens" are violent like neighbor Levesque or devoid of authority like Majid's father.

Not only is Majid drawn in opposition to his father; he sexually exploits other Maghrebi immigrant workers who occupy the same position his father had less than a decade ago, signaling that he carries no special allegiance to this displaced community. Just six years before the family joined the father in Paris, the latter lived alone for so long that on reuniting, Majid did not recognize his own father. Half a decade later, Majid and Pat target lonely, sexually frustrated Maghrebi and Portuguese workers who live in "yellow huts . . . like animals, excluded from the normal life of the city . . . in a work-camp surrounded by a wired-fence" (62). The two adolescents bring to this work-camp twenty-seven-year-old Solange, an alcoholic mother who at Maggy's bar turns tricks in exchange for a beer or a pack of cigarettes. Together, the trio knocks on the doors of the prefabs to sell her sexual services. The two young men have substituted actual factory work for this more lucrative business, but they enforce a similar efficiency logic by keeping an eye on their watch, "five minutes per customer and not a minute more" (64). They use Solange as if she were a "machine," ignoring her complaint about a pain in her kidney and goading more men to sleep with her. Though many workers at first appear sheepish or embarrassed, ultimately "the impoverished sex lives of immigrant workers make a good little earner" (64). In Chraïbi's novel, Algerian protagonist Raus entreats Waldick to share his lover with him, and in Charef's work we find several scenes whereby North African men hope to share the same woman. One of these scenes includes prepubescent boys lining up with their sex in their hand, waiting for their turn with Madeleine, an older and mentally delayed Breton girl who would meet them in the basement of a banlieue estate. Sexual acts in *Tea* are like this: a rushed affair that is public and exploitive. Majid and Pat also take turns having sex with Joséphine, a married neighbor, and with young women at a club, whom they swap as well. The clock, the line, and the swap all suggest ideas of speed and interchangeability of individuals, a capitalist logic the young men

embrace and the next section addresses more fully. Feeling dehumanized by
the young pimps' activities, an immigrant worker runs them out, shouting
"we're not bloody savages" (64). The epithet "savage," which Charef noted
describes how mainstream media have portrayed Paris banlieue residents,
signals various power dynamics that cut across the binary of city and periphery.

The titular harem invokes the mythical abundance of women languidly
awaiting the sexual attention of a man they share. While the novel includes
several passages where this image of the harem is reversed, with North African
men struggling to find sexual partners, other segments reinforce the image of
female sexual availability. Balou's father left his large family for a girl "he'd
picked up in a bar," shipping his "aging ex-wife" back to Tunisia and later
married "a poor kid from the mountain" (74). While older men's economic
stability may account for their ability to pursue younger women and marry
them, it comes at the expense of abandoning their original family. Balou seeks
revenge on his father by sleeping with his new wife. With such action, he under-
cuts his father's authority and signals his own sexual vigor. Unlike his father, he
can lure women without money.

Tea shows that sexuality is a means for banlieue youth to mark distinction
not only with their elders but also with middle-class men in the city, who in
Pat's words "are all poofs" (145). On one of their stealing adventures, Majid
pretends to be selling sexual favors on the Pont Cardinet, "a meeting place for
homosexuals" (126). He waits around, leaning against the balustrade until he
finds his "prey," an "obviously well-off" man, "not a hair out of place" (126). In
a matter of a few sentences covering less than half a page, the terms "homo"
(short for homosexual) is repeated five times and *pédé* (a derogatory term for
men who desire young boys) three times, as if the narrator could not stress
enough the difference between these two men. The city man smiles at Majid
and eagerly follows him toward a deserted square behind a hedge, where Pat
knocks him down across the back of the neck. Majid reaches into his jacket and
"relieves him of his wallet" (127). This relief, monetary rather than sexual,
brings the realms of class and sex together again. The swindle disrupts what
could have been a recognizable Orientalist script whereby French middle-class
men pay for the sexual favors of brown and impoverished younger subjects.
This implicit rewriting of a colonial dynamic establishes banlieue masculinity
in opposition to colonized men and city men. For Pat, city men are not after
women; they are too busy making money. In a fantasy scenario that reveals
much about class and sexuality, he describes to his friends how he and Majid
will be playing the gigolos for middle-class women on the Côte d'Azur in the
summer. The two adolescents would plant themselves on one of those terrace
cafés "where they go drink their tea"; after smiles are exchanged, the women

would wait for their husbands to get distracted so that they could slip the young men their phone numbers. Pat imagines the subsequent sexual encounter with the woman as class war: "You give her a good old proletarian ding-dong. You shag her till she drops [*crève*]. Give her something to remember you by . . . wad of banknotes into your pocket . . . her daughter, her mother, her sister, and you screw them too. No mercy!" (154). The colloquial verb "crever" carries the double meaning of "to exhaust" and "to kill." For critic Hélène Jaccomard, the Mediterranean coast is harem-like, proposing a reversal of roles, at least in Pat's imagination. It is a site where Pat can sexually compensate for his social impotence and take his revenge on an older well-off class.[59]

The story of Majid and Balou speaks to the declining relevance of the family in shaping these young men's identity. The youths' alienation from their immigrant families stems from a disconnect between the realities of segregation and poverty and the parents' cultural and social expectations. Malika wants Majid to work and contribute to the family's income, learn Arabic, and do his military service in Algeria. For Majid, who lives in Paris with no degree in a recession era, meeting these obligations is neither possible nor desired. Despite the overcrowded quarters and the fact that they cannot help their children with homework, many immigrant parents unrealistically expect their children to become "lawyers, schoolteachers and doctors," a hope the narrator qualifies as "the third world dream" (17). Whether the narrative touches on religious Muslim parents like Farid's or Algeria-centered mothers like Majid's, parents are out of touch with their children's world. What these young people know and understand is their immediate banlieue environment. Although the novel often depicts the youth as simply products of their environment, it develops their individual differences, especially Majid's ability to feel compassion for others in comparison to Pat. *Tea* discloses the youth's highly stylized performance of rebellion through the music to which they listen or the leather jackets they don à la James Dean. These myriad cultural artifacts drawn from British popular music and American film point to a fashioning of youth identity that hybridizes the local milieu.

Sexuality as Spectacle

As previously noted, sex in *Tea* is for sale, short-lived, and public. Portuguese and North African immigrants wait their turn to have sex with Solange just like Pat and Majid had lined up waiting for Madeleine to become available, "watching the one who was on the job" (10). This attentive line-up nevertheless evokes a mindless repetitive activity, like factory work. Balou drives into the banlieue with a blond semi-naked woman in a rented limousine, offering a spectacle to his male friends who gawk at their interaction through the closed window. Pat and Majid take turn having sex with their neighbor. At a nightclub, after the two friends "pull a pair," they operate a swap. What is the larger function of these repeated sexual encounters between one white woman and multiracial men? Why are they so public? What role do women have in these encounters? What can we make of the fact that white and Arab men are publicly sharing the same women? Do these portrayals mark a shift to previous encounters in *The Butts* that presented their rivalry for the attention of white female lovers in the metropole? For critic Carrie Tarr, the film adaptation of Charef's novel valorizes patriarchal sexual codes.[60] In contrast, I read the following scenes that display sexuality as a residual cultural artifact that contains traces of dominant ideology even as it attempts to articulate alternative possibilities. In other words, the novel does not simply indulge in heterosexual male fantasies; it explores and critiques rather than simply promotes the young men's actions.

While banlieusards boost their own ego and reputation by conquering their neighbors' wives or younger women, they consider their female relatives' sexual activity as crippling their power. The walls of flats in the suburbs function as a stage to shame families by publicizing young women's sexual reputations with graffiti that reads "Annie F. is on the pill" or "Fatima B. had an abortion" (20). The narrator sees such anonymous denunciation as part of life in the overcrowded suburbs, where "everyone [is] spying on each other" (20). But why are women the principal targets of such attacks? Why are expectations of virginity, modesty, or discretion only theirs? In contrast to the cowardly denunciation of allegedly sexually active girls, these same walls show "great long cocks and hairy testicles" spray-painted side by side with "raised fists," juxtaposing masculine sexuality with power (20). The long list of sexual encounters in *Tea* suggests that any woman in the suburb is up for grabs. However, when mates start looking up each other's female relatives, fathers and brothers feel threatened. Sixteen-year-old pregnant Naima is "the shame of the family," her older brother insults her, and her drunk father attempted to throw her through the window (113), an action she eventually executes herself (157). Young women's sexuality (outside of marriage) represents a threat not only for this traditional Algerian father who drove his daughter to suicide but also for young men of French stock like Thierry. After hearing insults from Pat about his sister's sexual favors, he waited for her outside school and "gave her a beating she would not forget. His honor vindicated, Thierry felt part of the gang again" (69). The collective's reintegration of Thierry reflects the young men's expectations and reproduction of patriarchal domination within families and beyond, in the neighborhood. This lopsided portrayal of sexuality evokes an alternative social order governed by peer pressure among young men and does not mesh with the traditional family unit. These youths embolden one another to engage in sexual promiscuity, even seducing their neighbors' wives in committing adultery. At the same time, they repress their sisters' sexuality and taint the names of sexually active women in their neighborhood.

Reminiscent of blaxploitation movies, the performance of Balou's spectacular return to the banlieue models powerful masculinity for Majid's gang. Growing up, Balou was an object of mockery in vocational school, ever since he misunderstood "Archimedes' theorem" for "tea in the harem of Archimedes." In the estate, youths knew that his father beat him up at home and his employer overworked him at the bakery. In short, Balou was at the bottom of the masculine hierarchy, and he knew it. His reappearances in the neighborhood seek to make up for his sense of emasculation. Once he arrived drunk and joined some youths assembled outside a flat. When the group started making fun of how drunk he was, he held a gun in the air and fired. The young men bolted away from him "like athletes off the starting blocks" (70). Triumphant, Balou beams at finally having "someone sit up and take notice" (70). His second return is more thought out, like a movie scene. That night, Balou drives a rented black car with blazing headlights right outside the Youth Club entrance. Dressed in a suit with a red carnation in its buttonhole, he puffs on a cigar, staring ahead with a half smile on his lips, "like the bad guy in a western" (71). On the windows of the car, he has pasted big denomination banknotes, and in the back seats a blonde girl is smoking a long cigarette, her "blouse unbuttoned, revealing small firm breasts" (71). In slow motion, Balou sets a 500 franc banknote (about $100) on fire to relight his cigar and throws the ruined banknote to the audience (Majid and friends) surrounding his car. The highlight of the spectacle comes as Balou turns toward the girl and has her open her legs with a gesture "from left to right with his forefinger" as one would gesture to an obedient dog (72). With his phallic cigar, Balou raises her skirt to show the crowd surrounding the car windows her "shaved woman's sex" (72).

Balou's masculinity is validated through the spectacle, which itself imitates the behaviors and adopts the postures and props of successful criminals seen in films: the tuxedo, the cigar, the fancy ride, and the young blonde. In addition to commodities that reveal Balou's anxieties about class and power, the young woman suggests a reversal of roles. Her unbuttoned shirt recalls endless images of Algerian women at the turn of the twentieth century and thus evokes another odalisque transposed to a new era. The young woman's desirability, in Patricia Erens's words, "becomes a function of certain practices of imaging, framing, lighting" (43). In this reconfiguration of the harem, Balou turns the tables by accessing white female sexuality. The woman's infantile-looking sex accentuates the power dynamic in a way that minimizes her sexuality so as to foreground that of the male spectators.[61] Together, this masquerade that hyperbolizes Balou's masculinity and the woman's femininity exhibits his power, but only if

he finds an envious audience to recognize and legitimate it. Balou's new status
is confirmed only when the young men declare "you're boss, Balou," celebrating
"the fact that one of their number finally made it" (71, 72).

The term "boss" (*chef*) here is revealing at several levels. The slang term
evokes an individual's superior status. The conventional meaning of the word
also conveys a leading position in the workplace. Balou performs a transformation from a subject exploited by his French boss to a boss who exploits French
women. This performative reversal offers an uncanny echo to Richard Wright's
sinister African American character Fishbelly, who in Paris is also able to turn
the tables in a similar fashion by pimping white women. The staged role of the
narcissist pimp reallocates bodies to their imagined rightful place. Yet at the
same time, the narrative does more than indulge in the performance. It emphasizes the artificiality of it all. Balou, we're told, "played the scene for all it was
worth" (71). "He'd planned this down to the last detail. He must have lain
awake day and night dreaming of this moment" (71). His relighting of the cigar
is "a showman's gesture that was slow, deliberate, and obviously rehearsed"
(71). The mention that the "show wasn't over yet" (72), or that the maestro
"wasn't quite right in the head," or that his smile is "sadistic" all point to an un-
nerving spectacle (73). The performance reinforces a dynamic in which the
banlieue youth are locked out and looking in, a similar dynamic in seeing the
city's display of riches from its periphery. Balou's show maintains exteriority
for the young men, the whole point being that they want the money and the
semi-naked girl in the car and they cannot have them. They have access to the
signs of power only through sight. But this is not simply a reminder of the great
divide between the haves and the have-nots.

Close attention to the text reveals a critique of the male youths as primitive
for their inability to question the display of power in this sordid spectacle.
While "pressing their hands against the windows and laughing nervously
among themselves . . . they circled the car in a mixture of awe and amazement"
(71, 72). Pat smiled at the girl, "stupidly, like a native seeing his own reflection in
a mirror" (71). Wonder maintains the young men in a passive state of admiration as if for an unfamiliar or exotic object. What this terminology evokes about
the meaning of Balou's performance is not only his masculine validation but his
ability to control these young men by exploiting their sexual desires. In this
scene the voyeurs are bewitched and manipulated by their inability to control
their libido. Similarly, another implausible scene of the novel shows how a female
teacher renders her student audience passive and malleable by exhibiting herself,
for "as long as their minds were on sex, things were quieter in the classroom"
(43). In these moments, Pat "became positively angelic," looking "like a choirboy
following the priest with a candle in his hands" (44). The narrative suggests that

the quasi-religious fervor with which the young men focus on sexuality degrades them to the state of animals as they "furtively, cautiously . . . approach the hole [in the teacher's desk] on all fours" (43).

With Balou's performance, *Tea* suggests something else about the spectacle. If the nude woman was from the neighborhood, her identity and reputation would ruin her the same way that other sexually active young women are held in contempt on neighborhood walls. Why is the reaction of the male audience to this woman in the back seat so strikingly different? Contempt is replaced here by awe and amazement, precisely because this young woman does not have a recognizable identity, nor do these young men have any for her. In this moment, she is not a person of flesh and blood but a docile sex object within reach and yet inaccessible. Balou's invitation to the young men to observe and explore is made possible through her abstraction and anonymity. In the end, the principal relationship is Balou's control over the men's voyeuristic lust and sexual desire. Even with no such oversight, we find an equivalent objectification of women when Pat and Majid go on their stealing adventure in Paris city center.

Descriptions of the city are interlaced with those of women on display, objects of consumption to be examined, bought for an hour, and even swapped. Pat and Majid spend the money on prostitutes and girls in a club. Reading the men's dialogue during their visits to the city is like eavesdropping on two young boys flipping the pages of a *Playboy* magazine, exchanging degrading observations on women and pointing to body parts as if they were unconnected to a person: "Look at the arse on that one" (144), "Look at those tits" (146), "Look at those lips. Imagine them sucking you off!" (146). When looking for a sex worker, Majid admits: "I can't decide which one" (146). Pat suggests, "What about that one over there! Built to last, that one!" (146). They look at women as products of consumption of varying quality. At a nightclub, Majid "devours the women with his eyes" (127) as he and Pat "check out the girls who are there in pairs. . . . Too much choice is the problem. They can't decide which pair to pull" (128). When they do decide, the new couples dance, and eventually the men accompany the women back to their apartment, where the respective couples have sex and swap partners. Pat and Majid's language posits women as utterly expendable, mere sexual objects as critic Carrie Tarr noted about the novel's adaptation into film. While the endless cast of sexually available female partners, from married neighbors to a teacher to city-dwellers, suggests the novel is tapping into the fantasies of a young heterosexual male readership, there may be more here than first meets the eye.

The novel ends on what appears to be yet another indulgent male heterosexual fantasy but turns out to be a powerful (if belated) critique of female objectification. After stealing money in the city and eating a sandwich, Majid and

Pat are now considering which sex worker to approach. Both spot the same one
with "tight-fitting black shorts and high-heel shoes" in the shadowed entrance
of a building (147). Since Majid likes the private location, he approaches her
only to discover that the long legs he admired belong to Chantal, Pat's sister
(147). Majid's sexual lust is suddenly deflated as reality replaces fantasy. He
can no longer look at the young woman's body as an object to be consumed.
With the distance between spectator and spectacle removed, Majid attempts to
protect her from Pat. He pushes her inside the building and warns her that her
brother is waiting for him outside. There is a clear shift in focus in this interaction from lust to compassion and a desire to protect Chantal from further
embarrassment. Interestingly, he mirrors her feelings, as "he was thoroughly
embarrassed too . . . he could only say 'I'm sorry'" (147). When Chantal attempts to buy his silence, Majid refuses the money. He had known of Chantal's
struggle in securing employment and had teased her that with her looks she
need not work. Now looking into her eyes, Majid is brought back to the dire
reality behind the performative façade. He questions his recent behavior:
"What a fuckup! . . . Why do I always end up in these situations?" (147). Here
Majid may be referring back to another moment when his masculine fantasy
about prostitution was debunked. After selling Solange's sexual favors in an
immigrant sector, Pat exclaims that after all this sex, she will get a good night of
sleep. Solange's response destroys his idea about sexual fulfillment and uncovers
her feelings of disgust. Pained by her plight, Majid (and later Pat) offers her his
share of the money.

In this final turning point in the novel, Majid's behavior changes following
this incident. If sex in the city used to be an escape for him and Pat, his recognition of and identification with Chantal unravels the sexual fantasy. This chance
encounter also demonstrates the relationship of dependence between the impoverished outskirts and the city. After all, this is where Majid pretended to sell
sexual favors, too. It is the place where banlieue youth like Pat and Majid come
to steal and partake briefly in what Paris has to offer. Pat's mother and Majid's
mother come to central Paris to work. With these journeys into the city, the
novel maps out a critique of commodity fetishism, whereby French and immigrant workers and women are reified into objects exchanged in market trade.

Beur fiction has been largely described as sociological in nature, and reviewers of *Tea* corroborate such function when they each highlight Charef's
authenticity as a banlieue insider. While his novel is principally autobiographical, it merits the kind of critical attention that showcases its author's creative
strategies to resist stereotypical portrayals of an other Paris. His displaced harem
mediates rather than mirrors sociological realities, in ways that bring together
the past and the present, the city and its periphery, citizens and foreigners. As

Balou's case exemplifies, identities are performed rather than simply expressed. Charef's titular harem evokes themes of containment and surveillance, of generational continuities and differences, and of exoticism and visual excitement. The foray into the spectacle brings together different experiences of class. Upon their arrival in the Paris slums, Malika and Majid feel reified as part of a spectacle of poverty offered to all. At home and in the city, Pat and Majid discuss their potential sexual conquests as if women were objects of consumption, comparing them to candy or auto parts. Both phenomena call attention to a distancing from these individuals as human beings. In the logic of capital, they are abstracted into objects for work production, sexual consumption, and exchange. Pleasure, whether qualified as exotic or voyeuristic, stems from detachment. In these scopophilic moments, identification would ruin the spectacle by calling attention to the spectator's relation to the subject on display, like in Majid's final meeting with Chantal. If the narrative calls attention to the city's reification of banlieue residents, it dislocates this binary by offering a critique of banlieue youth's sexual reification of women. The language of the spectacle ultimately provides a framework for articulating ideas of proximity and distance, a stage where one can diminish, increase, or perform power. With its use, Charef urges readers to abolish the distance with which they imagine Paris and its margins.

Other Queers

Since 2013, a couple of legal decisions carved a small but vital space in the French public sphere to discuss immigrant queer intimacies. On May 17, 2013, same-sex couples in France obtained the right to marry. Two weeks later, a Justice Ministry memorandum that described to civil servants how to apply the new law prohibited citizens from eleven countries from marrying same-sex partners. The circular stated that citizens from Algeria, Bosnia-Herzegovina, Cambodia, Kosovo, Laos, Poland, Montenegro, Morocco, Serbia, Slovenia, and Tunisia fall under the marriage laws of their countries of origin. Because France signed bilateral agreements with these countries, which do not recognize same-sex unions, the agreements take precedence over French law. But on January 28, 2015, the Cour de Cassation, France's highest court, overturned this exception in the case of a Franco-Moroccan same-sex union. The legal loophole that prevented Maghrebi queer subjects from marrying French nationals or other nationals, as well as its significant overturn for one Moroccan man, offered visibility for queer immigrants. I use the term "queer" to refer to nonnormative sexual contacts and desires in a French and Maghrebi context.

Sociologist Nacira Guénif-Souilamas explains that the French have long associated immigrants with Muslims from the Maghreb and therefore fail to fathom the experiences of those who are queer.[1] As a social phenomenon, Arab queer intimacy had been largely invisible until 2009, when two popular books on homosexuality in the impoverished suburbs were published: the memoir *Un homo dans la cité* (*Gay in the Projects*) by Brahim Naït-Balk, a Franco-Arab queer, and *Homo-ghetto* by Franck Chaumont, a white former journalist of the gay magazine *Têtu*. In his work written with Florence Assouline, Naït-Balk concludes that he has "suffered more from homophobic hatred by people who share my background, than from anti-Arab racism."[2] Chaumont describes gay and lesbians in the banlieues as the Republic's *clandestins* (illegals). Both texts have reinforced the association of Islamic cultures, the banlieues, and the repression of queer intimacies, offering a city map with clean-cut spatial and sexual politics.

Chaumont presents the Paris city-center as a place of salvation for banlieue queers and immigrant queers from North and West Africa. There, banlieue queers get to freely live their homosexuality. French cities are also an "Eldorado" for immigrant queers from Muslim nations. This triangulation encourages readers to perceive the banlieue as culturally foreign because it is burdened by familial Islamic traditions. For Chaumont, homosexuality evidences the outskirts's worrisome time lag in relation to the city at the turn of the twenty-first century, where stones are thrown in the direction of a queer woman, insults are daily, and where, we are told, some barely escape alive. Homophobia in the banlieue is allegedly singular in its intensity. What the author laments most, though, is not queer bashing in the banlieues but his interviewees' brand of homosexuality: secret, underground, and shameful (23). Though he announces that queer subjects are "clandestines" and "hostages" (103) in these "open-sky prisons" (106) that are the banlieues, he reserves his indignation for these subjects' complicity with the pathologically virile cultures of their milieu. Chaumont's expectations of exposure and transparency are precisely what his interviewees reject for the most part, preferring discretion, anonymity, and at times a double life.

Together the dozen interviewees draw another map of the city, where Paris is not quite the place of salvation Chaumont pictured. Majid, a twenty-seven-year-old French Arab, confides that he prefers going out with other *beurs*, conscious that he represents an "exotic sexual curiosity" as a "thug" from the banlieue for the city's white gay men (23). Similarly, Nadir, a French Arab journalist at *Têtu* who splits his life between the banlieues and the city, notes that a white city man has asked him to don sport clothes and reenact a rape scene in a basement. He has been refused entry into a city club by a doorman who said no sex worker could come in. Other Franco-Arab queers interviewed by scholars, such as Samir, corroborate feeling like "a sexual object" in Le Marais in Paris.[3] A white city dweller that Chaumont interviewed confirms this commerce of brown bodies, declaring that even if you have to pay a banlieue youth for sex, it is cheaper than going to Marrakech (187). This perception of Arab bodies as always already "foreign" in the city partly explains banlieue queers' rejection of the city gay cultures. Kader and Nadjib, a queer Franco-Arab couple who lived together for fifteen years, mentioned that they do not enjoy the effeminate gay milieu of Paris and therefore Le Marais (75). Revealingly, when Franco-Arab queer subjects like Farid choose to leave their familial cocoon for Paris, it is because the city's distance provides him with "anonymity" (133). For all the hype about the city as a site of escape and rescue, few of Chaumont's interviewees feel at home there or choose it as a space that allows sexual expression. To make room for these interviewees' experiences requires acknowledging the existence of a broader spectrum of homosexuality where the macho, the bisexual, and the man on the down low have a legitimate place and so do those who do not recognize themselves in "the imperative of sexual disclosure required in European sexual modernity."[4] Like in the colonial era, when "Oriental sex" was twined with homosexuality, Chaumont's study has "less to do with empirical description of an 'Oriental' difference than with normalizing what constitutes Western sexuality."[5]

A few politicians have played significant roles in drawing this map by stigmatizing not only Maghrebi immigrants but also French populations of Maghrebi descent as homophobic. Deploying a rhetoric of sexual and gender equality, Nicolas Sarkozy and Marine Le Pen have constructed Frenchness against the racialized banlieues. In his role as a 2007 right-wing presidential candidate, Sarkozy spearheaded a "sexual modernization of the right."[6] This included defining his party, Union pour un Mouvement Populaire (UMP), against populations of African descent in France, most of whom are Muslims. In his attempt to justify a Ministry of Immigration and National Identity, Sarkozy stated, "Here, women are free, free to marry, free to divorce, free to get an abortion." This freedom inscribes France as a nation where women can exercise choices in the private sphere, choices that other nations in the Global South do not guarantee. Sarkozy implied that immigrants and French populations who do not assimilate these principles pose a threat to French identity. Implicit in this statement is the existence of undemocratic cultures within the nation where women are forced into getting married, staying married, and bearing children. Though Sarkozy's endorsement of modern sexuality did not include homosexuality, it mobilized gender differences to mark Muslim populations as a menace to democratic values, a trend that other right-wing parties followed and expanded. Marine Le Pen, leader of the far-right party Le Front National, declared on May 1, 2010: "In some areas, it's not a good thing to be a woman, nor homosexual, nor Jewish, nor even French or white."[7] These areas where most immigrants and French *minorités visibles* reside are, in her view, "no-go zones." This spatial and rhetorical binary between sexually democratic and sexually undemocratic cultures hides mainstream France's own gender and sexual inequities by directing the focus exclusively on a segment of the population deemed misogynistic and homophobic.

These sexualized and gendered dimensions of immigration in Europe have seeped into the descriptions of the norms and lifestyles of the Dutch, the

French, and the Germans in naturalization documentaries and have influenced not only anti-immigration and naturalization policies but also exceptions to these policies. Anthropologist Miriam Ticktin uncovers the role of intimacy (particularly a relation marked by warmth, interest, and care) in how the French state grants some undocumented asylum, privileging the ill or violated bodies of women and homosexuals from the Global South. The decisions about who embodies the most suffering, who is the worthiest of care, are based not on "the mediation of science and medicine but of sentiment," and as such the subjects must be "recognizable as worthy of compassion."[8] Such recognition is mediated by gendered and racialized narratives that bind humanitarianism and the struggle against gender-based violence, foregrounding not just "physical pathology but cultural pathology."[9] Such immigration policies based on compassion and care, Ticktin notes, provide papers to "an HIV+ Malian woman, an Algerian child with cancer, and a gay Moroccan man gang-raped by Moroccan policemen and closes the door to most others, making these strangely desirable conditions for immigrants."[10] Ticktin learns in a 2001 conversation with the former president of ACT UP Paris (AIDS Coalition to Unleash Power) that the organization received phone calls from people inquiring how they could infect themselves with HIV to acquire legal status in France.[11]

The momentous and massive demonstrations in Paris and other French cities that preceded and followed the 2013 ratification of same-sex marriage known as *le mariage pour tous* ruined (at least temporarily) the tidy mappings of a north/south and city/outskirts cultural divide. An unprecedented number of Christians opposed equal rights for gay couples joining immigrant and French Muslims presumed to be sexually unenlightened. Tens of thousands of people took to the streets of Paris and large cities to demonstrate against gay marriage, surprising many. After all, France had never strongly opposed the recognition of same-sex couples. Its civil union laws known as Pacte Civil de Solidarité (PACS) have provided legal recognition to gay and straight couples without marriage since 1999. Nor are the French particularly attached to the institution of marriage. About half of couples are not married. Marchers came for different reasons. Some wanted a return to "a racially, religiously, and sexually pure France."[12] Others rejected *le mariage gay* because it opened channels of adoption, which the PACS did not.[13] Broadening the perspective beyond the banlieue and the Global South, these demonstrations and the bilateral agreements France signed with former North African colonies about their citizens' marriage clearly demonstrate ways in which antigay policies affect all, including immigrant queers.

Though immigrants and French minorités visibles are seldom thought of as queer in French society, a long string of films since the mid-1990s has centered on Arab queer intimacies, often casting Algerians or French individuals of

Algerian descent.[14] The Arab male queer on screen seemingly challenges Arab men's assumed heterosexuality in media and political discourses. He positions himself and is positioned in relation to his inherited and chosen family, in ways that reveal various forms of kinship (national, familial, racial). Against the critical consensus,[15] which holds that this genre of films expands our idea of Arab masculinity, I argue that it tends to contract Arab masculinity to a measure indicative of immigrants' and racial minorities' potential to fit in modern liberal democracies. Read against the grain, however, segments of these films transcend the lens of cultural difference to provide more productive windows for understanding the integration of immigrants from the Maghreb and minorités visibles, including socioeconomic deprivation, racial surveillance, and unequal treatment by the law. These lenses, though fleeting, can help us move beyond the dominant story of cultural pathology attached to racialized bodies in Paris (and France) to address the intersectionalities that shape their experiences.[16]

Whereas in previous chapters homosexuality plays a significant role in marshaling, defining, and policing Algerian and Franco-Arab masculinities, this chapter focuses on a genre of film that shifts attention from homoerotic allusions to the Arab male queer as a figure. This figure brings with him a new setting, taking us away from the banlieues to run-down sectors of Paris that gather sex workers, undocumented, and transvestites but have few French racialized residents. Included are films by directors of Maghrebi descent, such as Mehdi Charef's *Miss Mona* (1987), an important precursor of this genre; Ahmed and Zakia Bouchaala's hit comedy *Origine contrôlée* (*Made in France*, 2001); Merzak Allouache's blockbuster comedy *Chouchou*, seen by one million people during its opening week; and little-known dramatic shorts, such as Amel Bedjaoui's *Un fils* (*A Son*, 2003). The Arab queer also appears in numerous films by white French directors, such as *Drôle de Félix* (*The Adventures of Félix*, 2000) by Olivier Ducastel and Jacques Martineau, *Vivre me tue* (*Life Kills Me*, 2003) by Jean Pierre Sinapi, *Tarik el hob* (*The Road to Love*, 2003) by Rémi Lange, *Wild Side* (2004) by Sébastien Lifshitz, and *Change moi ma vie* (*Change My Life*, 2001) by Franco-Albanian director Liria Bégéja. Both sets of films predominantly cast either a young undocumented subject from the Maghreb or a French youth of Maghrebi descent prostituting himself in the central city. I give special attention to *Made in France*, which distinctly cast both an undocumented subject from Algeria and a French young male *banlieusard* of Algerian descent, in ways that disclose the overlap in the cultural fashioning of Algeria and the Paris periphery as oppressive spaces to women and queer subjects.

Queer studies as an academic field has traditionally defined the contours of its investigation to what lies outside the sexual status quo. Since the development of queer theory in the late 1980s and early 1990s, critics have moved away from an essentialized view of sexuality by historicizing its intersection with race and other facets of identity, in ways that interrogate the idea of sexuality as a given. In *Saint Foucault: Towards a Gay Hagiography* (1995), David Halperin famously defines "queer" as "whatever is at odds with the normal, the legitimate, the dominant. There is nothing in particular to which it necessarily refers. It is an identity without an essence."[17] This prevailing notion that queer is an opposition to hegemonic social forces has been called into question in the past decade and a half. Scholars such as José Esteban Muñoz, Jasbir Puar, Marie-Hélène Bourcier, Mireille Rosello, Sudeep Dasgupta, and Mehammed Mack have pointed out that queerness can be deployed for hegemonic, assimilationist, and exclusionary purposes. In a US context, Puar coined the term "homonationalism" to describe "an analytic category deployed to understand and historicize how and why a nation's status as 'gay-friendly' has become desirable in the first place."[18] Following suit, European critics pondered on homonationalisms at home,[19] and in particular on the sexualization of national debates about immigration, religion, and cultural diversity. Contributing to this conversation, my analysis of the Arab queer cinematic genre illuminates the relationship between discourses on queer intimacies and the integration of racialized populations.

As Didier Eribon notes, France has been at best meek in its interest in queer theory, translating key works by Judith Butler or Eve Sedgwick more than a decade after they were published in the United States, and at worst hostile to its tenets at odds with its Universalist principles.[20] In the past decade, however, constructions of sexuality in French cinema have received much critical attention, including Arab queer intimacies.[21] This chapter builds on this scholarship and specifically attends to a repeated but unexamined observation. In his analysis of *A Son*, which casts as its central protagonist Selim, a young queer man of Maghrebi origin, Darren Waldron notes that the film "succeeds in constructing an image of its Beur hero as having integrated a non-Maghrebi milieu. Selim established new relationships away from the family home."[22] While Waldron explains that Selim's racial difference is diluted, "his queerness— through his occupation, sexuality, and lifestyle—is constantly maintained."[23] Similarly, Murray Pratt and Denis Provencher remark that films like *Drôle de Félix* and André Téchiné's *Les témoins* (*The Witnesses*, 2008) that focus on sexual difference deal less with racial difference.[24] In these narratives, the assimilated beur citizens have no families, or "ties to the Maghreb, or violent image of the *banlieue*."[25] In general, these three scholars note the dominance of sexual orientation or race in shaping masculine persona as models of integration but seldom the relationship between the two. Yet their dynamic is revealing of how cinematic narratives have deployed queerness and racial difference as adversative. By remaining attached to a mode of analysis that frames queerness as antihegemonic and anti-assimilationist, this critical discourse does not address its mobilization in processes of racialization. The use of sexual tolerance to discuss Arabs' modernity and assimilability (or lack thereof) is strikingly familiar to the use of gender during the colonial era to reject the assimilation of colonial subjects. In laying bare the association of racialized men with homophobia and male chauvinism in the contemporary period, this chapter also articulates links and ruptures with Orientalist narratives, which often foregrounded Orientals' homoeroticism.[26]

In his study of the dynamic between family on the one hand and ethnicity, immigration, and race on the other, Werner Sollors provides a useful framework of consent and descent: "Descent relations are those defined by anthropologists as relations of 'substance' (by blood or nature); consent relations describe those of 'law' or 'marriage.' Descent language emphasizes our positions as heirs, our hereditary qualities, liabilities, and entitlements; consent language stresses our abilities as mature free agents and 'architects of our fates' to choose our spouses, our destinies, and our political system."[27] Relations of descent seem oriented toward the past and traditions, whereas relations of consent orient toward the future and modernity. This grammar of descent and consent took specific declination in French colonial discourse. France saw its role as a colonial power to move its colonies from retrograde traditions (hierarchical structures, community-oriented rationales, religion, attachment to place and time) to modernity (democratic processes, individualism, secularism, detachment from place and time). In colonial Algeria, the *sénatus-consulte* law of 1865 made it possible for the native population to submit individual requests for access to the rights of French citizens, if they relinquished their personal status as Muslims.[28] Access to equality, which was conceded only to a few, depended on natives' adaptability and assimilation to French cultural values. When those whom colonialism sought to modernize reversed the direction of travel and settled in Paris, they and their offspring embodied their foreign provenance and alleged traditions. In Sarkozy's previously mentioned statement, the immigrants' origin determines perceptions about their cultural baggage, religious belief, and familial organization. This relationship to consent is overdetermined by descent.

Central to understandings of "descent," family has been at the heart of representations of the *minorités visibles*, particularly their inassimilability. In her analysis of beur and banlieue filmmaking, Carrie Tarr deplores that in films that do not refer to banlieue stereotypes such as *L'Honneur de ma famille* (*My Family's Honor*, 1997) by Rachid Bouchareb or *Karnaval* by Thomas Vincent,

> the acceptability of the *beurs* seems to be directly related to their degree
> of commitment to their Maghrebi origins. The films' depictions of the

immigrant Maghrebi family maintain the view that the values and attitudes of first-generation immigrations are the primary obstacle to the *beurs'* desire for integration and settlement in France, and suggest that integration is possible only for those who choose to isolate themselves from their family and culture of origin. . . . None of these films, then, is able to imagine a truly multicultural French society, in which the majority culture would be able to accommodate and incorporate difference (not evacuate or assimilate it) and in which difference would be an asset rather than a disadvantage.[29]

Similarly, in films set specifically in the banlieues and which focus on young women of Maghrebi descent, Tarr deplores again the fact that "they identify the oppressive immigrant *banlieue* family and the patriarchal violence of young men of immigrant origin as the chief obstacles that stand in their way" (113). Some films avoid such stereotypical views, but generally Tarr identifies a connection between spatial and sexual politics. At home, these women are "the victims of the oppressive patriarchal Arabo-Islamic sex/gender system" in *Pierre et Djemila* (Gérard Blain, 1986) and *Chaos* (Coline Serreau, 2001). In public spaces, including city streets, they are sexualized women: from prostitutes to exotic dancers in *Grand frère* (Francis Girod, 1982) and *Clubbed to Death* (Yolande Zauberman, 1997). Tarr concludes that these mainstream representations of young women of immigrant origin represents them as either sexualized or submissive.

Film critics too often label female or queer Franco-Arab protagonists as successfully assimilated if they have left behind their familial milieu and culture. Their language emphasizes choice or freedom based on building new ties. This imagined chosen family based on consensual relations contrasts the inherited family associated with relations of duty and oppressive expectations. In other words, the critical focus is overwhelmingly on cultural difference. For example, Darren Waldron calls queer protagonist Selim, who prostitutes himself in the city center to save money for his father's surgery, "integrated" because he left his Maghrebi family home. However, if we adopt other lenses beyond cultural difference, such as class and race, clearly Selim had no place in the city. His actions there are "criminal" and render him a sexual exotic commodity. Other categories of difference such as segregation can not only complicate our readings of integration but also uncover how relations of consent are not equally available, especially to those whose descent renders their bodies marked.

In analyzing interracial queer intimacies in French and Francophone cinema, this chapter seeks to answer the following questions: Why do these intimacies overwhelmingly take place in the central city, when Arab families have been principally located in the poverty-stricken banlieue? How does queerness (often in the shape of prostitution) affect the integration of the racialized subject?

If ideas of violent patriarchy and uncontrolled libido permeate representations of Algerian men in Paris across decades, what kind of ideological work does the belated arrival of Algerian male queers perform? By interrogating the presupposed heterosexuality of Arab men, do queer Arab protagonists modify previous imaginaries of the Paris margins or the Maghreb? Portrayals of belligerent Algerian men helped solidify a racial category. Does queerness help question it? If other portrayals of Arab masculinity weave in the disintegration of the traditional family, how does the Arab male queer position himself vis-à-vis his inherited family?

From the Banlieues to the City: Recasting Marginal Masculinities

Unlike Citébeur video production, specializing in gay porn and erotic films such as Christophe Honoré's *L'homme au bain* (*Man at Bath*, 2010), mainstream films in the banlieue have either ignored or portrayed a hostility toward queer intimacies. Despite their unique stories, banlieue films often revolve around hypermasculine men in poor sectors who devalue women and homosexuals in everyday talk. Charef's 1985 adaptation of *Tea in the Harem* into film paved the way for a certain treatment of banlieue male youth: school dropouts who are as tough as the concrete jungle where they grew up. Majid, Pat, and Balou exemplify the aggressive proletarian male youth prone to petty crime in the central city that later became emblematic of banlieue films. In one of their city adventures, they visit the Bois de Boulogne, a park of Paris reputed for same-sex activities. Majid waits for a wealthy client, whom he slowly leads behind a bush, where his friend Pat knocks him down and relieves him of his wallet. The casting of overly masculine racialized men who fight, steal, get in or out of prison, do and sell drugs, rape women, harass people, confront police, and riot inevitably caricaturizes the impoverished outskirts in films such as Mathieu Kassovitz's *La haine* (*Hatred*, 1995), Jean-François Richet's *Etat des lieux* (*Inventory*, 1995) and *Ma 6-T va crack-er* (*My City Is Going to Crack*, 1997), and Thomas Gilou's *Raï* (1995). The converging emphasis on seemingly inassimilable aggressive multiracial men shores up "the ways banlieue youth are demonized in dominant media discourses," and this belligerent virility serves as a synecdoche that rehearses fears about this urban space.[30]

Departing from the subject matter of banlieue films and its consistent treatment of masculinity, Charef's second film, *Miss Mona* (1987), represents one of the earliest portrayals of Arab queer intimacy in French cinema, a significant though unacknowledged precursor. Like later narratives, it is set in distressed sectors of Paris, in this case a trailer by the canal, rather than the banlieue. Carrie Tarr states that the film offers "a challenge to the masculine heterosexual identity of its protagonists" (38). While *Miss Mona* still focuses on protagonists struggling to make a living, it follows the downfall of Samir (Ben Smaïl), an undocumented Algerian immigrant, who after losing his job in a fabric sweatshop is driven into same-sex prostitution, scams, and eventually murder. An older transgender woman, Miss Mona (Jean Carmet), introduces Samir into this world with the promise of fake papers so as to escape frequent police *contrôle d'identité*. She, too, would benefit from their alliance by saving enough money for a sex change operation. In his first encounter with Mona, Samir warns her that he is not attracted to men, but his own desire, he learns, is not necessary to turn tricks. Samir's virility is emphasized by his clothes, which include leather pants, a cowboy belt with a large buckle that direct the eye to his midsection, and a long coat that accentuates his towering height and broad shoulders. Regardless of his Western dress, Miss Mona knows that youthful "bazanés" are particularly sought after by older European men wanting to fulfill Orientalist fantasies. We find this motif of the Maghrebi heterosexual man resorting to prostitution to survive or send remittances to his family back home in *Change My Life*, Bégéja's long feature film, and Lifshitz's *Wild Side*.

According to Carrie Tarr, Charef's *Miss Mona* ultimately redraws the line between Samir's Algeria and "a corrupt and degraded" France "through its representation . . . of transvestites and gays" (39). In Tarr's words, Charef's film shows that "it is the perverse, feminized French who are responsible for [Samir's] downfall" (41). A couple of scenes corroborate her conclusion: Samir's bewilderment when he sees sexuality on display, his nausea after meeting a male client in a bathroom, and his inability to enter a mosque after sex acts with men. These segments gesture to moments when Samir's cultural difference chafes against his Parisian experiences. There are other significant moments when the film blurs the differences between Samir and French queer protagonists. Samir, who had been exploited in a sweatshop, invites a manipulated French male stripper to spend the night with him in Miss Mona's trailer. Previously a client had paid to watch Samir have sex with this young man. Now, Samir rescues him from his aggressive boss and invites him to share his bed. This invitation intimates a solidarity among economically deprived individuals regardless of sexual orientation. This young French man turns out to be a thief who stole Miss Mona's money, but the film paints other gay men mainly as lonely and the lead character as a woman trapped in a man's body. Samir kills someone to protect her. Though his relationship to her is formed in dire economic circumstances and tainted by scams to exploit other *sans papiers* or older white homosexual city dwellers, these experiences unite them. Samir may be left with few options after he loses his job, but he is not simply a victim of his host society. Like his partner in crime, his questionable actions are the price he accepts to pay to live "freely" in the future. Several scenes portray Samir, Miss Mona, and her father as a reconstituted family having a picnic in a park and meals at home. This is the first site in Paris that offers Samir warmth and recognition. For Mona, living with her senile father, Samir represents a nurturing companion. This Franco-Algerian intimacy is rooted in the two individuals' understanding of their marginal status and commitment to one another. The film ends on Samir's untimely arrest during a routine identity control that targets people who look like him while Miss Mona waits for him at home with iced champagne and a newly purchased fake identity card.

By taking sectors of Paris as their setting rather than the family-oriented banlieues, movies about immigrant and Franco-Arab queer intimacies indicate that these different locations matter. Clearly, the city offers anonymity and is where the greater number of clients reside. But beyond this economic factor, these spaces differ in allowing or suppressing queer expression. Echoing the queer-bashing scene in Charef's film adaptation of *Tea* (1985), Amal Bedjaoui's short *A Son* (2003) reinforces the geographical binary when four banlieue Arab-looking men violently beat a queer Franco-Arab youth in the city, driving an already depressed Selim to suicide. The short enlarges on the tension between Paris and its urban periphery by pointing out relations of economic dependence. The story is organized spatially around the family locale of a housing project, where Selim visits his ailing widowed father, and sections of Paris city, where he prostitutes himself to save money for his father's back surgery. In the city, Selim dresses in a pink sequin top or flowery shirts, sartorial choices he never adopts in the outskirts, but in the city prostitution circumscribes his sexual desire for other men. When he falls for Max, a middle-class white client, the latter refuses to see him as more than a sex worker.

Whether they address economic differences between the banlieue and the city or France and the Maghreb, Arab queer narratives repeatedly map out class relations between white and brown through the prism of prostitution. *Change My Life* also weaves the spheres of family, poverty, and sex work, but in a broader north/south context. Sami (Roschy Zem), an undocumented hetero-sexual Maghrebi sex worker, sends remittances to his mother. Sami's virile postures and clothing play up his virility that contrasts with the femininity of his transvestite roommates. He professes to his clients: "men, women, all you want, but no one buggers me." His refusal to be penetrated fits the homosexual cliché in Maghrebi cultures, whereby "Arab men, as long as they are penetrators, even with men, are still manly; the passive partner is either a boy or is feminized."[31] In spite of this measure to retain his masculinity, Sami takes drugs (which eventually kill him) to cope with his emasculation at the hand of older

Max pays Selim for sex (*Un fils*, 2003)

French male clients, one of whom asks him, for example, to dress as an Arab female maid and prepare couscous. Sylvie Durmelat reads this moment as "the staging of a complex scene of postcolonial domination."[32] In the emptied Oriental restaurant, a white client in a wheelchair watches as Sami dresses in traditional Algerian garb, dons a wig, and pretends to prepare couscous. This client's request suggests a sexuality aroused by racial domination.[33]

The leitmotif of prostitution in narratives of Arab queer intimacies encourages us to consider economic differences between France and its former colonies and between the city and its racialized periphery. In *Change My Life*, homosexual interracial contacts are traversed by differences of class, age, nationality, and even sexual orientation. In Rachid O.'s fictionalized autobiography *Chocolat chaud* (*Hot Chocolate*, 1998), adapted to the screen, and Ben Jelloun's novel *Partir* (*Leaving Tangier*, 2006), too, sex with other men is a ticket to Europe for those excluded by neoliberal prosperity. Similarly, homoerotic encounters in the metropole organize power relations between the city and the suburbs, white and brown, old and young, and rich and poor. As Chaumont's interviewees indicated, Franco-Arab gays in public housing projects do not fit into the Paris homosexual community, because many white gays see these youth as their opposite: uneducated, poor, and aggressive. Franco-Arab banlieue queers serve as a site of sexual fantasies for some white middle-class gays who are attracted to eroticized figures of aggressive masculinity. This sexual exoticism positions the Franco-Arab subject as exotic because he remains foreign regardless of his country of birth and nationality.

The prevalent framework of prostitution in films treating the subject of same-sex relations seemingly criminalizes homosexuality, but it also serves as a metaphor for economic marginalization, a queering of poverty that echoes the colonial period. As such, Arab queer sexuality in Paris recalls sites in North Africa, site of fantasies and tabooed pleasures. In *Colonialism and Homosexuality*, Robert Aldrich explains that the French "widely believed that all Arabs enjoyed homosexual contacts, both with each other and with foreigners" (329). He quotes from André Gide's travel journals that detail how in North Africa "sexual opportunities abounded . . . he was 'satiated' with propositions."[34] What gets lost here is the uneven power that made Gide, and later Roland Barthes and Frédéric Mitterrand, find an abundance of young Moroccan men willing to offer them sexual favors. Prostitution in the cinematic narrative of the Arab queer in Paris establishes clear demarcation of power between those who pay and those who service sexual favors, those who can fulfill sexual desires and those who play assigned roles. Maxime Cervulle, Nick Rees-Roberts, and Richard Dyer encourage us to consider how films—by Sébastien Lifshitz, Gaël Morel, François Ozon, and André Téchiné—on the Arab boy position the audience as "class tourists" in storylines where social misery becomes a spectacle.[35] Marginal figures par excellence, the Arab queer (French or undocumented) often disappears from the Parisian setting by the epilogue. Both *A Son* and *Change My Life* close with the tragic death of the central protagonist from a drug overdose, conveniently ending their struggle to fit in. Also found in *Vivre me tue* (2003) by Jean-Pierre Sinapi, this death pattern represents a failure to make room for racialized sexual minorities.

Set in Paris, films about Arab queer intimacies have mainly dealt with either a local or a global context, either the Franco-Arab or the undocumented sex worker, but *Made in France* (released in January 2001) brings these figures together in a story that complicates the spatial binaries examined thus far. Directors Ahmed and Zakia Bouchaala counterbalance representations of Arab masculinity in the housing projects by introducing an Algerian transgender character and a budding same-sex interracial romance. Like other Arab queer films, the action takes place mainly in the city. Yet this Paris is not homogeneous. In *Made in France*, the belly of Paris inhabited by prostitutes, Arabs, and the undocumented is imagined as a different world within the capital. The Paris outskirts are absent, at least as a setting. This highly entertaining comedy revolves around a case of mistaken identity. Patrick Maurel (Patrick Ligardes), a white, Parisian, middle-class man is dressed for a costume party as a female hooker when Zoubida, an Algerian transgender sex worker, swaps handbags with him in a seedy Arab café. The police arrest Patrick as an undocumented alien based on the contents of the handbag. Awaiting his day in court, he shares a cell with Sonia (Ronit Elkabetz) and Youssef (Atmen Kelif), two allegedly undocumented Algerians. During the transit to Lyon where the threesome is to take the next flight on Air Algérie, they escape. Now the colorful trio has to learn to get along. Their hiding gets complicated when the media disseminates their pictures and labels them terrorists, collapsing their escape with their presumed nationality in a context of civil war in Algeria opposing the government and Islamic groups.

Made in France contrasts bourgeois and underground Paris by following Patrick's travel from well-lit corporate Paris, a serene apartment, to a dark and dingy alleyway, a seedy Arab café, a prison cell where jailers violate inmates' basic rights, dark tunnels, and underground basements where the court presides. In the first half hour of the movie, Patrick, dressed as a hooker, joins his girlfriend, Marie, at a costume party held in the corporate building where she works. The second level of the lobby serves as a stage where black and brown drag queens dance to the rhythm of an electric soundtrack. They perform for Marie and her media advertising white coworkers located on the ground floor, who are amusingly pretending to be of the opposite sex for one night. This entertaining spectacle is quickly followed with a scene about the struggles transgender individuals encounter in Paris. Leaving the party and his cheating girlfriend, Patrick, dressed as a woman, struggles to find a cab. In dark alleys of the city, Zoubida, a transgender sex worker, walks the cold streets with mace, condoms, and a deportation notice in her bag. The narrative focuses on Patrick, whose unfortunate and unwanted crossing of the lines between spectator and wanted subject touch off his expulsion from bourgeois Paris. His entry into the Arab café leads him to jail, deportation, and unfounded accusations of being undocumented, a terrorist, and later a serial killer. Like Pat in *Tea*, Patrick's mere presence in a bar frequented by Arab customers puts his Frenchness into question. After being processed by the police as Ali Berrada, Patrick is locked in a cell with three Arab individuals, despite his claim that he should not be there, because he is not "like these people . . . not a transvestite, or a prostitute, or an Arab. . . . It's a mistake." The film follows his transformation as his forced proximity to Youssef to whom he is shackled and Sonia, a fellow runaway, forces him to see the world from their perspectives.

Sonia and Youssef shed light on racialized Parisian experiences differentiated by status and sexual orientation. Through these protagonists, *Made in France* weaves together national anxieties about the banlieue, illegalized immigration, and Islamic terrorism. Although it does away with the banlieue as a setting, in

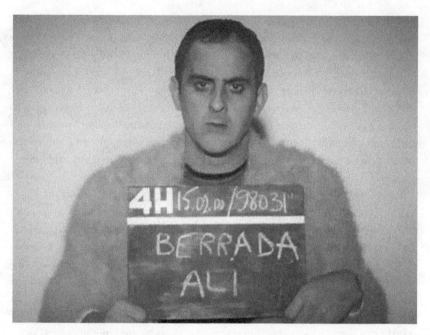

Patrick is arrested as "Ali Berrada" (*Origine contrôlée*, 2001)

other ways the film summons this locale with its multiracial trio,[36] though only Youssef hails from there. He represents its worst clichés. Self-centered and loud-mouthed, this French youth of Algerian descent hates the police, steals money and cars, and threatens people with violence to do his bidding. He stands out in an otherwise sympathetic group. Sonia, an Algerian sex worker, shares his familiarity with anti-Arab racism and the French justice system but not his vulgarity or his thuggishness. And white middle-class Patrick, a mismatched newcomer with whom the majority audience can identify, has almost nothing in common with the protagonists of banlieue films. Through Youssef, the narrative filters discourses about the banlieue. The press has designated this site as a foil to the Republic's ideals of democracy, civility, and respect. Since 2000, media outlets have hyped "insecurity," a catchphrase for the generalized fear of a French white majority for a working-class racialized minority, allegedly ever more criminal. Algeria, recently torn by a civil war and a site of advancing Islamic fundamentalism, also serves as a foil for France. Sonia must escape it to live safely as a transgender woman. It is also the place an older undocumented Algerian man the trio meet will not return to, choosing instead to walk into a grisly death in the whizzing highway traffic. Only Youssef, who has never set foot there, volunteers to go, in hopes of finally fitting in. His arrest for lack of documentation although he was born in France evokes the unstable nature of

French minorités visibles, profiled and stopped daily by the police as potential aliens.[37] Sonia's arrest also calls attention to the ruthless and blanket deportation of the sans papiers that in her unique case may constitute a death sentence.

Ahmed Bouchaala said the spark for the film came when he read in a newspaper that four Algerian transvestites were brought back to the border dressed as women in an Algeria torn by Islamic radicalization in the 1990s. Zakia counseled him to avoid the "mistake" of their first film, *Krim* (1995), set in a banlieue of Lyons, which she felt had not found a broad audience because it was "too political, too socially conscious, too dark."[38] Making their protagonist a French character, she suggested, would provide "comic relief."[39] The formula interested at least five producers, and as a final touch to make the subject, in Zakia's terms, "light, entertaining, accessible," famous Rai singer Cheb Khaled agreed to contribute a song for the film.[40] All the major French newspapers, including *Le canard enchaîné*, *L'express*, *Le Figaro*, *Parisien*, *France-soir*, *Libération*, *Le Nouvel observateur*, *Sud-Ouest*, and *Télérama*, recommended the film, and it sold forty-three thousand tickets in one week. It won the Prix de la critique et du public à l'Alpe-d'Huez and was recognized at the Florence Festival. Reviewers called it a "funny and smart comedy," and "thoroughly like-able";[41] the *Sud-Ouest* said it addressed "social positioning and the unfailing hierarchy of identity values that goes with it" (January 28, 2001). Brigitte Baudin called *Made in France* a "joyously entertaining modern fable on tolerance" that examines the "themes of appearances, tolerance, right to difference in the lighter register of comedy."[42] Only Jacques Mandelbaum disparaged the film, saying it turned "into a rhythm-less stampede full of didactic dialogues whose principal asset is the right to difference."[43]

The right to difference refers to an idea first articulated by the leftist administration of President François Mitterrand. In a 1981 speech, Mitterrand proclaimed that "to deliver a blow to a culture and language is to hurt a people at its very core. We proclaim the right to difference." His statement and the following Giordan commission report (1982) recommended the acknowledgment and promotion of France's regional differences, including languages and traditions. Based on such statements, immigrant and antiracist groups from the banlieues sought to claim the right to difference through a series of marches, including the 1983 March for Equality and against Racism. The visibility of immigrant families increased on the radio, the news, and cultural productions such as films and literature. But French multiculturalism was short-lived, as political parties quickly shifted gears to condemn a model of ethnic identification deemed closer to US "community logic" than to French universalism.[44]

In a nation generally opposed to multiculturalism and identity politics, *Made in France* plays on ideas of French authenticity. The French title, *Origine contrôlée*, refers to the protection of wines and other goods produced in specific soils and climate and according to traditions. Literally the phrase means "controlled origin," a label the Ministry of Agriculture bestows to mark the authentic origin and quality of French agricultural products against inferior or competing products from the global market. Broadly, this title also calls to mind police and officials' contrôle d'identité, or verification of identity. The narrative points out a certain French anxiety about personal origins and categories of difference the *Français de souche* consider disqualifications for "authentic" Frenchness, including Arab ethnicity. The film's trailer captures French attachment to labels beyond the supermarket. In fact, Patrick, "the trannie," is an accountant, and Youssef, the "Arab," is French. Victims of profiling, the trio learn to subvert labels others imposed on them and transcend their own in the course of the film.

Queer Integration and the Revamped French Family

Displacing the bromance of the banlieue trio and the Arab male prostitute discussed above, the romance plot in several Arab queer films indicates the pervasiveness of sexual encounters as a lens to filter the integration of characters of Algerian descent. Family has been a principal avenue for queers and immigrants to gain citizenship and rights. Within the familial rubric, cinematic representations of interracial or same-sex intimacies (including marriage) stage significant cultural conflicts in ways that critique, reinforce, or transform the French integration narrative. Integration, as Sylvie Durmelat and Vinay Swamy note, has mainly been a state injunction that delineates acceptable forms of belonging for subjects seeking naturalization.[45] Despite the abstraction of republican universalism, the concept of integration is largely understood as requiring the erasure of foreign cultures.[46] This model puts the burden of integration squarely on the shoulders of immigrants and their families, who are constantly scrutinized for evidence of adaptation to French mores, including dress, choice of names for their children, and secular beliefs. Films by Maghrebi or Franco-Arab directors give voice to a larger array of cultural concerns surrounding the idea of integration, for instance, invoking ways state agents and urban policies thwart the integration of racial minorities or how mainstream French culture remains attached to racialized understandings of Frenchness. For Hamid Naficy, this "accented cinema" tends to represent experiences of exile and diaspora as marked by claustrophobia, confinement, and control.[47] In these narratives of containment, forms of intimacy, amorous and nonamorous, broadcast often-competing articulations of kinships. How the Arab male queer protagonist navigates his inherited and chosen families marshal old and new ideas about French integration.

   At first sight, *Made in France* has little connection to the intimate imaginaries of interracial families in Driss Chraïbi's *The Butts* or Algerian families in Mehdi

Charef's *Tea in the Harem*. Patrick's cellmates, Youssef and Sonia, have no relatives; there is no Maghrebi familial space. They circulate rather than live anywhere. The absence and invisibility of Maghrebi families and residents is striking. The Arab queer genre frequently conveys this absence, which in some cases works to translate the queer protagonist's integration potential. Olivier Ducastel and Jacques Martineau's *The Adventures of Félix* addresses the question of family in explicit ways. Félix, a Franco-Algerian mixed youth who battles HIV, decides to leave Paris for Marseilles after the death of his French mother, parting from his older white boyfriend, to look for the Algerian father he has never met. Along the way, Félix meets a wide range of characters that the narrative introduces like the title of would-be chapters—"my brother," "my grandmother," "my sister," "my father"—suggesting an alternative kinship that ultimately replaces the search for blood ties. In the end, Félix abandons the search for his father and reunites with his boyfriend. The chosen French family seemingly compensates for and excludes the search for the Algerian family. While the white characters trust and welcome him, at times into their homes, Félix witnesses a racist murder on his journey, and he is afraid to report it to the police because of his "gueule d'Arabe" (Arab face). Félix's road trip introduces a new register of Arab masculinity on the screen—a well-spoken, generous, and confidently homosexual individual—and two sides of France. In one, a young Arab-looking man can connect with a truck driver, an older lady, a young gay man, and a middle-class mother, all of whom are white; Félix avoids the other, which consists of cities, either too big or with far-right mayors. Passing connections with a large and diverse group of Franco-French individuals counterbalances Félix's absence of roots, but interestingly he does not meet with any racial minorities. This demarcation is all the more flagrant given Félix's countless encounters. One may conclude that he already represents racial difference on the screen, or that affiliations with other racialized subjects is precisely what he overcomes.

Nick Rees-Roberts notes that *The Adventures of Félix* fails to fully explore its protagonist's mixed-race origin and as such fits this cinematic genre of films that privilege either race or sexuality.[48] But the pairing of Félix's confident homosexuality with his ambivalent relation to his Algerian lineage is not co-incidental. Addressing the intersectionality of race, gender, and sexuality, Judith Butler advises us to "resist the model of power that would set up racism and homophobia and misogyny as parallel or analogical relations. The assertion of their abstract or structural equivalence not only misses the specific histories of their construction and elaboration, but also delays the important work of thinking through the ways in which these vectors of power require and deploy each other for the purpose of their own articulation."[49] *The Adventures of Félix* indeed deploys the absence of Arab ties to articulate a successfully assimilated queer Arab individual. As a racially unaffiliated and family-free Arab queer, Félix embodies the idea of French republicanism, which promotes the sameness of individuals regardless of their different origins. David L. Eng describes the forgetting of race or the denial of racial difference as "queer liberalism," that is, the logic in our color-blind moment to oppose a politics of intersectionality that reveals the coconstruction of race and sexuality.[50] Since the film opens with the search for the Arab father and replaces it with a French family of choice, either the journey cannot accommodate both families, imagined and real, or having found the nurturing relations he was looking for, the need for the father, a figure that traditionally evokes authority, may unravel Félix's chosen French family.

The hit comedy *Chouchou* by Algerian director Merzak Allouache is a rags-to-riches fantasy that also casts a Franco-Arab queer intimacy that reconfigures the French family, albeit less rigidly. The opening rai song, "salam alicoum ya lahbab" (hello family), follows Choukri, nicknamed Chouchou, an undocumented immigrant from Algeria who just arrived in Paris. A generous priest offers this *blédard* lodging and helps him secure work as an assistant in a psychoanalyst's office. At work, he can cross-dress as a woman. A fortuitous meeting with his queer friend Djamila and his nephew Hamid, who also relocated to Paris, leads Chouchou to perform as a drag queen at a gay club, where he meets and falls in love with a French aristocrat, Stanislas. Chouchou's illegal status provides conflict, but the same-sex couple in due course reunites and marries. In the last scene, Chouchou in a white wedding dress and red hair runs toward Stanislas wearing a blue shirt, and their embrace is the color of the French flag. Their wedding guests, including rowdy banlieue youth, stern aristocrats, and flamboyant transvestites of La porte de Clichy, clap in celebration, representing a larger, approving France. But unlike Félix, Chouchou retains an Algerian family rather than losing it to accommodate Frenchness or queerness. Granted, *Chouchou* is a utopia that presents an unlikely romance and friendship across class and national lines, and it models the possibility of cross-racial intimacies while still showing the significance of Chouchou's family ties, Maghrebi culture, and the Algerian transvestite community. Chouchou's friend Djamila also evokes a clear attachment for Algeria, tearing up when she hears news of her family, whose pictures are pasted on her wall alongside a map of the country. Together, this small Algerian queer community visits Hamman, where they sing in Arabic and reminisce about the past. These sustaining bonds disrupt the common narrative that the Arab queer can only find acceptance from the tolerant Français de souche or that to gain sexual freedom he must sacrifice his family and Arab culture. Rémi Lange's film *Tarik el Hob* is also remarkable in publicizing the

Djamila and Chouchou, two transvestite Algerian friends, run into each other on the streets of Paris (*Chouchou*, 2003)

coexistence of queer expressions and Maghrebi culture through the figure of Karim. A Franco-Arab graduate student, Karim (Karim Tarek) researches the same-sex unions among Zelaga men in Egypt's Siwa Oasis and similar rites amongst the Beni Brahim men of Algeria while slowly reconciling himself with his sexual desire for men.

Critic Denis Provencher contrasts *Chouchou* with *Made in France*, implicitly addressing the question of family. He calls films like *Chouchou* "tales of good sexual citizens who find their way into a socially acceptable (white) middle class milieu" while films like *Made in France* show "'queer sexual citizens who continue to survive outside that dominant French social space but who are still able to create meaningful friendships and often times new forms of kinships and queer affiliations."[51] For Provencher, *Made in France* disrupts the utopia of *Chouchou* as it points out that the traditional family is inaccessible and also undesirably normative. But these two films may have more in common than first supposed. Both present new kinships through the budding romance between an undocumented and impoverished Algerian transvestite or transgender person, and either a French bourgeois or an aristocrat. The re-creation of families provides another lens for reading these films and shows that *Made in France* demands the abandonment of blood ties before immigrant subjects can become integrated into the Gallic family.

Again, queer intimacy mediates the integration potential of protagonists of Algerian descent. In *Made in France*, courtships help juxtapose Youssef's misogyny and homophobia with Patrick's respect and tolerance for difference. A Maghrebi wedding song, "Dor biha Chibani," known as the bride's dance, provides a leitmotif for the narrative. It is heard when Patrick first enters the Arab bar in women's clothing. Later, when the police apprehend the trio, Sonia and Youssef sing it in a prison cell. The meeting and escape that come between these instances of the wedding song feature Youssef and Patrick attempting to seduce Sonia in ways that illuminate deep differences in how they treat women and queer subjects. Youssef seeks sexual favors, and Sonia is the means. Following Sonia's rebuke, he stands in his boxer shorts and socks facing her and fondles a gun he stole from a cop. Sonia shoos it away like a fly, dismissing both this symbol of phallic power and his sexual desire. For about half of the film, Youssef plays with the gun, using it mainly to threaten others, until Patrick yanks it out of his hands and throws it in the Seine. The gun is symbolic not only of Youssef's sexual immaturity but also his desire for authority. Like the beur male archetype, Youssef cannot "assume a mature masculine identity" until Patrick forces him into adulthood.[52] Written by two directors of Maghrebi descent for a broad audience, *Made in France* reproduces a patronizingly colonial relationship between the French adult and the Arab child. In the end, Youssef tags along with the other two, happy to be included—even if marginally. It is interesting to note that in narratives about banlieusards like Youssef, romances, interracial and endogamous, family life, and stable employment are strikingly absent.[53]

When the possibility of interracial romance emerges, it is Patrick who is open to Sonia's different background, despite his initial impression that she may belong in jail. After Youssef makes insinuations that a sexual relationship exists between Sonia and Patrick, she considers leaving, too, but Patrick begins to court her in his turn. He pleads with her to continue their travel together on the grounds that the authorities are looking for "three Arabs, not a badly shaved man and a top model." Sonia dismisses his evident feelings as "the story of the rich guy who falls for a whore." She reminds him that he has a job awaiting him and that she is always struggling to survive. Patrick responds by accusing her of prejudice: "That's it! I'm not Arab. I come from a rich country. I didn't do the war, so I cannot understand, nor love." Patrick insists that she tell him why she is going to Geneva on her own. In lieu of an explanation, Sonia kisses him and directs Patrick's hand on her crotch to reveal her sex. The secret impedes the romance, but Sonia later confides that she seeks to undergo a sex change in Geneva, renewing the possibility of a relationship.

Made in France reiterates the belief found in *The Adventures of Félix* that Arab familial bonds and queer expression cannot be reconciled. Sonia's family story justifies her flight from Algeria. She embodies all the differences in *Made in France* at once. She is Algerian, undocumented, homosexual, and transgender. Leaving Algeria, where male relatives and neighbors ridiculed her when she was a child, she changes her original name Abdelkader to Sonia. The name, as Butler notes, "is a token of symbolic order, an order of social law, that which legislates viable subjects through the institution of sexual difference and compulsory heterosexuality . . . the name secures and structures the subject named."[54] Revealingly, some descriptions of the films mistakenly name Sonia "Samia," an Arabic name, but Sonia's selection of her name contests not only the masculine gender assigned in her original name but also its ethnicity. The Western name embraces assimilationist expectations by erasing cultural difference, an element that advantages candidates in naturalization cases. Abdelkader, interestingly, recalls the founding father of the Algerian nation, a heroic figure who resisted French colonial conquest in the nineteenth century. This double and symbolic contestation further suggests the incompatibility of queer and Algerian identities. To enter sexual modernity, Arab queer (and women, as Carrie Tarr noted) must let go of their families and cultures. This omnipresent model evidences presumptions about immigrant and Maghrebi cultures as already and always oppressive.

On hearing of the murder of four transvestites on the radio, Sonia calls the victims her "sisters," evoking a reconstituted family, one based on identity politics rather that descent. Her chosen family expands traditional affiliations of blood, nationality, and ethnicity though it still borrows the traditional language of familial kinship. In *Sexual Strangers*, Shane Phelan argued that "lesbians, gays, bisexuals, and transgendered people in the United States are strangers . . . a figure of ambivalence who troubles the border between us and them."[55] Sonia's figure shows that queerness can also work to mark the foreigner as less foreign and thus worthy of being "saved." By leaving Algiers for Paris, Sonia established the polar differences between these two locations, inscribing the French capital as a space of refuge for transgressive Algerian subjects. While she also confronts race and class prejudice in Paris, the narrative foregrounds mainly her desire to live freely as a woman. Her escape lends credence to the gendered and sexualized narrative of rescue that have underpinned policies on asylum and Western military interventions in the Middle East, bolstered by symbolic gestures such as the proclamation of an International Day of Action against Homophobic Persecution in Iran by French and British LGBTQI organizations on July 19, 2006.[56]

Although her life may be at risk in Algeria, Sonia does not pose any threat to Parisians, but then again, she is the Algerian exception. When Paris is unsafe for queer subjects in *Made in France*, the threat comes primarily from Algeria. A serial killer has killed four transvestites, and all the clues point to one perpetrator, Zoubida, the Algerian prostitute who stole Patrick's handbag. This would explain why Patrick's papers were found in one of the crime scenes. It would also explain the method the murderer used to cut the throats of his victims, the so-called *sourire Kabyle* (Kabyle smile), which recalls graphic images of the Algerian revolution and civil war, as well as terrorist acts. By implying that an Algerian man, perhaps posing as a transvestite to approach his targets, is the murderer, the narrative casts Algerians as the perpetrators of violent hate crimes. The narrative does, however, acknowledge the risks transgender people face in Paris, but they are less consequential: the police insult, mistreat, and even exploit transvestites, and a Frenchman at a bar casually remarks that the murder of queers is good riddance, calling Jews, blacks, homosexuals, and transsexuals collectively "scum." Yet even if Paris is safer than Algiers, it is nonetheless merely a way station for Sonia on her way to Geneva.

As a story of mistaken identity, *Made in France* relies on the misunderstanding of "real" and "stable" identities, particularly French blood ties. Patrick insists at the police station, "I'm as French as can be," and then, to the judge: "Your honor, I was born May 15, 1968, in Lille, I am French! My mother's French! My father's French! Generations of French! My granddad fought for France!" In asserting his nationality, he states: "I am French. . . . I am not a homosexual, I am not Arab." His radical statement suggests that Frenchness excludes homosexuals and Arabs, evoking in passing whiteness and heterosexuality as privileged identities. French and white male police officers corroborate this when they rename cross-dressed Patrick "Cindy," an Anglo-Saxon name that evokes transvestism and transgenderism as foreign importations. These claims suggest that gradations exist and that accordingly, some French people are more authentic than others. Sensitive to the same gradations, the judge inquires whether Patrick's grandfather was a *harki*, that is, an Algerian auxiliary soldier who fought on the side of France during the Algerian War of Independence. His question traces back to a larger France that included Algeria. The judge and Patrick's vision of Frenchness as blood tied, inherited generation after generation, and only extended nominally to colonial migrants from Algeria was discussed by Chraïbi in 1955. That we find it again in *Made in France* illustrates the persistence of this belief five decades later.

Patrick's defense does not accommodate the integration of racially marked foreigners and their French descendants. Youssef is a case in point. Though he has never set foot in Algeria (as we learn toward the end of the film), speaks no Arabic, does not know how to pray, and eats pork, he laments that in the global and French imaginaries, he is an Islamic fundamentalist and a thief. For Youssef, only international French soccer player of Algerian descent Zinedine Zidane escaped this racial essentialism, but the rest of his generation, he remarks, have remained *bougnoules* whose allegiances and faith are suspicious.[57] In a rant, he ironizes, "when I'm in a store, I pat myself down to check that I didn't steal anything. You never can tell, with my instincts." His statement plays on the idea of an unalterable Arab essence. In turn, his hostile environment leads Youssef to sympathize with other victims of anti-Arab racism. In a bus ride to the tribunal, he reassures Patrick: "Don't listen to [Sonia], cousin. Be cool in front of the judge. . . . If he throws you out, do as I did. They threw me out four times, and four times I came back. It's like a vacation. They pay for your plane ticket. You see family and when you get tired of it you come back to France." Youssef's fantasy of a street-smart foreigner able to play the system to his advantage conjures up French alarmist discourse about hordes of foreigners pouring in with ease. In fact, Youssef has never left France and knows little about the realities of expulsion, officially known through the euphemism of éloignement (distancing).

In addressing Patrick as "cousin," Youssef asserts racial solidarity with an alleged undocumented Algerian, summoning a metaphorical racialized family that fills the absence of a national one. When Sonia retorts that Patrick is not Arab, Youssef challenges her focus on physical appearance. "What does a French person look like? How do you recognize one? . . . I know lots of Arabs who look French and I know even more French people who look Arab." It is not clear here whether Youssef is referring to the fluidity of race, which makes it possible to perceive white French individuals as racialized "others," or if he is pointing out the tension between nationality and race, when some French, like himself, appear to be foreign. The film's conclusion confirms the view that some French can look Arab. In this scene set in a Paris airport at the gate for Air Algérie, Patrick forces the police to free Sonia and Youssef by pretending to be an Algerian terrorist affiliated with the Armed Islamist Group (Groupe Islamiste Armé). Concocting a story, he warns the two officers that if they do not release the two prisoners, "there'll be a river of blood." He indicates among the travelers several men who are allegedly ready to fire. Each of these travelers suddenly appear threatening to the white officers (and perhaps to the viewer seeing the men through their point of view). The scene breaks into snapshots of men, some in white robes and white caps, others in jeans and leather jackets, referring to how race often intersects with suspicion of criminality. The smile of a middle-aged Maghrebi man at the police officers who stare at him comes across as sinister rather than friendly.

Together, the trio presents us with various understandings of intimate bonds that are based in queer identifications (Sonia), blood ties (Patrick), or race (Youssef). Each of the protagonists exemplifies a form of *communautarisme*, that is, they give priority to groups based on these ties over the national collective. France has a long tradition of rejecting communautarisme, identity politics, and multiculturalism associated with US national fragmentation. As historian Joan W. Scott explains, "French universalism insists that sameness is the basis for equality. To be sure, sameness is an abstraction, a philosophical notion meant to achieve the formal equality of individuals before the law. But historically it has been applied literally: assimilation means the eradication of difference."[58] In practice, the investment in universalist discourse stigmatizes any attempt to make racial inequalities visible. Fouad Zeraoui, president of Kelma ("words" in Arabic), an association for LGBT Arab people, points out the contradictions between the assumption of equality and the realities of discrimination: "How is a [gay] *Beur* supposed to think that he is just like everybody else? Because he is *beur*, no one will hire him, and because he is gay, no one will rent him an apartment. In France, no one is doing anything [to help him] since everyone is supposedly integrated in society."[59] For sociologist Éric Fassin, the danger of communautarisme today comes from the French white majority rather than racial minorities;[60] as such, we can read the investment in universalism as an investment in white communautarisme, that of the invisible majority.

Together, the trio represents France. The long shot that frames them by the Eiffel Tower and the nationalist blue, red, and white colors of their clothes as they squeeze together on a Vespa in the final shot encourage us to read these subjects as a new national configuration that incorporates Sonia even without legal papers. *Made in France* may make room for an Algerian or for transgender individuals but not communities. The absence of North African families, places of residence, or LGBTQ communities further promotes the republican idea of abstract individualism that refuses to allow such groups to become visible. It is as if the film is trying to have it both ways: unravel the French universalist thread and expose it as faulty and weave in the French dislike for identity politics by showing a trio that ultimately closet their identity politics for the benefit of the group. Said differently, the film critiques French manufacturing of racial difference, yet reinforces the status quo about the invisibility of queer and ethnic communities.

In this story line that promotes the interest of the micro-nation on the run above the so-called special interests of each individual, "queer" is mobilized as an opposition to identity rather than a term of identity.[61] *Made in France* registers an opposition to labels and communities from which they derive. Patrick, who was at first stuck in his costume, ultimately dons new ones to perform multiple identities, while rejecting identity labels. By espousing "queering" or a refusal to identify, he works against French racist and homophobic labels that depend on unchanging legible bodies. Similarly, Sonia's transgenderism triggers "a category crisis" that is "a failure of definitional distinction, a borderline that becomes permeable, that permits border crossings from one (apparently distinct) category to another."[62] While their bodies challenge heteronormativity, the narrative elsewhere suggests that their nonnormative romance needs to stay in the closet. As the film draws to a close, Patrick follows the police van taking Sonia and Youssef to the airport to be sent back to Algeria. There, he pleads with a parking enforcement officer to give him five minutes to run inside after the love of his life, who is pregnant with their child. Moved by a story that reinforces the heteronormative sexual script, she agrees not to fine him for illegal parking. While Patrick's queering adapts to whichever role serves him best—he impersonates a transvestite, a French lovelorn businessman, and an Algerian terrorist—brown subjects like Sonia and Youssef cannot pass for white. They cannot camouflage their visible difference and retain throughout the narrative the same "Arab" role. Whether Youssef wears a business suit or Sonia wears slinky clothing, they both end up sharing a prison cell.

Foreigners, Laws, and Manners

In *Made in France*, it is not only Arab prospects that are blighted by increasing French hostility toward perceived foreigners, but also those of born and bred Frenchmen like Patrick. Individuals read as "Algerian," as well as those read as "poor" or "queer," deal with a justice system and public attitudes that are markedly different from those that organize the idealized French national family. Patrick's outrage at his new treatment reveals his rights have been revoked once he is mistaken for an Algerian cross-dresser. In turn, accused of being a terrorist and a serial killer, mocked by the average Franco-French person, denied basic rights by the police and the court, Patrick gets a firsthand account of what Paris looks like from the other side of the tracks. *Made in France* goes beyond exposing the gap between universal pretensions and marginalizing realities. In taking Patrick as its focus, it shows his loss of white privilege, highlighting in the process the nation's urban and racial frontiers (and class values associated with them). When opportunity comes, the latter refuses to simply reclaim his privilege while his marginalized friends remain trapped. At the same time, Patrick is a foil for Youssef's aggressive masculinity, which reasserts the stigmatization of the banlieues. Yet even as the film solidifies stereotypes of the Arab male outsider with the character of Youssef, it turns the discourse of *insécurité* upside down by displacing the lawlessness associated with the outskirts on the justice system itself, thereby addressing other forms of lawlessness. Perpetrators of insecurity are embodied by white police agents, immigration officers, and everyday individuals.

Made in France expands homophobic behavior beyond the cartography of the banlieue by portraying queer subjects as exotic, foreign, or "out of place" in Paris. White male officers bully Patrick when they arrest him in the Arab bar, they later deny him a phone call, and one of them attempts to sexually exploit him. When he exits the bathroom of the seedy café frequented by Arabs, Patrick faces insults from two white male police officers who perceive him as foreign (based on the bar's clientele) and a transvestite (because of his costume): "Where's this beauty from? You have your papers Cindy? Come on, hurry up!" In addressing Patrick informally with the "tu" pronoun instead of the polite "vous" and nicknaming him Cindy, like Cindy Crawford the model, the officers deride him and question his femininity by measuring it against an icon whose image (though airbrushed) still evokes authenticity. The Anglicized name Cindy also interrogates Patrick's Frenchness, illustrating Phelan's claim that states and their agents read queer subjects as strangers. Looking inside a bag Zoubida left by Patrick's seat, the officers find a resident permit, with an expired date. Despite the officers' assumption that he is Algerian, transvestite, and a sex worker, Patrick's politeness as he explains the circumstances of his dress and his stolen handbag (and papers) contrasts their incivility. Later, another officer's sexual request frames the transvestite as a sex worker. The officer's justification that he's "never tried with a transvestite" also summons up Patrick's exoticism. The Franco-Frenchman's mistaken identity buys him and the viewer entrance into an unfamiliar world and awakens our consciousness about the existence of two justice systems—one for normative French subjects, and one for perceived outsiders.

Other segments of the film give a damning portrayal of the police as racially prejudiced. Patrick's assertion that "this is France, I have rights" falls to pieces. The judge has already made up his mind when he first meets Patrick and pays little attention to the evidence. The court members display condescension and mockery toward him. Even his lawyer thinks him guilty and simply asks that he be given time to bid farewell to his friends before departing for Algiers. As the police are forced to realize their mistake when presented with Patrick's French passport, the chief of police later refuses to apologize, dismissing the blunder as "a sand grain in the machine." We also learn from Youssef that the police killed his friend Sami, taking him for a car thief because he drove a BMW. At the same time, the film carefully presents details that nuance this portrayal. Two police officers, for example, trustingly unshackle an old Muslim man and let him walk away from the police van to go pray by some trees, accommodating his religious duties. They soon see him walking into the busy highway, and one of the officers aims his gun when the man refuses to stop. The same policeman later aims his gun at Sonia when she runs away. Interestingly, this young officer is black and a rookie, two facts that complicate the meaning one may attribute to these shooting attempts.

Male bullies are everywhere, including the police force in *Made in France*. White men with violent proclivities include a trucker who ejects Sonia out of his cabin when she reveals she is a transgender woman, a vigilante bar owner who hold Youssef and Patrick at gunpoint after learning they are on the run from the police, and a customer in a bar who applauds Patrick for his alleged murders of transvestites. These incidents do not limit violence to the impoverished outskirts or to an ontological Arab masculine nature. Yet these instances of white male aggression pale in comparison with Youssef's macho posturing, homophobia, and bullying of innocent passersby. In its focus on Youssef, the narrative tilts toward the problem of behavior rather than denied rights. In a scene that captures Youssef's conduct, he knocks a policeman to the ground and continues kicking the unconscious and defenseless man until Patrick stops him. His comportment distinguishes the Franco-Arab man as a menacing figure, particularly in contrast with his fellow runaways.

Some scenes call attention to a sort of culture-based misogyny and homophobia, suggesting that Youssef may display a specifically foreign masculinity after all. From the outset his harassment of Sonia is based on some vague interpretation of Islam even though he is not himself religious. When she refuses to eat pork, Youssef explodes: "She does not eat pork, but playing whore she does not mind. It's authorized by the Koran, I imagine." This statement echoes multiple discourses broadcast in French mainstream media. First, it highlights Youssef's hypocrisy and sense of entitlement in judging Arab women against his own imagined cultural standards. By invoking Islam, the film may hint that Youssef's misogyny is a derivative. Second, Youssef's self-assigned policing calls to mind the so-called *grand frères* (older brothers) of the banlieues, self-appointed neighborhood men who control women's action and reputation. Youssef's expectations that Arabo-Muslim women be chaste contradict other statements he makes that characterize women as sexually available and pliable. For example, when Sonia refuses him, he declares that he felt "something was off," because "a real woman" would have accepted him, "no woman ever refused [him]. Never." This variance may point out Youssef's hypocrisy, but it may suggest that the directors are combining different masculine roles often given to Franco-Arab male youth from the outskirts: the hypocritical Muslim patriarch and the macho thug. Youssef reacts unsurprisingly to the news that Sonia is biologically male by ridiculing her as "twisted" and "completely crazy." Other white men also deride cross-dressed Patrick, but their homophobia does not appear to have any specific cultural origin. Youssef, however, the only character who openly mistreats both women and queer subjects, reinforces associations of the banlieues with Islamicized cultures. By branding his misogyny and homophobia as distinct, the narrative fails to connect these issues across racial, class, or cultural lines, as if masculine domination in the banlieue was exceptional.

Masculine violence, radicalism, and homophobia mark the banlieue as a space unlike mainstream France. Though he was raised in Paris, Youssef is the person in greatest need of domestication in the film. Toward its epilogue, as if it were a second thought, the film attempts to soften his image by gesturing toward Youssef's tough guy posture as a mask that hides a deep social wound. Youssef had planned to go to Algeria with his friend Sami and remake the country before French police killed Sami. The film only mentions this, but does not explain why these men wanted to go to Algeria rather than stay in France, and hence the implied condemnation of their exclusion is muted. *Made in France* not only fails to add dimension to the Arab male archetype; it insists that Algiers stands as the principal site of terrorism, sexual violence, and Islamic fundamentalism. Potentially the Parisian outskirts are another Algiers, the nation's foil within. The film casts characters with deep social differences, only to dismiss the question of their inequality. The manners of the protagonists take center stage, particularly their treatment of women and queer individuals. In contrast to Patrick, Youssef and various police officers are ideal candidates for a sexual civilizing mission. Unlike Charef's *Tea*, where the politics of recognition centers on class struggle and urban segregation, *Made in France* presents masculine aggression and intolerance as shared by all men, with Youssef's behavior rooted in Islam and standing out as the most offensive. The focus on gender and sexual exclusion by a banlieusard stifles the fact that they pervade French culture.[63]

Like *Chouchou* and *The Adventures of Félix*, *Made in France* promotes tolerance as the appropriate response to the presence of Third World immigrants and their French children. In *Regulating Aversion*, Wendy Brown asserts that tolerance presents itself as a "universal value," or an "impartial practice," but it has been framed as part of "a civilizational discourse" in which the West determines what constitutes tolerance and what is tolerable.[64] Tolerance talk conceals its own designation of the civilized and the barbaric, the subjects imagined as tolerant and intolerant, the ones eligible for tolerance and "certain cultures or religions . . . marked in advance as ineligible for tolerance."[65] Of course, tolerance is the prerogative of those in power, and "in France, just as in many other western countries with minority populations, tolerance is demanded of the marginalized, not very well tolerated minority."[66]

The line drawn between the tolerable and the intolerable operates both domestically and globally. Youssef, a markedly intolerant subject, evokes a nonliberal society located within and outside of France, even though he himself is a so-called product of the French banlieue. Youssef's antisocial behavior makes it difficult to sympathize with his claim that he is not wanted in France. The narrative has worked so hard to justify his exclusion that viewers are more likely to attribute it to his conduct rather than to racial exclusion. His stereo-typical attitude toward women and queer subjects is shorthand for an essential-ized Franco-Arab male identity. Patrick's example as a tender man who "would not hurt a fly" renders Youssef's virility all the more deviant. Though *Made in France* evokes contemporary social issues such as insecurity, the Algerian civil war, the ruthless deportation of illegalized immigrants without due process, and violence against racial and sexual minorities, it turns them into stories of civility and good conduct, as if the right attitude would produce justice for all. Of course, some of this light register is a function of the comic genre. Nonetheless, this chosen lens offers a behavioral solution to political problems. By erasing sites of political conflicts like the *banlieues* and focusing on individual behaviors, the film ultimately depoliticizes these issues by making them the subjects of manners rather than power struggles.

In his 2007 novel *Visceral*, French writer of Algerian-Sudanese origins Rachid Djaïdani denounced white French filmmakers for the clichés they produce about the banlieues, comparing these artists to followers of right-wing extremist politi-cian Marine Le Pen. Djaïdani's young male Franco-Arab character, Lies, hails from a housing project like his author. When he shows up for a role in a film, he refuses to play the drug dealer, interjecting, "here, you give me the main role as a drug dealer, tomorrow a role of an Islamic terrorist, and then a hoodlum prostitute. . . . That's your cinema? . . . You only portray us as clichés, respect us, give us a more positive image, you're artists, not Lepénistes [followers of Le Pen]" (105, my translation).[67] These limited roles for Franco-Arab actors, highlighted by Djaïdani, mirror equally limited treatments. Darren Waldron observes this in his discussion of Franco-Arab and Maghrebi queer figures in French cinema, noting that these protagonists face two options: assimilation or removal through death.[68] However, while Waldron and other critics observe the dominance of sexuality or race in the portrayal of assimilated or nonassimi-lated subjects, they do not examine their entanglement. My hope is that this chapter has interrogated this formulaic genre in ways that make visible the mo-bilization of queerness for assimilationist and racialist purposes. One leitmotif that emerges clearly from these films (with the exception of utopic *Chouchou*) is that Maghrebi families have a nefarious influence on their offspring. Critics do not fail to celebrate evidence that youthful protagonists move away from its influence, but they seldom extend this treatment to white families, though as Patrick Simon, director at the National Institute for Demographic Studies, has shown, the latter are overwhelmingly more exclusive in their choices of partners and friends.[69]

Films like *Made in France* by filmmakers who openly identify with Maghrebi immigrant communities show that white French filmmakers do not have the monopoly on hackneyed portrayals of Arab masculinity. Maghrebi and Franco-Arab productions are equally traversed by dominant ideologies about integration, individualism, and universalism. These ideologies may reflect the filmmakers' own beliefs or a careful calculation for a film's commercial viability given the French public's shared aversion to identity politics. In 2012 Djaïdani's first feature film, *Rengaine* (*Hold Back*), includes the role of a Franco-Arab queer in a sensational narrative that mainly explores family tensions surrounding an interracial marriage between a French woman of Algerian origin and a French man of West African descent. The queer subplot reinforces the construction of an exclusive Maghrebi family that opposes the union of Sabrina with Dorcy, a Christian theater actor, so vehemently that some members consider murdering the future groom. In the absence of an Algerian patriarch, Slimane (one of Sabrina's many brothers) solicits the help of his siblings to track down Dorcy. To solve this family affair, Slimane confronts his gay older brother, whose name has been literally erased by the family (even the viewer does not learn it). The queer brother points out Slimane's hypocrisy since the latter has been secretly involved with Nina, a Jewish female singer, for many years and yet seeks to put an end to Sabrina's relationship with a Christian man. As Slimane threatens his repudiated brother with a gun, the latter encourages him to shoot, explaining that for thirty years he has been dead. In invoking his exclusion from his family as a form of death rather than salvation, this man condemns the religious and cultural taboos on homosexuality but also crucially seeks to challenge them to make room for himself, Sabrina, and even Slimane. Here the Arab male queer's departure from his family is not celebrated, as it is commonly the case in mainstream films we have examined, but is instead a vicious and avoidable loss. Djaïdani's film also avoids his predecessors' tragic endings, tracing out the survival of the Franco-Arab queer.

Embodying the City

Building on the two previous chapters' attention to the visual, this chapter foregrounds the deployment of graffiti in the central city, in ways that disrupt fearful depictions of the banlieue found in landmark films, such as Matthieu Kassovitz's 1995 *La haine* (*Hatred*). By turning to the use of graffiti and street art by postcolonial novelist Leïla Sebbar and internationally known contemporary Paris-based artists of African descent—Princess Hijab and JR—this chapter argues that through spray-painting and flyposts, protagonists and artists politicize the relation between racialized bodies and central Paris. They do so by rehumanizing the abject and the abstract. Armed with red paint, Omer and Amel, two youth of Algerian descent, literally mark sites of colonial bloodshed on the Parisian landscape in Sebbar's novel *The Seine Was Red* (1999). The red paint reminds the Parisian passersby of where Algerians' blood covered cobblestones and where the police hurled the unconscious bodies of peaceful Algerian demonstrators into the Seine on October 17, 1961. Graffiti artist Princess Hijab spray paints black veils and niqabs on advertising posters that line the Paris metro, dressing models with clothing that is outlawed in some public spaces. Her images invoke the criminalization of religious difference and plays it up against omnipresent nudity in advertisements. *Photograffeur* JR flyposts giant images of racialized youth from the banlieue on walls of a fashionable neighborhood in the city center (Le Marais). His photoposting of young men in aggressive postures returns these stereotypes back to their senders. By inscribing colonial and contemporary forms of violence on the city itself, these creations frame in vibrant visual terms universalism as the city's operative fantasy. The illegal and transient nature of their work powerfully rewrites the idea of Paris as an open site of artistic expression. Together, these street interventions make the *minorités visibles* central to the capital, in ways that interrogate Paris's exclusionary cultural expressions.

The graffiti is itself a mark associated not only generally with crime but also with the urban culture of the banlieues. As such, JR's photographs of brown and black faces from the multiracial ghettos projected onto the walls of a middle-class Paris neighborhood speak of the spatialization of race. They evoke how bodies are read as spaces. Photographed or determined by cultural signs of difference (like the hijab, long beard, urban street gear), the body summons the space in a metonymic association. Sebbar's Arab protagonists cross spaces to bring traumatic memories of colonial violence from the urban margins to the Paris center. Princess Hijab symbolically frustrates state policies that banned the veil in some public spaces by donning models with the hijab on the metro billboards, displacing this sartorial practice from the racialized banlieue to the city center. Whether these artists critique cultural, religious, or historical erasures in central Paris, they foreground the emotional value of space. Their graffiti calls attention to layering techniques whereby the public space is coated with the private and the intimate, the local with the transnational. For Silvia Loeffler, "This critical visio-cultural perspective urges the viewer to look at the inscriptions of public space as forms of longing and a dimension of the social."[1] Emotions, sociologist Sara Ahmed reminds us, are not about the individual's interior states but about social and cultural practices formed in the relationship between bodies, objects, or subjects.[2]

In a much-commented scene of *Black Skin, White Masks* first published in French in 1952, Frantz Fanon, a black man from Martinique, travels by train in the metropole and is interpellated by a child, who points him out: "Mama, see the Negro! I'm frightened!"[3] In that moment, Fanon is "taken out of the world" and transformed into a "crushing objecthood."[4] He suddenly becomes conscious of his body as perceived, "woven . . . out of a thousand details, anecdotes, stories."[5] His appearance here represents an entire race associated with stigmatizing ideas about cannibalism, intellectual deficiency, fetishism, and slave ships. Fanon describes this moment as a violence, "an amputation, an excision, a hemorrhage that spattered my whole body with black blood."[6] This embodied experience of place, which Fanon refers to as "racial epidermal schema," challenges the universalism of many spatial theories associated with Paris, from Walter Benjamin's notion of the flâneur to Michel de Certeau's wanderer.[7] It signals the different experience of bodies "overdetermined from without," bodies that have been hypervisible and have been deemed out of place in European cities.[8] The fear of the young white boy for Fanon mirrors a socialization, whereby the white gaze reads racialized bodies as dangerous. The boy's naming denies Fanon from being "a man among other men" and informs the latter's anger.[9]

This train scene disturbs not only a universal understanding of phenomenological experiences in Paris but also the abstract equation of the city with topophilia, that is, "the affective bond between people and place or setting."[10] In *Poetics of Space*, Gaston Bachelard called topophilia "the quite simple images of *felicitous space*. . . . They seek to determine the human value of the sorts of space that may be grasped, that may be defended against adverse forces, the spaces we love. For diverse reasons, and with the differences entailed by poetic shadings, this is eulogized space."[11] In the train scene, Fanon contrastively relates the repulsion felt toward him in a white environment, which in turn shapes his sense of himself in the metropole as someone to be feared. What this important scene renders visible is the previously unspoken boundary of skin that conditions everyday life in the capital.

Just like the boy's fear of Fanon "eating [him] up" seems to emerge from comic books such as *The Adventures of Tintin* by Hergé that portrayed black men as cannibals, images about racialized bodies appear frequently in the form of cartoons in Paris newspapers or political tracts on city walls. Historically, the perceived "Arab" has been a scapegoat in Paris, from the 1920s, with spikes during the Algerian War of Independence (1954–62), the 1973 oil crisis, the early 1980s economic recession, the 2005 urban riots, and the terrorist attacks in 1995 and 2015. Disseminated by far-right political party Le Front National, the tract in the photograph shows a drawing of a warrant for a fictional character "Mohamed Ben Zobi." The first name is one of the most common Muslim names, "ben" signifies "son of," and "zobi" means "penis" in Maghrebi spoken Arabic, making this figure a sexualized archetype. Featured donning a fez in a mugshot that exaggerates his ears and nose, he also appears in a series of actions underneath, one of which uncovers his head to reveal tightly curled black hair. The tract notes in capital letters that "this man is dangerous, likely to kill, rape, steal, burglarize. To find him, no need to go very far . . . there are 700,000 like him around you." Le Front National does not have the monopoly on encouraging this sort of racist typology. A large portion of the media has shared this practice, particularly *France-soir* and *Le Parisien Libéré*.[12] In September 1980 the weekly *Le Jour du Dimanche* headlined "200 Arab killers" with no further information.[13] Other sensational titles refer to other labels such as Algerians, Arabs, North Africans, Maghrebi, or Muslims.[14] In contrast, images that portray the coexistence of various religious communities in Paris have been censored. For example, in 2012 the photograph of an assemblage of men and women in various religious garb (Jewish, Muslim, and Christians) proposed by the Collectif Contre l'Islamophobie en France (Collective Against Islamophobia in France) was

Tract distributed by the far right in the early 1980s (*Gastaut, L'immigration et l'opinion*)

rejected by the Paris transit authority for its "religious character" and "political demands."[15] Nine years before, portraits of secular racial minorities were on spectacular display on the Palais Bourbon in central Paris on the occasion of the women's march for equality on July 14, 2003. This publicized and well-attended event was organized by Ni Putes Ni Soumises (Neither Whores Nor Submissive, NPNS), a banlieue association that sought to protest the living conditions of women in the city's outskirts, particularly their lack of sexual freedom.[16] The march dovetailed with the national debates over the headscarf in public schools, which NPNS vehemently opposed. Symbolically placed on the site of the national assembly, the *Mariannes d'aujourd'hui* (*Today's Mariannes*) exhibit featured overblown pictures of women from the *cités* donning the tricolor revolutionary *bonnet phrygien* and *cocarde*. In this context of controlled visibility, the graffiti bypasses the gatekeepers while still evoking images and views deemed illegitimate.

Images from Kassovitz's iconic film *Hatred* have played a crucial role in fixing ideas of racialized bodies as out of place in central Paris and linking the graffiti to banlieue vandalism. *Hatred* was the first popular film to shine a light on the multiracial banlieues that heretofore had been largely ignored in French cinema. It was showered with prizes: best director at Cannes in 1995, César for best film, César for best producer, César for best editing, and Prix Lumières for best film in 1996. Jewish director Kassovitz was incensed by the death of young Zairian Makome M'Bowole, shot in the head while handcuffed to a radiator in a police station, and that of Malik Oussekine, a French student of Algerian descent who was beaten to death by riot police after the repression of a 1986 student demonstration. He decided to make a film about police brutality against French youth of color. Shot in black and white, *Hatred* chronicles nineteen hours in the lives of three young male friends in an unnamed Parisian banlieue: Saïd (Saïd Taghmaoui), a loud-mouthed Arab; Vinz (Vincent Kassel), a wiry quick-tempered Jewish youth; and Hubert (Hubert Koundé), a cool-headed black boxing coach. All are unemployed, living in overcrowded apartments with their parents and siblings, and dealing hashish on the side. The film opens on the aftermath of a riot in their neighborhood following the vicious beating of their friend Abdel in a police station, which landed him in a coma. In the riots, Vinz recovered a police gun lost in the scuffle and promises to shoot a police officer if Abdel dies. Each encounter with the police — in their neighborhoods, the hospital where Abdel is, and the central city — carries the potential to become tragic.

The highly stylized opening scene of *Hatred* shows images of confrontation between the police and banlieue demonstrators and closes on Saïd creating graffiti on an occupied police van that reads "Saïd fucks the police." This act of

"The World is ours" (*La haine*, 1995)

bold vandalism is followed by the young man and his friends dealing drugs and verbally attacking others, marking the outskirts as precarious sites. Halfway through the film, the graffiti invades the central city. Having missed the last train to return home, the young men wander the dark streets of Paris central city discussing children's comic books until they come across a gallery opening. They enter this brightly lit space, where they find an art exhibit: white painted plastic bottles encrusted into white walls. Their bewilderment at the art and their skin color, urban clothing (track suits), and uncouth behavior all mark them as different from the white guests in shirts and dress pants and the waiter in white uniform, whom they mockingly call "Charles." After they pilfer the food at the tables, Saïd and Hubert turn their attention to two young women. After the women reject their sexual advances, Saïd gestures as if he were going to slap one of the women, making her flinch. A middle-aged white man intervenes by asking the young men to calm down. They leave, but not before insulting the attendees, throwing food in the direction of the two women, stealing someone's credit card, and turning over a table. As the white rescuer closes the door, he turns to the visitors and the camera, announcing, for explanation, "the malaise of the banlieues." Now in the streets again, Saïd picks up his spray paint and alters a commercial poster that read "The World is yours" into "The World is ours."

The mise-en-scène of this segment offers a Paris of contrasts revealed through different cultural expressions: on the one hand, the underclass represented by the unruly young multiracial youth who break into a *vernissage* they cannot understand and spray-paint onto Paris's commercial signs; on the other hand, the middle class embodied by the city's quiet modern art aficionados. Emerging from the dark streets into the brightly lit white room of the art exhibit, it is these youths who are on display. They are allegedly not where they belong, and their class and cultural difference become legible. The scene suggests these men are invading a space in which they cannot fit, ultimately justifying the closed door that ends the commotion. Where elsewhere the film interrogates the media sensationalism of the outskirts through banal everyday domestic scenes and a critique of opportunistic journalists hunting juicy stories about the riots, here, the downtown gallery scene contrasts bodies, cultivating long-established ideas of racialized men from the Paris margins as primitive and dangerous.

Framed through their different cultural expressions, the differences between the banlieue and the city highlight this youth as rapacious and criminal. Without any reference to racial difference, this scene nevertheless offers a racial grammar for understanding the relationship between the city and its "no-go zones." This cinematic segment constructs the young men as figures of abjection, which functions as substitutes for their place of residence. By rehearsing people's fears about specific bodies and spaces, *Hatred* summons a topophobia. The youth constitutes the prosthetic arm of the banlieues or the embodiment of the apprehension, dislike, and revulsion associated with this space.

As a cultural practice largely associated with the banlieues in France, the emergence of the graffiti in the city disturbs the order of place by representing people, traumatic memories, and concerns located at the margins. The site of display is integral to the politics. By desegregating the political graffiti, the artists claim Paris streets as a public sphere for the dissemination of postcolonial knowledge. Ulrich Beck's notion of subpolitics is helpful in thinking about the role of graffiti in this segregated context. According to Beck, subpolitics

> refers to politics outside and beyond the representative institutions of the political systems of nation-states . . . subpolitics means direct politics—that is, ad hoc individual participation in political decisions, bypassing the institutions of representative opinion-formation. Subpolitics means the shaping of society from below. It sets politics free by changing the rules and boundaries of the political so that it becomes more open and susceptible to new linkages—as well as capable of being negotiated and reshaped.[17]

Transposed to the city center, graffiti marks an affiliation with the urban racial-ized margins while also conveying a desire to participate in the public sphere. That this participation takes the shape of the graffiti, a criminal act, is all the more symbolic in terms of figuring unequal access to the public sphere. Impor-tantly, the graffiti makers who inscribe messages about their family or commu-nity experiences have different statuses (citizens, undocumented), suggesting desires of inclusion regardless of citizenship.

Graffiti, Street Art, and the Banlieue

With documentary films and increasing magazine coverage on artists like Banksy, Jean-Michel Basquiat, Shepard Fairey, or Keith Haring, street art has been gaining visibility beyond its subculture origins. In the late 1970s, Jean Baudrillard labeled New York's graffiti as a radical invasion of "the ghetto in all the city's arteries."[18] They do not participate in the white city's architecture; to the contrary, they taint it. Graffiti are the exclusive domain of the spray-painter, from the quickly drawn graphic signatures (tags) to their oversize versions that take longer to accomplish (throw-ups), to the more sophisticated sprayed (sten-cils) or stuck (paste-ups) versions. Labeled at times a postgraffiti movement, street art, on the other hand, tends to integrate city walls, similar to the way a painter might use a canvas.[19] It comprises a larger variety of techniques and styles, placing "less emphasis on lettering with spray-paint and more weight on fashioning varied interventions into the cultural landscape of a city."[20] JR, for example, uses flyposts that consist of billboard-size posters glued on city build-ings, bus stops, and trash cans, featuring mainly distorted black and brown male faces from the impoverished Paris suburbs, shot up close in a fish-eye lens. In his "street gallery," JR includes photographs of Parisians pausing to consider these images, creating an encounter with the "other." Unlike the indecipherable tags, this genre of street art has reached a broader audience, receiving attention from other artists and journalists.

As street art grows and becomes incorporated in public spaces, the meaning we attribute to it in the city has evolved. Public art now assists places in gaining a positive image as creative, even "transgressive or overtly critical public art, such as graffiti and street art (operate) as signs that attract rather than repel in-vestors."[21] Yet graffiti and street art simultaneously continue to be criminalized and interpreted as a sign of an urban malaise. The scholarship on criminology considers graffiti a sign of urban decay, clustering in some locations, and devises means for its prevention.[22] Graffiti and street art both illicitly and anonymously appropriate the public space as their temporary communication medium. This appropriation without permission renders these visual eruptions political acts, regardless of the content. As Marshall McLuhan puts it: "the medium is the message."[23]

There is also, as Baudrillard notes, a racial undertext to graffiti.[24] French journalists associate this urban phenomenon with banlieue delinquency, alongside shoplifting and drug dealing, one sign among others that evidences "resistance to assimilating mainstream French cultural values."[25] In the 1980s, graffiti was everywhere in Paris, especially in the subway system.[26] Right-wing figures would lump this urban phenomenon together with crack, rap, and immigrant hordes.[27] Decades later, in the aftermath of the 2005 suburban riots sparked by the death of two French *minorités visibles*, Minister of the Interior Nicolas Sarkozy referred to the rioters, mainly teenage youth of color, as "scum" and vowed to "power wash" the banlieues with a *kärcher*, a high-powered hose used to clean off graffiti.[28] This insulting language that reads rioters as dirt by invoking graffiti redrew the line between the clean and ordered city and its peripheral nemesis. This configuration of the boundary, physical and social, is what street artists and postcolonial authors have sought to publicize and undermine. As a trace of the "other," the marginal, and the rowdy, graffiti alters sanitized and exclusive images of Paris. Illegal as it may be, these visuals claim a right to the city by altering how passersby read its various sites.[29] Real and fictive street artists construct the city's landscape, refusing its current organization, inserting cross-racial dialogues and symbolic encounters in high-circulation spots. Their tags are, in Alain Milon's words, "the sign of a presence, the presence of anonymous authors, inhabitants."[30] Whether they use the city or the pen as their medium for expression, graffiti artists and postcolonial authors unveil spaces as political, transforming our Paris imaginary by helping a large audience experience it anew.

In postcolonial novels, graffiti is generally created by banlieue youth for a banlieue audience, as illustrated in Charef's *Tea in the Harem* (1983) and the best-selling novel *Kiffe Kiffe Tomorrow* (2006) by Faïza Guène, a French novelist of Algerian descent. In *Tea*, Majid and Pat's neighborhood consists of "concrete walls, covered with slogans. . . . cries from the heart . . . anti-racist graffiti in the form of raised fists . . . great long cocks and hairy testicles spray-painted down the walls" (19–20). Published two decades later, *Kiffe Kiffe Tomorrow* takes place in the same neighborhood, Le Paradis, where fifteen-year-old Doria navigates life at home with a struggling single mother and at school where she does not fit. She describes her neighborhood as separated from others by a wall

worse than the Maginot line or the Berlin wall. On the project side, the divider is covered in tags, drawings and concert posters and flyers for

different eastern-themed evenings; graffiti praising Saddam Hussein or
Che Guevara, patriotic signs, VIVA TUNISIA, SENEGAL REPRESENT, even
rap lyrics with a philosophical slant. But me, what I like best on the wall is
an old drawing that's been there for a really long time, long before the rise
of rap or the start of the war in Iraq. It's an angel in handcuffs with a red
cross over its mouth. (41)

A "symbol of the margins,"[31] graffiti is nevertheless ideologically impossible to
pin down. In the above passage, we can read it as a celebration of national
pride by subjects with origin in Tunisia and Senegal, or the absence of it by
youth that are in large part French. It can stand for juvenile immaturity, revolutionary or dictatorial ideals, geopolitical or religious partiality, and feelings of
disempowerment. What is clear is that despite its multivalent meaning, it is a
synecdoche for the banlieue.

When we find graffiti outside the immediate setting of the outskirts in
Mohamed Razane's short story "So Far, So Close By" (2011), it is a weapon
used by its residents to get revenge on the city. The story is set following the
historical death of Zyed Benna and Bouna Traoré, the two young men accidentally electrocuted as they sought to avoid a police identification check and
whose tragic fate sparked the 2005 banlieue riots across France.

> Several meters away, a group of twenty or so hooded young men, their
> faces covered with black scarves, stand at the bottom of a building. The
> leader is talking to his followers: Does everyone have his red stick? You've
> got red sticks because the color red is for the blood of our brothers? OK?
> Let's take out the maximum number of windows, the windows of this
> consumer society made for bastards who're killing our brothers. Let's fuck
> everything up and put up graffiti everywhere: "Ziad and Bouna, we'll
> never forget." Got it? OK. Let's go. After the tears comes revenge.[32]

In this context, the graffiti is part of a logic of property destruction, a tool of
blind revenge that takes businesses as its target. Despite its association with
vandalism in Razane's narrative, which differ from Guène's depiction, graffiti
is again the stuff of the banlieue.

In the works that follow, the graffiti and street art are located in the central
city of Paris rather than the banlieues, and their primary objectives are to represent concerns and populations of the urban periphery. These graffiti that break
Paris's "Maginot line" are instructive rather than destructive. Already in November 1961, graffiti appeared on the Pont Saint-Michel following the massacre of
peaceful Algerian protesters by the Paris police. Captured by Jean Texier in a
black-and-white photograph, it marked a site of violent bloodshed on the side
bank of the River Seine. The walls of the bridge read: "here Algerians are

"Here Algerians are drowned" (© *Le Paris Arabe*, Editions de la Découverte, Paris, 2003)

drowned." In a context where journalists and photographers were prohibited from attending the demonstration (which was itself unauthorized), the graffiti makes visible both the act of police repression and the site where it took place, identifying central Paris as a theater of colonial brutality that jars with dominant representations of Paris as a place associated with high culture or romance. Similarly, the postcolonial street art of Sebbar, JR, and Princess Hijab undermine the passerby's sense of place, by projecting memories, symbols, and faces associated with the racialized urban margins.

Sebbar, Graffiti, and Memoryscape

In *The Seine Was Red*, the graffiti addresses a mainstream Parisian public, unaware of its colonial past in the mid-1990s. This short postmodernist narrative is split between two time frames: the tragic night of October 17, 1961, when about one hundred peaceful Algerian protestors were massacred by the Paris police, and October 17, 1996, the anniversary of the massacre. On this commemorative occasion, Amel, a French adolescent of Algerian descent accompanied by Omer, a young undocumented Algerian journalist, retrace the steps demonstrators took that tragic night. With red paint, Omer marks sites of colonial bloodshed on the Parisian landscape. The novel goes back and forth between the night of the tragedy and 1996. The 1996 narrative follows and is constituted principally of a documentary film about October 17, 1961 made by young French student Louis. The text represents a story within a story with a splintered structure that assembles multiple perspectives, mirroring Louis's film, which relies on a collage of family photos and documents (newspaper clippings, correspondence with Algerian militants), archives, and testimonial accounts by family contacts. Louis distrusts the official state narrative, whereby his parents are "traitors" who betrayed France by assisting in Algerian nationalists for independence. He tells his mother that he wants to explore "your truth, Dad's truth, what you thought, experienced, suffered through . . . your life" (12). This conflict between official and personal and familial is precisely what the second generation, who had not witnessed the event, seek to reveal in the city by super-imposing, literally through graffiti, memories of the colonial repression to French official history.

Born in Algeria to a French mother and an Algerian father who were teachers in Aflou, a small town of the high plateau, Leïla Sebbar left her country of birth soon after its independence to study literature in Aix-en-Provence and later in Paris.[33] Her family history, as she describes it in *Lettres parisiennes: Autopsie de l'exil (Parisian Letters: Autopsy of Exile)*, has made her an outsider to both French and Algerian cultures, a "division" that has nourished her fiction.[34] This out-sider position may account for Sebbar's ability to discern the multiple relations individuals bear toward the Algerian War and their complex motives for want-ing to remember or forget it. Louis's film based on his parents' photographs, documents, and friends' testimonies represents his attempt to understand his family's active role in the decolonization of Algeria and to educate Amel, the Franco-Arab high school student with whom he is enamored. Amel is baffled by her mother's participation in Louis's film because she had repeatedly refused to tell *her* about the family's involvement in the Algerian War. On the anniver-sary month of the 1961 massacre and after watching Louis's documentary, Amel runs away from home with Omer to retrace the steps her mother took that fate-ful night. Though Louis, Omer, and Amel have different personal motivations to recover memories of the Algerian War of Independence, they all have to over-come not only the state's silencing of the event but that of their families. Their graffiti expose another image of Paris—that of colonial violence.

On October 17, 1961, about thirty thousand Algerian workers and their families left the isolated slums of the Parisian periphery and took to the streets of central Paris to demonstrate for an independent Algeria. The peaceful march expressed opposition to Prefect of Police Maurice Papon's discriminatory curfew, which forbade Algerians' presence on the streets of the capital after 8:00 p.m.[35] Opposed to the demonstration, the Paris police broke the proces-sion as they charged and killed nearly one hundred demonstrators.[36] "The bloodiest act of state repression of protesters in the modern history of Western Europe,"[37] this police brutality against Algerians in France during the Algerian War remained an ellipsis in French official history until 2001 when Bertrand Delanoë, the socialist mayor of Paris, accepted a proposal to install a small plaque on a barely visible corner side of the Pont Saint-Michel in remembrance of this event. The plaque does not attribute responsibility to the Paris police but simply reads that Algerians were killed in a repression. In 2012 President François Hollande officially recognized the event in a similar and very brief statement that eschews the responsibility of the state and particularly the Paris police.

The setting for *The Seine*, 1996, is also the year when President Jacques Chirac unveiled a monument to the dead in Paris dedicated to the memory of civilians and military who died in North Africa. At the official unveiling, Chirac spoke of the French colonial enterprise as a national accomplishment, concealing the brutality of the colonial encounter in a discourse of French exceptionalism: "Peacekeeping, uplifting territories, spreading education, founding a modern medicine, creating administrative and judicial institutions, these are many of the traces left by the uncontestable works the French presence contributed. . . . Hence, thirty years after the return of the French [of Algeria] to metropolitan France, it is noteworthy to recall the important and rich work France has accomplished there and of which it is proud."[38] The same year the state erects this monument to colonial accomplishment, the instigator of "black October," Maurice Papon, awaits a press-crazed trial (1997-98) for his complicity in the false arrest of thousands of French Jews during the Nazi occupation.[39] The Papon trial provided the crucial context through which French Jewish testimonies could be heard.[40] *The Seine*'s polyphonic structure is reminiscent of this courtroom setting with its testimonials, its confrontation between survivors, witnesses, archives, historians, and perpetrators. It is a trace, albeit unofficial, of what happened.

The new *lieu de mémoire* inaugurated by President Chirac is part of a proliferation of official monuments and other commemorative practices that increasingly disseminate the illusion of a common memory by creating common mnemonic spaces at a time when France experiences a "crisis of identity."[41] As Gerardus Van der Leuuw observes, "a politics of exclusion might be an integral part of the making of a sacred space."[42] The exclusion of memories of colonial violence from Paris's public monuments is not accidental: the coherence of the republican historical narrative requires it, for as Ernest Renan notes, national cohesion requires forgetting.[43] France's increasing demands of conformity is a reaction to the cultural diversity of its population, originating mostly from the former French colonies. Instead of loyalty, the institutional demand for mnemonic conformity has generated a strong culture of dissent, where works of fiction like *The Seine* play a central role in constructing less glorious versions of French colonial history. Since the 1980s and increasingly after 1996, a slew of literary texts and films have preserved and transmitted memories of "black October." Listed in Sebbar's dedication, these fictional and journalistic works show that generational and cultural memories are strongest where national memories are either weak in their representation or violent in their censorship of countermemories.

As a medium of expression, graffiti has been "historically represented as peripheral and subversive and (related) to contents (such as characters, narratives, sceneries) that exhibit criticism or dissidence."[44] By deploying graffiti, Sebbar calls attention to forms of representation deemed illicit and illegitimate. She does not seek to insert censored voices of the past into a national narrative that would thus become more pluralistic. Their presence does not celebrate the nation. Instead, graffiti represents unequal access to the public sphere and a tenacious collective desire to publicize conflicting stories of the past. Through its use, the author calls for a model of commemoration that is participatory, risk-prone, and dissonant. By contrast, the sanctioned Parisian mnemonic landscape appears as an institutionalized consensus of the past achieved through exclusion.

Sebbar's novel, the first to focus entirely on October 17, 1961,[45] calls attention not only to this momentous event during the Algerian War (1954–62) but to the fact that accounts of it and other colonial atrocities were made illegal by the state. Below the dedication to the Algerian victims of the massacre, *The Seine* lists authors who resisted state censorship during the Algerian War, giving them an honorary place in a "family" constituted by its memories. The acknowledgment of the Comité Maurice Audin; historian Jean-Luc Einaudi; photographer Elie Kagan; publisher François Maspero; journalists Paulette Péju and Anne Tristan; novelists Didier Daeninckx, Nacer Kettane, and Mehdi Lallaoui; and the activist George Mattei directs the reader's attention to a long alternative historiography of the Algerian conflict. Beyond the Parisian police repression, the text also reinserts titles of censored books during the Algerian War, such as Jean-Louis Hurst's *Le déserteur* (*The Deserter*, 1960), which depicts a French soldier's refusal to fight Algerian revolutionaries, and Henri Alleg's *La question* (1958), which describes the author's experience of torture by French paratroopers during the war. The dedication and these texts inscribe Sebbar as a participant in a French anticolonial tradition that has produced a competing and at one point illegal archive to the national one.

The novel, like the graffiti, offers a rereading of Paris. *The Seine* exemplifies the circulation of memories from the private to the public spheres, highlighting in particular differences of power in the representation of the past. The novel is spatially organized with locations as subtitles that take the reader from the low-income periphery of Paris, which includes the 1961 slums, and Amel's 1996 Algerian family home in Nanterre—where witnesses' testimonies are heard and domestic archives found—to the center of Paris and the theater of the massacre: Rue de la Santé, Défense, République, Concorde, Bonne Nouvelle, Saint-Michel, Rue Saint Séverin, and Orly. The title, *The Seine Was Red*, evokes the massacre of Protestant noblemen in Paris on St. Bartholomew's Day (August 24–25, 1572) whose slaughtered bodies were thrown in the river, rendering it red, and the bloody repression of Algerian demonstrators. The title, like the graffiti, denotes the superimposition of memories of colonialism onto French history and icons. The two protagonists reread common sites and monuments where demonstrators gathered as spaces of commemoration and mourning. At République and Défense, meeting points for Algerian demonstrators in 1961, Amel observes the statue of Marianne, "a giant woman, standing, as if she were poised to face the enemy," and asks Omer, "Who defended [the Algerians] when the police charged on the Neuilly bridge? You heard the reports, the panic, bodies trampled, the wounded, the dead . . . baby carriages turned upside down, lost shoes of adults, children" (39, 40). In reassessing this symbol of the republic and the ideals of the revolution, the novel contrasts abstract ideals and the betrayal of these ideals on October 17, 1961. Amel's reinterpretation of Marianne challenges the image of a revolutionary Paris frozen in time.

The official memoryscape provides national subjects with a common past, erected into monuments, legitimated and maintained by the state. In contrast, the graffiti is considered an act of vandalism punishable by law and will be cleaned off. The two protagonists' illegal appropriation of the public space denotes how the state's exclusion has led individuals to develop compensatory strategies to represent themselves and their collective memories. Omer's hope that his inscription "won't come off, etched in the stone" (14), relays his wish that his family's story become part of the Parisian landscape, timeless and visible to all. Omer explains as he places graffiti on the wall of the Prison de la Santé, a site of remembrance for French resistance to the Nazi occupation and the unacknowledged site where Algerian nationalists were guillotined: "I just want to acknowledge what happened in these walls" (15). By marking this site, Omer influences how passersby might experience the place anew.

Omer's graffiti adjoined to official lieux de mémoire challenge hegemonic French collective memories through juxtaposition and mimicry. Homi Bhabha called (colonial) mimicry "the sign of a double articulation . . . , which 'appropriates' the Other as it visualizes power."[46] Omer's inscription appropriates and reproduces the official plaque on the wall of La Santé. Critic Anne Donadey remarks that the graffiti by Amel and Omer "create[s] a historical palimpsest

that subversively sheds light at once on the Algerian events and the lack of official commemoration on the subject in France."[47] Indeed, their graffiti literally
exposes unequal access to representation of memories. As a reproduction of
official plaques, the graffiti crucially compete with and contest the French view
of the colonial war as "peacekeeping" and a battle against terrorists by appropriating the frame and the wording of memorialized French events to reframe
memories of colonialism. One piece of Omer's graffiti mimics the plaque in
form (capital letters and centered), genre, and wording, juxtaposing the similar
resistance of the French during World War II and Algerians during the War of
Independence, but the outcome differs for these freedom fighters.

ON NOVEMBER 11 1940	1954–1962
IN THIS PRISON WERE HELD	IN THIS PRISON
HIGH SCHOOL AND UNIVERSITY STUDENTS	WERE GUILLOTINED
WHO, AT THE CALL OF GENERAL DE GAULLE,	ALGERIAN RESISTERS
WERE THE FIRST TO RISE UP	WHO ROSE UP
AGAINST THE OCCUPATION. (14)	AGAINST THE FRENCH OCCUPATION. (15)

Representing the Algerian War through the prism of foreign occupation, Omer
attributes legitimacy to the Algerian struggle, claiming German occupation of
France during World War II as a sort of equivalent. If the French students in-
carcerated for resisting the Nazis deserve commemoration, so do Algerians
who were killed for resisting French occupation. The juxtaposition also functions
to highlight the extreme measures taken by the French state to execute Algerian
revolutionaries. Mimicry here helps rethink the Algerian War by presenting it
through the trope of nationalist liberation, illustrating how the language we use
to describe historical events shapes our understanding of these events and the
legitimacy we grant their participants. Using graffiti as a revisionist tool that
competes with official accounts, Omer's inscriptions function as captions in
that they help read the Parisian public space. They identify sites scarred by colonial violence and bloodshed as they superimpose the postcolonial vision onto
the republican one. Omer and Amel's peregrination in Paris and Omer's graffiti
highlights the second generation's sense of responsibility to reveal the violence
of October 17, 1961, to Parisians.

Through their public commemorative practices, Louis, Omer, and Amel
do not attempt to enter a nationalist narrative; rather, they become "memory
entrepreneurs" who resist it. Elizabeth Jelin calls "memory entrepreneurs" individuals who seek to intervene in the public realm and gain public recognition
for their collective past. Beyond the association with enterprise for private
profit, Jelin reminds us that "entrepreneurs" also refers to actions of a "social"

or collective character; the term signals individuals' commitment, organizing efforts, creative initiatives, and the social hierarchies that they navigate. "The important point," Jelin claims, "is that the entrepreneur becomes personally involved in his or her project; in addition, he or she generates commitment from others, fostering participation and organizing efforts of a collective character."[48] Unlike official memory, memory entrepreneurs undoubtedly help describe a more democratic relationship with the past. Entrepreneurs' efforts highlight the agency and investment of individuals in fashioning their own history. In *The Seine*, such participation in memory making illuminates a crisis of identification with a nationalist model that is monolithic, exclusive, and imposed. In the novel, protagonists find in their families a rich warehouse of memory to be tapped and participants to be broadcast. Sebbar's dedication to actors in and historiographers of the Algerian War betrays her intention to promote the cultural sphere as a stage on which the new generation can publicize and legitimate alternative narratives of the past. Cultural works thus represent a surrogate form to the official archive, a source of knowledge for generations to come, and a repository of truths suppressed by the state.

More than any other novel about the massacre of October 17, 1961, *The Seine* focuses on the forms of memory transmission, marrying both archival documents and descriptions of historical photographs with family photographs, individual recollections, film editing, graffiti, and references to French popular culture. In addition, the cacophony of testimonial accounts marks *The Seine* as a different kind of novel from those by French writers of Algerian descent. Texts such as Nacer Kettane's *Brahim's Smile* or Mehdi Lallaoui's *Nuit d'octobre (October Night)* have framed the event as a foundational moment for postcolonial France. By reconstructing an event they had not themselves experienced or witnessed, what Marianne Hirsch calls a postmemory,[49] these writers underscore their strong emotional ties with the decolonization struggle and its cultural importance for Franco-Arab identities. Sebbar, on the other hand, illustrates the legacy of October 17, 1961, for a broader range of participants and their descendants who are French, Franco-Arab, *pied-noir*, and Algerian. Against a nationalist consensus model of collective memory, *The Seine* models dissonance as an approach for inventorying the past, producing, in turn, a dissonant narrative. The competition between different memories questions the state ownership over collective memory and faults state universalist pretentions to represent all views. The presence of 27 blank pages out of 125 pages total calls attention to gaps and absences in the overall recounting of the event, suggesting that the full story remains inaccessible. The collage of multiple perspectives on *octobre noir* undermines the French and Algerian official narratives on the Algerian War, enabling the recuperation of neglected participants: Algerians fighting on the side of France, French fighting on the side of Algerians, and the role of women activists on both sides.

Three years after the publication of *The Seine*, on October 17, 2001, a small commemorative plaque was installed on the left bank of the Pont Saint-Michel to mark the fortieth anniversary of the event. The association Au Nom de la Mémoire, founded in 1990 by journalist Samia Massaouid, writer Mehdi Lallaoui, and historian Benjamin Stora, advocated for the state public recognition of October 17, 1961, which now finally appears in school history books. The socialist mayor of Paris, Bertrand Delanoë, accepted a proposal by the council of Paris to commemorate the event.[50] "In memory of the many Algerians killed during the bloody repression of the peaceful demonstration of 17 October 1961," reads the plaque's inscription. The contestation surrounding the plaque, which is mirrored in its small size, placement, and residue of vandalism, emblematizes the formidable conflict over memories of France's colonial past or the "memory war." Placed on the least visible side of the Pont Saint-Michel and featuring bronze letters on a bronze background and attractive golden frame, the plaque raises the question: what does it mean to publicly acknowledge a massacre with a plaque, only to place it in a nearly invisible location? Traces of vandalism and remnants of red paint below the plaque's left corner further encapsulate the tension between impulses of commemoration and suppression. Though out of sight, this gesture of recognition has not left all Parisians indifferent. Unlike the graffiti of Sebbar's protagonists, the plaque does not name the Paris police as perpetrators of the massacre. But for some, this memorial is a blemish on those who fought for a French Algeria and the plaque has been defaced, damaged, and replaced several times since its 2001 installation.[51]

Princess Hijab's Graffiti:
Layering to Unveil Difference

In contrast to this plaque's relative invisibility, twenty-one-year-old anonymous street artist Princess Hijab chooses advertising images in high-traffic locations and transforms them with black spray paint and marker pen. Her altered models don uniform black niqabs, like the ones in Iran. By selecting areas of the Paris metro, Princess Hijab addresses a broad audience of lay people, who may not be familiar with graffiti codes.[52] Since 2006, this self-described "racial outsider" has layered media advertising posters with veils and niqabs. Like the graffiti in Sebbar's novel, her artwork provides a layering that encodes racial difference and the space of the urban outskirts. She provocatively labeled her artwork "artistic jihad." This rhetorical inflation is reminiscent of graffiti theorists who have called graffiti a semiotic "guerilla warfare," "a form of aesthetic sabotage," and a guerilla tool,[53] with the difference that "jihad" also signals religious and racial difference in the French context. In her online manifesto, Princess Hijab rejects ties to any lobby, movement, or political, religious, or advertising group. In an interview for the German newspaper *Der Spiegel*, she confided that she was not a Muslim, countering many bloggers' accusation that she is an Islamic fundamentalist bent on covering signs of female nudity and encouraging women to submit to Islam. Practices of covering up skin on posters by blacking out bare skin happen daily in Saudi Arabia (Aburawa). In the United Kingdom, activists behind Muslims Against Advertising also cover undressed models in street ads with paints.[54] The idea that Princess Hijab dresses up nakedness because of a Muslim conservatism does not stand deeper examination. As other commentators note, she does not fully cover models, often leaving legs uncovered. She also hijabizes her subjects indiscriminately of gender.

These blog comments locate Princess Hijab's work in an overdetermined debate over the hijab. In 1989 three high school girls were suspended from public schools in the suburbs of Paris for wearing headscarves in class. Celebrated Tunisia-born feminist Gisèle Halimi wrote in favor of these expulsions in an article in *Le Monde*, where she describes the veil as "the flag of fundamentalism."[55] Over the next fifteen years, decisions to suspend or not suspend future Muslim girls who cover their hair were left to the discretion of school principals. In 2004, following years of mini-affairs regarding this sartorial practice, the national assembly and the senate passed a bill banning "ostentatious religious symbols" in public schools on the grounds that they go against the French principle of *laïcité*, or the separation of state and religious institutions. Previously in 1998, the high court settled that the headscarf was not incompatible with secular schools, unless, "in its ostentatious or political character, [it] constitutes an act of pressure, of provocation, of proselytism or of propaganda."[56] In 2009 both legislative bodies voted to ban full face covers, a law that targets the niqab. Prior to this additional law, the national assembly launched a study that revealed only 367 women wore the niqab in France.[57] In 1995 Gaspard and Khosrokhavar also noted the rarity of girls wearing the headscarf.[58] Women who wear the niqab are fined €150. The law stipulates that those who force a woman to wear it will be fined €30,000 and one year in prison, revealing assumptions that this sartorial practice is imposed by fathers, brothers, or husbands rather than chosen by the wearer.[59]

As an artist name, "Princess" calls up Orientalist tales often focused on aristocratic beauties and "Hijab" marks the reduction of the Orient to a demonized sign of Islam in the West. Together, the name merges various fantasies linked to the Maghreb. The veil or hijab has long been understood in French cultural discourse as the symbol of women's repression par excellence: repression of their desire, their voice, and their femininity. It erupts here, where it is least likely, on advertising posters where models, male and female, routinely appear as sexualized commodities. Beyond its religious symbol, the hijab evokes Muslims and the spaces they inhabit. Its graffiti presence in the Paris metro paradoxically summons its absence from advertising images, which beyond selling products naturalize which bodies and sartorial practices belong in the city through iteration and which do not through exclusion. What makes bodies "out of place" in the French public imagination is increasingly coded through Islamic practices (hijab, niqab, skullcaps, and khamis) rather than exclusively skin color. Because Muslim symbols of dress have been generally isolated from the public imaginary and criminalized in schools, hospitals, and other places by law, their presence invokes an identity that chafes against the city's ubiquitous images. By using the graffiti, a criminalized medium, to cover models in commercials, Princess Hijab superimposes two layers of crimes in the public space: the graffiti and the Muslim headdress. The Parisian landscape, remade by these graffiti, interrogates the common notion of "Le vivre ensemble" (a phrase that encourages citizens to embrace diversity) by unearthing the silent language of clothing.

In her semi-biography cowritten with journalist Sylvia Zappi, Fadela Amara, a staunch advocate of secularism and the founder of the banlieue association Ni Putes Ni Soumises, had boxed banlieue women into a mere three categories according to their sartorial practices: "the submissive, the mannish, and the invisible."[60] Each problematic sartorial expression relays a hidden and stunted femininity in the virilist banlieues. As Mehammed Mack explains, the hijab is for Amara "a protective armor" that "virilizes" the submissive woman who wears it.[61] Amara's surface understanding of veiled Muslim girls speaks to a tacitly shared postfeminist mainstream culture in the 1980s that limits expressions of femininity to feminine desirability. Exposed skin and tight-fitting clothing become signs of mature sexual agency and women's freedom in an era that dehistoricizes and decontextualizes sexual desire. In postfeminism, Angela McRobbie explains that women "are encouraged to embrace their own objectification as form of self-making: Sexual objectification is (re)presented not as something done to women by some men but as the freely chosen wish of active, confident, assertive female subjects."[62] Drawing on McRobbie, Patricia Stuelke explains that "freedom becomes defined as a woman's ability to participate in her own sexual objectification—to choose it, and to understand it as always empowering."[63]

Princess Hijab's altered billboards deconstruct not only Paris's visual language but also the commodification of sexuality. In the transformed fashion advertisement for Virgin Records, a hijabized model is captured full shot in a comprehensive framing. With her buttocks peeking out of the length of her headdress, the side view figure turns her gaze, confronting the viewer. In the original poster, a youthful white woman appears naked holding a little Virgin brand bag with the slogan of "la culture du plaisir" (the culture of pleasure) hiding parts of her buttocks. The graffiti covers the word "plaisir" with the hijab, which outlines an "r," so that the eye reads "durcir" (harden) instead. The caption of the dressed-up version presents the female body as an object of masculine sexual arousal, a selling tool for Virgin music, elsewhere for Joker orange juice, or Guerlain perfume.

The other billboard for Galleries Lafayette, an iconic Parisian department store, displays one of Jean-Paul Goude's fashion photos. In a front, medium shot, a white, youthful female model dons an oversized and inverted cone-shaped hat, mid-arm black gloves, and a strapless crop top with the colors of the French flag. Princess Hijab placed a triangular niqab to cover part of the model's face. This superimposition of the French colors, with a sign associated with Islam, is provocative in and of itself. The image is reminiscent of photographs of young veiled girls who donned headscarves the colors of the French flag in a December 2003 demonstration against the proposed headscarf ban that gathered 3,000 to 4,000 people in Place de la Bastille.[64] Their sartorial choice questioned the idea that they could not be simultaneously French students in public schools and Muslim girls. This Gallicization of Islam can also redraw the national line between an Islam practiced by the urban and literate French and the backward traditional practices of their immigrant parents as Mayanthi Fernando notes about her interviews with French Muslims.[65] In other words, some French Muslims recycle the binary of moderns and antimoderns, in an attempt to argue legibly for their inclusion in a nation that has defined them as outsiders. By redeploying the codes of exclusion, they perform their membership into Western modernity, bypassing other questions such as residential segregation, the imperative of secularism, and racial difference.

These Muslims' emphasis on their membership to the nation excludes those who are not citizens, creating a binary of good and bad Muslims, those who are modern and use reason versus those who are foreigners from underdeveloped countries and blindly submit and follow.[66] We see a different symbolism of the colors of the French flag in the films *Chouchou* by Merzak Allouache and *Made in France* by Ahmed and Zakia Bouchaala, discussed in chapter 4. Both films end with French and Algerian protagonists whose embrace is tricolor. These epilogues intimate that without the Franco-Arab or undocumented subjects, Paris would be incomplete. In Princess Hijab's image, the running paint dripping on the model's chest and clothing projects an aggressiveness absent in the Virgin advertisement or JR's stylized photographs that look like a billboard without a brand. On the Galleries Lafayette poster, the messy running edges remind us that we are looking at a criminal act. It is an image that projects both difference and illegality at the same time, suggesting that these are dangerously conflated as one and the same in today's France.

Princess Hijab states that her painting over billboards is an act of resistance against "the visual terrorism" of advertising. By hijabizing bodies, she hopes to rehumanize embodiments rendered distant by capitalist messages. The body is no longer instrumentalized in the abstract but represents a lived experience. She tells Arwa Aburawa that "her work attempts to remove the hijab from its gendered and religious context and convert it into a symbol of empowerment and re-embodiment."[67] On another level, by appropriating a sign of "outsider" status and layering it on public figures, she asserts that she is "trying to create a connection with and between people." By presenting minority-coded images in the heart of the city, she also presents counterhegemonic embodiments of femininity. This may be her distinguishing feature from anti-ad groups such as Adbusters, a movement she followed as a teen. Inherent in the altered Virgin poster is a critique of the exploitation of the female body for the profitable benefit of the fashion industries. These hijabized female bodies present alternative expressions of femininity, too often demonized as symbolic of female oppression in the West. Princess Hijab's work interrupts French hegemonic views of femininity by interrogating the supposedly "natural" or "normal" feminine sartorial styles. Her graffiti disrupt the femininity exalted by the advertisement machine and the fashion industry, as well as that constructed by French hegemonic culture.

In the aftermath of the new law banning headscarves in public schools, many minority women were invited on television, and their autobiographies were published by prestigious presses, all in support of the new law. Invisible and unheard were the dissenting voices of those actually affected by the law: the veiled girls. In fact, only two veiled girls were invited to the hearings of the Stasi Commission on whether to ban the headscarf and only as an afterthought on the last day of its proceedings at the request of Jean Baubérot, who was surprised that they were not already on the commission's list of people to consult.[68] In *Voices and Veils: Feminism and Islam in French Women's Writing and Activism*, Anna Kemp notes this glaring absence.

From reading the media, one would believe everyone agrees with the headscarf and niqab bans: the left, the right, the intelligentsia, the politicos, and the Muslim girls from the banlieue. For this consensus to emerge, veiled girls were shunned by the media; moreover, "the Education League—the largest federation of French educators, with over two million members—opposed the law." Like memorial consensus, the manufacturing of political consensus based on censorship foments dissent. It shows that far from being a reality, the French secular state is a social construction dependent on reiterated projection of social unity, censorship of tension and dissent, and a constant negotiation of borders. By politicizing visuals in the metro, Princess Hijab works at the ground level to create a conversation in the public space about the imagined other.

Occupying Central Paris:
JR's Portrait of a Generation (2004–6)

In October 2010 the little-known French photographer–graffiti artist who goes only by his initials, JR, was dazed to hear he won the $100,000 TED prize for humanitarian work. The TED website includes a link to JR's virtual page, where one can see some of his work and its coverage in a half-dozen newspaper articles in French, Italian, and English. Self-described "photograffeur," JR fuses photography and graffiti in unexpected ways, using various street surfaces to flypost enormous black-and-white photocopies of his portraits. Many of the close-up portraits of individual faces are shot with a 28 mm lens that covers a 180-degree perspective and gives subjects a distorted appearance. He prints his monochromes in billboard sizes and pastes them on vertiginously high buildings at the end of blocks of flats in the housing projects, or on city walls, where he drapes construction site barricades and bridges, bus shelters, and trash cans. After selecting the location to display his subjects, JR at times captures an encounter between the photographed subject and the viewer who stops to observe what could have easily been mistaken for a billboard without a brand. In the banlieue, some of his prints include the building number and names of his subjects, restoring the individuality of subjects too often invisible. A "clandestine" photographer, JR's anonymity has the practical advantage of protecting him from being sued for illegally pasting his artwork, first in Paris suburbs and central city, then a favela of Rio, the wall between Palestine and Israel, and a slum in Kenya's Kibera. Cities are JR's canvas and open-air gallery. He never asks permission to display his work to the public.

With some poster brushes, paper, and pots of glue, JR's keen eye for spatial politics literally puts a human face on places that national media caricature as lawless, pathological, or subhuman. Traveling to areas deemed dangerous, JR approaches residents and enlists them as collaborators in his project, building relations of trust with communities. The end results are portraits that cannot be ignored and that intimately interpellate audiences in unexpected places. Close-up faces of the multiracial suburban youth appear in Paris's bourgeois sector, Palestinian and Israeli faces who share the same profession are paired indiscriminately on both sides of the wall that divides Israel and Palestine, and faces from the favela Morra da Providencia pasted on its walls return Rio's gaze. Though his photography reveals "forgotten communities,"[69] JR insists his work's "intention is artistic not political."

Born in France to immigrant parents from Tunisia and Eastern Europe, JR professes to make free art for the kind of people who do not go to the museum. Quickly his provocative artwork was noticed by an urban culture magazine, *Wad*, and *Photo* magazine named him a young talent in 2002.[70] In 2005 the self-taught artist had already published "carnets de rue," a book that gathers urban art photographs taken in Paris, New York, and Amsterdam following street artists. Prints of his monochrome images sell for €900 in Paris's art galleries.[71] In 2016 JR was invited to create two huge photo collage installations for the Olympic Games in Rio.

JR's first "official" street gallery was not located in the gentrified neighborhood of central Paris where he lives, Le Marais, but in Les Bosquets, a poverty-stricken mass housing area in Montfermeil, a suburb of Paris. "Cliché de ghetto"[72] started with neighborhood youth nagging him into taking their pictures and materialized into a full-fledged artistic project that saw the end of blocks of flats covered by a six-by-eight-meter picture of their residents. With the proud faces of its inhabitants displayed for everyone to see, Les Bosquets no longer fit the uniform line of faceless decrepit buildings found in the Paris periphery. On one of the mid-shot super-sized pictures of "Ghetto cliché," a young black man with glaring eyes aims a camera like a machine gun at the photographer, equating media cameras with deadly violence. Other images include a low-angle shot of a young man in street gear leaping out of a crowded balcony and another of a family making faces against fenced bars, behind them a wall covered with graffiti. These pictures of desolate and disintegrating high-rise buildings frame banlieue residents as victims of social relegation, instead of violent perpetrators as often cast in news media. Among these images of squalor and overcrowdedness, conviviality and warmth emerge as in the image of a black toddler receiving a kiss from a white friend. For one night, JR and his collaborators turned one of the poorest sectors of the city into a gallery by inviting other Parisians and providing drinks, but only a couple of journalists came. Parisians do not go to places like Les Bosquets.

But in October 2005 countless Parisian journalists did come to the banlieue of Clichy-sous-bois, next door to Montfermeil, to capture boys and young men torching cars, setting buildings on fire, especially schools, and breaking into businesses in their own neighborhoods.[73] Scenes of hooded angry young men—black, brown, and white—hiding their faces with scarves, and throwing bricks and other objects at the police ran around the clock on television news. With the riots spreading like wildfire from the periphery of Paris to virtually all working-class outskirts in the country, TV screens ran and reran scary long-shot views of a mass of angry and anonymous banlieue youth, but the reasons behind their protest were never heard. Like in previous significant riots in 1981, 1990, and 1998, politicians and intellectuals took the front stage to interpret, explain, and speak for the banlieue. Without their voices or context, images of the *minorités visibles* burning and vandalizing buildings, causing more than $290 million (in 2007) in damaged property, confirmed stereotypes about the "badlands of the republic."[74] The government took extraordinary measures to curb the riots, resorting to a state of emergency with curfews, police searches, and mass detention of suspects. On November 30, 2005, almost five thousand young men were questioned and detained according to the Ministry of Interior. Yet there is little record in the public sphere of what these youths had to say.

Blending photographs from Les Bosquets and La Forestière in Clichy-sous-bois before and after the revolt, JR's street gallery "28 Millimeters, Portrait of a Generation" (2004–6) captures inhabitants who live at the gates of Paris up close, literally an inch away from their faces, consciously contrasting the distance with which the media depicted the riots with long shots from the edge of the neighborhoods. With this intimate collection of mostly black and brown male faces pasted across central Paris, racialized individuals from the banlieue greet sites they seldom frequent: municipal buildings to fashionable cafés and shops in the trendy bohemian neighborhood of Le Marais. For JR, the faces are those of friends, not of thugs or criminals. He explains further the rationale behind the flyposts and their location in the eastern part of central Paris: "Parisians, even liberal, left-wing people often regard these kids as extra-terrestrials, sub-humans. . . . I wanted to show them as they really are, as I know them, with a kind of violence, sure, but also great humor and great energy. A creative violence."[75] The distorted oversized images from the invisible margins, now relocated in the affluent city, project back to the center the perverted representation of banlieue residents it had constructed for decades. In one photo, a black youth wearing a baseball cap sternly approaches the camera, biting his upper lip as if he were an attack dog ready to jump at its prey. Another photo features a black man wearing a woolen hat and a hoodie, head slightly bent with ferocious eyes frowning menacingly at the camera. In contrast to these angry postures, other photos include children making funny faces. JR notes: "When you look at the banlieue now, they look back." Certainly, the banlieues have long been objects of scrutiny by the media and politicians, its inhabitants, mere aggressive caricatures: "terrorists," "scum," "Muslim fanatics," "delinquents," and "rapists."[76] JR's photo-graffiti creates a hyperreality that, in Baudrillard's words, substitutes the signs of the real for the real.[77] We may wonder, however, whether passersby might be able to recognize these images

Still shot of poster in Le Marais (JR, "28 Millimeters, Portrait of a Generation")

as returned to the sender. Without context, one might wonder whether disfiguring images of racialized masculine violence help interrogate them. One particularly poignant image is a photograph that indexes victimization rather than violence. It captures a city worker removing the poster of a black child's face with a high-powered water hose. Here, the image recalls another transatlantic history of racial domination and violence through visual association with the repression of African American civil rights protesters with water cannons. Such a parallel encourages us to frame the riots in the banlieues in terms of a more globally visible and available history of struggle for racial equality. These encounters may be deemed safe since the racialized others continue to be subjected to the city's gaze while being kept at a safe distance. But these visual interventions in the city mark the artist's ability to participate in an environment, particularly to play on affect to demonstrate how Paris's topophilia depends on the creation of a topophobia.

The narratives we have examined in previous chapters touched on the lack of access to modes of representation. Driss Chraïbi's *The Butts* casts an Algerian writer who seeks in vain to publish a book about the miserable existence of his compatriots in Paris, treated as pariahs by the general public. The editor he meets rejects the manuscript and warns him that the line between indignation and deportation is thin. Perceived as a threat, Waldick's book remains unpublished. In William Gardner Smith's *The Stone Face*, Algerian experiences are also largely invisible. For example, Ahmed, a young, gentle Algerian student in Paris, is outraged to hear that Simeon did not know about the internment camps in France where Algerian National Front suspects are sent. While self-referential characters aspiring to write (or paint) a collective experience virtually disappear from later postcolonial plots such as Mehdi Charef's *Tea in the Harem* or Ahmed and Zakia Bouchaala's *Made in France*, discussions of the forms of racist oppression, economic segregation, and resistance have remained. For critics Odile Cazenave and Patricia Célérier, this means that the notion of engagement (or commitment) "has not gone away; it has changed its genres and forms."[78] By "engagement," they refer to the political or social action of artists and the notion of moral responsibility attached to such commitment. These scholars do not fail to note that a few Western publishers oversee African writers' work, which is read mainly by a Western audience, with themes of masculine violence and immigration dominating their fiction.[79] Street artists, indeed, bypass the selection process entirely, never asking permission to display their work for the public. Princess Hijab and JR's graffiti convey the invisibility of the urban margins in the city, while at the same time claiming a right to this public space, a right to recompose social bonds and participate in constructing the city they inhabit.

The postcolonial authors and filmmakers I have examined nurture a similar desire to participate and shape our Paris imaginary. Their Paris reminds us that identities and feelings of membership shape and are shaped by the politics of space. Their creation powerfully writes back and challenges negative meanings imposed on specific places and bodies. It becomes clear that the periphery is not just an impoverished place; it is a dynamic laboratory for rethinking restrictive understandings of identity and fostering cross-racial solidarities. Again and again, their stories expand our understandings of who and what is Paris. In the process, they revisit and revise tired clichés of the city as a space of liberation for the African diaspora or a moving feast for expatriates. Today, more than ever, we need to recognize the existence of this other Paris.

Coda: Everyday Islamophobia

In the course of writing this book, a wave of terrorist attacks shook Paris in January and November 2015. On Bastille day 2016, a man rammed into a crowd with a truck, killing 86 and injuring more than 400 people in Nice. The state of emergency declared after the second Paris attacks was extended multiple times until a new antiterrorist law signed by Président Emmanuel Macron on October 30, 2017, enforced and augmented its measures. This context intensifies the questions of race, Islam, and the banlieues discussed in previous chapters, making it plain that these will remain hot issues for twenty-first-century France and Europe. As previously noted, debates surrounding terrorism are not contained to perpetrators of violence but extend to whole communities suspected of harboring them or of sharing their faith and ideologies. Discourses about terrorism, then, risk justifying the expansion of the logic of securitization that targets the *minorités visibles* and the banlieues as well as France's laws restricting the visibility of Islamic sartorial practices. Today more than ever, the myth of French universalism needs to be unraveled to face the risky institutionalization of everyday islamophobia, racial exclusion, and state violence that further mangle national cohesion and foster resentment. I thus close this book by returning to elements eschewed by fictions of intimacy: French exceptionalism, selective securitization, and the gendered rescue narrative of Islam's victims in public debates surrounding terrorism.

On January 11, 2015, Paris was "the capital of the world" as more than fifty world leaders assembled there for an unprecedented march of solidarity against terror attacks.[1] In the wake of the bloodshed at *Charlie Hebdo* and in a kosher supermarket that left eighteen people dead, presidents, prime ministers, and state representatives joined a silent march of 1.5 million people to honor the victims.[2] This event—the largest show of unity and solidarity in the West since events following the September 11, 2001, terrorist attacks on the World Trade Center and the Pentagon in the United States—brought together world leaders including Palestinian Authority President Mahmoud Abbas and Israeli Prime Minister Benjamin Netanyahu, Chancellor Angela Merkel of Germany, Prime Minister David Cameron of Britain, Prime Minister Matteo Renzi of Italy, and UN Secretary-General Ban Ki-moon. Arms linked around French president François Hollande, they formed a symbolic line that stretched from Europe, to Africa, to the Middle East that would stand up to the terrorists. Assembled at the Boulevard Voltaire, named after the French philosopher renowned as a staunch advocate of freedom of speech and freedom of religion, the dignitaries walked to Place de la Nation. They joined demonstrators who carried banners that read "We are Charlie."[3] People of different ages and political affiliations united to call for an end to violent extremism.[4] They paused on the boulevard for a minute of silence and later when the name of the seventeen victims were read over a loudspeaker.

Other European capitals marched in solidarity, too, joining the 3.7 million who marched across French cities that Sunday. Around the world, cities donned the colors of the French flag. While a few signs at the Paris demonstration read "partout contre la barbarie" (Against barbarism everywhere), other countries that suffered cataclysmic loss due to terrorist attacks (such as Turkey, Syria, and Mali) have not seen such large-scale solidarity. Nor have other tragic deaths in Paris—such as Zyed Benna and Bouna Traoré, who were electrocuted as they tried to escape a police identification check in October 2005—received much compassion in mainstream France. This unequal demonstration of sympathy reminds many that some lives are, in Judith Butler's words, more precarious than others.

Four days before the march, two gunmen (Saïd and Chérif Kouachi) had entered the Paris offices of *Charlie Hebdo*, a controversial satirical weekly paper, killing nine people inside and a police officer of Algerian descent dispatched to the incident. One person survived the shooting by finding protection behind a desk, and another was told by one of the perpetrators: "we don't kill women." The gunmen said they were avenging the magazine's derogatory portrayals of the prophet Mohammed. The following day, another gunman (Amedy Coulibaly) shot a black policewoman and killed four Jewish customers in a kosher supermarket. All three instigators were eventually shot and killed by the police. The death toll made this the deadliest attack on French soil since World War II, until it was exceeded by the November 2015 terrorist attacks that claimed the lives of 133 people. This more recent murderous wave of attacks included suicide bombings outside the Stade de France and mass shootings at cafés, restaurants, and the Bataclan concert hall. The Kouachi brothers had pledged allegiance to Al-Qaeda Yemen and Coulibaly to ISIS, but they planned and funded their own operations.[5] Foreign terrorists had conducted attacks in the name of Islam in France before, but for anthropologist Alain Bertho, the relationship between France and these perpetrators is "older, deeper, almost more intimate."[6]

For French citizens, the days of terror in Paris reactivated the specter of the "interior enemy," conjuring memories of the Algerian struggle for independence and a wave of terrorist attacks mainly in Paris since the 1990s organized by "djihadists made in France,"[7] including Khaled Kelkal in 1995 and Mohammed Merah in 2012.[8] The men behind the attacks are products of France, sometimes petty criminals. They lived with family, friends, and neighbors. Unlike conspicuous Islamists, the Kouachi brothers and Coulibaly did not display beards or long garments; they shaved, dressed in jeans and basketball sneakers, showing no outward indication of their beliefs. Merah dressed in punk clothes at one point. Saïd's wife said he liked to play video games. Chérif's neighbors remembered he would carry their groceries up the stairs when the elevator broke. Coulibaly's neighbors described him and his wife, Hayat Boumedienne, as "nice, good people."[9] Born to an Algerian family in the village of Treignac in central France, Chérif and Saïd were orphaned at the ages of twelve and fourteen but did well in school. One classmate reminisces that "if they had a religion, it was Paris."[10] They left their small town for the capital around 2000 and settled in a North African working-class neighborhood in the Nineteenth arrondissement. Chérif delivered pizzas; Saïd mainly had short-term jobs. After the US invasion of Iraq in 2003, Chérif decided to go fight the US forces after seeing images of Muslims degraded at the Abu Ghraib prison. Arrested hours before his flight on January 25, 2005, he was sentenced to three years of prison for terrorist association.

Representing only about 12 percent of France's population, Muslims fill about 60 to 70 percent of the country's prison system, indicating the nation's failure to integrate its postcolonial population, according to sociologist Moussa Khedimellah.[11] Prisons, especially those in cities with large concentrations of racial minorities, have been described in the media as key sites of radicalization. During his last jail stint, Coulibaly used a smuggled camera to document the miserable conditions of Fleury-Mérogis, footage that later aired on French television.[12] Before meeting Chérif in prison, Coulibaly had already been convicted five times for robbery and once for drugs.

Born into a large family of immigrants from Mali in a banlieue south of Paris, Coulibaly became radicalized in prison in his early twenties. He was cited for robbery when he was fifteen and at age eighteen, his best friend and accomplice, Ali Rezgui, was shot to death by police right in front of him. The authority's refusal to open an inquiry about the circumstances of Rezgui's death as requested by his family led to several days of riots in Grigny and surrounding banlieues.[13] Before being killed in the police raid ending his hostage taking, Coulibaly conducted a phone interview with French television, where he referred to shooting the police woman before he took hostages in the Jewish supermarket, declaring: "I got started by taking out cops."

These events have turned public debates about terrorism from long-distance chaos to homegrown urban carnage, marshaling fear about enemies within, a discourse that is not new. Since the 1970s, the French media has deployed Islam as a religious factor to explain global politics and economic and social realities, from the oil crisis (1973), the Renault factory strikes (1982–83), the terrorist violence of 1986 and 1995, and suburban riots since the 1970s and especially in 2005.

In the 1980s, the mainstream media questioned the "real" identity of a large Muslim population by whipping up fears that behind everyday faces of Muslim neighbors, coworkers, teachers, or customers may hide a terrorist. Reading media headlines and politicians' provocative statements since the 1980s in the aftermath of the 2015 attacks suggests the concretization of the Islamic plot, making a reality of what were alarmist or shocking rumors. Consider the following titles: "Islam's new conquerors," "Between France and Islam, will there be a war?," "Are 'our' religiously organized and indoctrinated immigrants and our young *beurs* becoming a shadow army, mobilized against us in the name of Allah?," and book titles like Gilles Kepel's *Islam's banlieues* (1987).[14] In these titles, Muslims, whether French or immigrants, are never part of "us." Rather, they are France's problem.

Careful studies of Islam, such as *Être musulman en France* (Being a Muslim in France, 1994) by historian Jocelyne Césari, and more recently *Only Muslim: Embodying Islam in Twentieth-Century France* by Naomi Davidson and *The Republic Unsettled* by Mayanthi Fernando, belie the reiterative media fantasy of an Islamic takeover of the nation. Already in 1994, Césari noted that "in the western, and particularly the French imaginary, the term Islam is associated with conquest, violence, and fanaticism," a totalizing view of Islam that has little to do with how the generation born to former colonial migrants perceive it.[15] According to Césari, their relation to Islam functions more as a cultural reference than a fervent religious practice.[16] Almost two decades later, Davidson notes the striking essentialized view of Islam in France. Her study *Only Muslim* traces the origin of a "French Islam" to the turbulent 1920s and 1930s. Bringing together police reports, billboards, films, and other documentation, she demonstrates how "racial difference was encoded in the language of religion."[17]

In this context of everyday sensationalized islamophobia, *Charlie Hebdo* was merely a small platform for a much more widespread and profitable bigotry.[18] While the magazine used to take powerful right-wing politicians in its line of sight (especially in the 1970s), after 9/11, Muslims, which represent a large and vulnerable population in France,[19] became the principal butt of jokes, selling to a mainly leftist audience the idea that Islam is a problem for France. Olivier Cyran, who used to work at *Charlie Hebdo*, wrote a 2013 article condemning the post-9/11 Islamophobic turn of the magazine. He notes the quasi obsession of the cartoons with the "barbus" (the bearded) often surrounded by flies, the women in veils or burkas kneeling in prayer with their buttocks exposed, or cutting hair on their legs with scissors, which lost the magazine a lot of readers and gained them new members more in tune with the war on terror. In a 2011 video posted on the *Charlie Hebdo* website, the publication director, Stéphane Charbonnier, mimics the Muslim call to prayers, while his friends are heard laughing in the background. The magazine opposed the civilized (Europeans) to the barbaric (Muslims), naming those who questioned such binaries as "useful idiots" or "Islamo-lefties." There is no attempt in *Charlie Hebdo* to distinguish between Muslims and radicals or Muslims and terrorists. Among the jihadists interviewed by journalist David Thomson, one of them referred to the difficulty of living as a Muslim in France, stating, "Every day we are humiliated by blasphemy, like the Charlie Hebdo cartoons. It's too humiliating to live here. It's a dishonor for us, really."[20] The lawyer for *Charlie Hebdo*, on the other hand, conveyed the magazine's view of itself as a defender of French values. He said, "The veil is the death, the burial of the republican triptych: Liberty, Equality, Fraternity," an illusionary motto for too large a section of the French population. This protection of French values such as *laïcité* is also at work in the 2004 law banning headscarves in public schools and reinforced in 2010 with a national law banning Muslim women from wearing the full face veil (niqab) in public, criminalizing other Muslim sartorial practices.

These exclusionary laws, no matter their universal wording, intensify the exclusion of a population already socially and culturally marginalized. In theory, everyone is equal in France. In practice, being accepted as French depends on the extent you conform to a Westernized ideal in your appearance, religion, dress, diet, postal code, and name. For veiled women who can no longer work in day care, volunteer in soup kitchens (*les restos du Coeur*), or enjoy the beach; for mothers who can no longer attend their children's school activities or even enter their school gates; for girls prohibited from attending public school, those warned that their skirts are too long, or those expelled because their bandanas on their hair were too large, French universalism is a terrible joke.

Far from preventing future violence, the criminalization of Islamic practices in France appears as a key explanation for increased terrorist activity. The nation's policies created fertile conditions for ISIS recruitment, according to a 2015 study by the Brookings Institution.[21] A few weeks before the attacks, Chris Meserole and his team of researchers found a striking result in the data they assembled about ISIS: "The most powerful variable by far in predicting how many jihadis a country would produce was whether the people in that country spoke French."[22] Meserole and McCants attribute this finding to the antiveil campaigns in France in 2010 (Tunisia in 2006, and Belgium in 2011). The French/ISIS connection reappears in a disputed poll released on June 26, 2015, right before the waves of terrorist attacks. According to an inquiry led by Gallup in France, Germany, and Great Britain for the Russian group Rossia Segodnya, 16 percent of the French have a rather positive opinion of ISIS jihadists in Syria and Iraq, with 27 percent of favorable responses among those between 18 and 25 years old. By comparison, only 7 percent of Britons and Germans have a positive view of ISIS.[23] These results are deployed variously, at times as fodder in logics of heightened surveillance, to criticize France's dictatorial cultural uniformity, or as evidence of the radical beliefs of French Muslims.

Given the spatial distribution of immigrants and racial minorities in French cities, it is not surprising that the banlieues became a flashpoint of discussions about Islamic radicalization. The Islamophobic discourse superimposed itself to the discourse on criminality and insecurity in the outer cities. Chérif Kouachi referred to himself as a "ghetto Muslim," a designation the press has cultivated since the early 1990s when Islam started to be described as a banlieue phenomenon.[24] Newspapers frequently discussed the radicalization of Muslims in ghetto basements, without any structural explanations, such as local authorities' reluctance to provide sites of worship for Muslims. With the 1995 terrorist bombing of the Paris metro perpetrated by Algerian immigrant Khaled Khelkal, a young delinquent from a banlieue of Lyon, this space has become a target of antiterrorism actions, with heightened policing in the cities, arrest of suspected Islamic militants, and racial profiling in subway and train stations.[25] Youth with Kelkal's lineage and social itinerary of small banlieue delinquency have been (according to media and television show pundits) the privileged recruits of Islamic fundamentalist. Films such as *100% Arabica* (2000) by Algerian director Mahmoud Zemmouri and *Made in France* (2016) by Nicolas Boukhrief reproduce this narrative about Islamic radicalization of the banlieue. Yet in his important study, *French Jihadists* (2014), published after a year of interviews with more than fifty participants, journalist David Thomson interrogates such assumptions. Among the eighteen who agreed to discuss their lives, beliefs, philosophy, and aspirations in detail, nine are from Christian families. The ones from Muslim families had not inherited their radical religion from their surroundings, nor had they been converted in prisons or mosques. What little they typically know about Islam, they learned from the internet and social networks. The interviews corroborate sociologist Farhad Khosrokhavar's notion of an Islam-free Islamism—an empty shell in which the young Islamic fanatic places his revolt against society, being attracted less by Islam than by violent struggle.

The logic of securitization has been in place since 2002 with the rise of Jacques Chirac's government to power. The *idéologie sécuritaire* (securitarian ideology) consists of increased police power and, more broadly, a repressive penal turn. As geographer Mustafa Dikeç explains, "this ideology has a very precise spatial referent: 'la banlieue.'"[26] Nicolas Sarkozy, in his role at the Ministry of the Interior, increased the publication of statistics compiled by the police from once a year to every month, encouraged press releases, and initiated twenty-one laws and twenty-one decrees on security between 2002 and 2009.[27] Denis Salas refers to this unprecedented repressive turn as "penal populism."[28] In this logic of securitization, arrest numbers determine the allocation of resources, resulting in prison overpopulation for nonviolent crimes, mainly related to drugs. In 2009 Amnesty International released a damning report about police violation of citizens' rights in France, including homicides, excessive use of force, torture, and other nefarious treatments with racist motivations.[29] The report concludes that the French police continue to benefit from total impunity enabled by weak legislation and an unwillingness on the part of the police, the public ministry, and tribunals to conduct exhaustive investigation that may implicate police agents.[30] The suspicious death of Adama Traoré in police custody on July 19, 2016, and the sodomization of Théo by a policeman's truncheon on February 8, 2017, led to massive public demonstrations in Paris against police *bavures*, but with no justice for the young black men and their families.

While politicians have urged us not to make dangerous generalizations (*amalgames*) that conflate Muslims with terrorists, Didier Fassin notes that government policies treat all Muslims (and racialized bodies associated with Islam) as suspects. These institutional policies written into law are much more worrying than what the press has focused on: that is, the 223 percent increase of aggression against Muslims in 2015 compared with the previous year.[31] These included the desecration of places of worship with dozens of mosques vandalized and even fired upon.[32] Since November 2015, Muslims in the banlieues have been targeted for house searches and house arrests. Other less tractable discriminatory practices have also increased, including the stop and search of people in train and metro stations based on their appearance. Enforcing the measures of the state of emergency, which limited individual liberties, the 2017 *loi antiterroriste* renders what were exceptional and temporary police practices into common law. The law differs from previous measures with its increased punishment for violation of house arrests, extension of the order of house searches to prefects, new grounds for closing places of worship, and the expansion of border controls in airports and train stations.

Journalists too have warned against amalgames at the same time they produce them. For Thomas Deltombe, who studied the French media construction of Islam from 1975 to 2005, the denunciation of the amalgames is really a preamble to their introduction.[33] In the aftermath of the January 2015 attacks, the mainstream news media circulated a pair of pictures of Amedy Coulaby and his wife, Hayat Boumedienne. In one picture, they pause in a side hug in front of the ocean. Coulibaly's body is muscular, Boumedienne looks like a model in her bikini: slim, golden tones, with her hair down to her shoulders. On the other picture, a selfie that frames their faces, Coulibaly is wearing a white T-shirt and a dark coat, while Boumedienne is donning a niqab (prohibited in France since 2010). This before-and-after picture released after the attacks re-centers the niqab in a coverage about terrorism. Boumedienne is now "the most wanted woman in France," "armed, dangerous, and at large." As discussed in chapter 5, the absence of the niqab in the French public sphere makes this appearance striking in its rarity and ties this garment to questions of national security and violent threats. With this sensational visual association of the niqab and terrorism, it is not surprising that many veiled girls and women were harassed following the terrorist attacks. This image and context corroborate the media consensus on the veil and niqab as symbols of patriarchal oppression or indoctrination. Another popular juxtaposition was the beach picture with one of Boumedienne in full-face veil aiming a crossbow at the camera. Three days after the attacks, the women's magazine *Terrafeminina* republished these pictures in an article titled "Hayat Boumeddienne: From the Bikini to the Cross-Bow." The author selectively drew on a short interview given by a childhood friend of Boumeddienne in the newspaper *Le Parisien* to describe the twenty-six-year-old as "impulsive," "emotionally frail," and "a little childish." She had lost her mother when she was eight and had gone from one foster home to another for four years. She was passionately in love with Amedy and married him in 2009. The following year they went on a pilgrimage to Mecca. Visually, the pictures project a radical transformation, from the tanned smiling young woman in a bikini, a symbol of her Westernization, to the menacing terrorist in full-face veil holding a weapon at the viewer. The written narrative focuses not so much on Boumedienne, who remains an elusive figure, but on a radicalized Amedy who connected with a network of terrorists while in prison and then indoctrinated his wife.

In this story, the Muslim woman's body is scripted as the battleground between good and evil, Western pseudo-feminism and Islamic fundamentalism, freedom and enslavement. Boumedienne's full-face veil supposedly evidences that she is the passive conduit of an oppressive masculine ideology (but not the bikini picture). It may be too late for her, the narrative suggests, but other women can be saved from Islam's propensity to violence. This battle to protect "freedom" at home and to bring it to Muslim women elsewhere hides and condones other forms of violence. In France, such discourse obfuscates a large and growing underclass, wherein youth of color feel especially stigmatized and alienated. By covering exclusively women's victimization and Islamic fundamentalism in the banlieues, the French media and publishing industries posit that one cannot be a law-abiding French citizen and a Muslim. Yet as women demonstrators wearing French tricolor veils clamored after the 2004 ban on Muslim headscarves, they are both.

Since the early 1990s, the mainstream press and politicians have focused on spectacular forms of subjugation of women in the Middle East (genital mutilation, child marriage, honor crime, forced veiling, and acid violence) and in the French outskirts (crime, riots, gang rape) and interpret them as offshoots of a violent Islamic culture. Together, popular narratives and the press coverage surrounding these violent acts have created a cultural script of rescue for understanding the plight of Muslim women in the Middle East and at home. In this script, Muslim women—whatever their context, history, or customs—are eternal battlegrounds between Islamic patriarchy and Western feminisms. The architects of the 2004 French law that banned the veil in public schools claimed they sought to protect Muslim women from patriarchal coercion.

The few years preceding the 2004 law saw the harmonious imbrication of politics, literature, and mainstream media. Buttressing a neo-Orientalist emergence, an onslaught of memoirs by Iranian women in exile in France, like Djavann Chahdortt and Majane Satrapi, focused on women's oppression under Islam. These writers were invited to speak on numerous television shows, the radio, and other venues. Alongside the heavy marketing of their stories, the film *La Squale* (2000) by white director Fabrice Genestal drew a sensationalist portrait of Muslim girls in the banlieues as vulnerable to beatings, gang rape, and daily humiliations by Muslim men.[34] Two years later, the movement Ni Putes Ni Soumises, presided over by Fadela Amera, mobilized around two events. Sohane Benziane, a young Franco-Arab woman, was burned alive by a jilted adolescent in the basement of a Paris suburb,[35] and Samira Bellil published an autobiographical book, *Dans l'enfer des tournantes* (*In the Hell of Gang Rapes*), that documents her hellish experience at the hand of some banlieue men. Ni Putes Ni Soumises launched a call against machismo and masculine violence in the banlieues and later organized a women's March Against the Ghetto and for Equality. The news media's coverage of these memoirs and of the murder of Benziane has fashioned the banlieues as a site of Islamization. As critic Hassiba Lassoued explains, the mainstream media imposes a vision of France as a republican model, while at the same time depriving French racial minorities a voice by assigning them a controlled space of dialogue. When these French citizens are solicited, it is always in relation to stereotypical themes such as forced marriage, banlieues, violence, and delinquency.[36]

Amara and Djavann, spokesperson against the veil, were sought after by the Stasi commission (the government-appointed group that investigated the question of the headscarf in public schools). They provided private testimonies to the commission, while their books garnered support against the ban and Islam more generally. In *Bas les voiles* (2003), Djavann denounces the fact that she was compelled to wear the veil for ten years in Iran. From this personal experience, she claims that this sartorial practice shames women and compares it to rape and to the yellow stars shaming Jews who had to wear them. A common characteristic of these memoirs is, as noted by Saba Mahmood, the "abhorrence of everything Muslim and sheer exaltation of all things Western."[37] In these texts, the mainstream audience is legitimized in its Islamophobic views. As such, they reproduce Orientalist ideas about Muslims' religious zeal, oppression of women, and propensity to violence. Djavann received the Grand Prix de la Laïcité in 2003 and became a Chevalier de l'ordre des Arts et des Lettres in 2004, the highest French honor awarded by the Ministry of Culture to recognize distinguished artistic or literary merit. Amara's memoir *Ni Putes, Ni Soumises* (2003), cowritten with Sylvia Zappi, a journalist at *Le Monde*, received Le Prix du livre politique and Le Prix des députés. Authors like Djavann comfort the French public, which has long constructed the veil as a sign of women's oppression under Islam. To do so, they must also silence elements that go against an essentialist portrayal of an oppressive religion. For example, Djavann does not address the fact that a feminist press was established in the decades following the Islamic revolution in Iran, that Iranians produced films that were internationally acclaimed, that the literacy rate for women more than doubled under Islamic rule, and that more women were elected to the Iranian parliament than to the US Congress.[38] These developments may explain why many women have supported Islamic movements in which they are key participants.[39]

The narrow focus on Muslim women's lack of freedom has long served as a smokescreen for other factors that affect the lives of these women, such as poverty, war, corruption, and, in the French banlieues, massive unemployment and racial discrimination. As Saba Mahmood eloquently warns, "unless feminists rethink their complicity in this project, which requires putting our most dearly held assumptions and beliefs up to critical evaluation, feminism runs the risk of becoming more of a handmaiden of empire in our age than a trenchant critic of the Euro-American will to power."[40] In the aftermath of the French terrorist attacks, with the public support of a law that targets the banlieue and residents of color, the status of the minorités visibles has never been as precarious. Even decades before, inhabitants of the banlieues bitterly lamented the fact that the media was only interested in reporting crime, violence, and terror in their neighborhoods rather than the everyday lives of its inhabitants. Films, too, from *La Haine* to the recent celebrated *Bande de filles* (*Girlhood*, 2015), reinforce these stereotypes.

There is another long-standing and rich cultural archive of novels, films, and art installations that has long served to expand what it means to be French and a minorité visible as well as a Muslim in the hexagone. Some of these works have found room in prestigious publishing houses, such as les éditions Denoël (Driss Chraïbi's 1955 modernity novel *The Butts*), Mercure de France (Mehdi Charef's *Tea in the Harem*), and Hachettes Littératures (Faïza Guène's *Kiffe Kiffe Tomorrow*). Some visual art, like that of JR, can be found in the Louvre and prestigious galleries across the world, while films queer Frenchness, like Merzak Allouache's *Chouchou*, an all-time classic. This cultural production challenges beliefs that Islam is a threat, that Muslim women are always subjugated, and that the acceptance of homosexuality distributes itself according to race, faith, or geographical location. It also keeps central what the nation would like to forget: colonialism and its legacies of racial inequities, police violence, and relentless discrimination. This postcolonial Paris challenges us to decolonize French cultures and its assumptions about who or what is French, to catch up to its cities' rich diversity and the ordinary lives of its residents.

Notes

Introduction

1. Loïc Wacquant explains that despite the French media association of banlieues with American ghettoes, the French banlieues' size, multiracial population, and the virtual absence of gun violence mark them as singular entities. Wacquant, "Banlieues françaises," cited in Hargreaves, *Multi-Ethnic*, 67.

2. In France, ISIS (Islamic State of Iraq and Syria) or ISIL (Islamic State of Iraq and the Levant) is referred to as DAESH, an acronym derived from the Arabic transliteration of ISIL (al Dawlah al-Islameyah fi Iraq wal-Sham).

3. Zappi, "Manuel Valls, l'apartheid et les banlieues." Quotations are from published translations except where noted; other translations are mine unless otherwise noted.

4. Said, *Orientalism*, 54.

5. Pinçonnat, "Le Paris Maghrébin: une capitale invisible?," 276.

6. Ireland, "Les banlieues de l'identité," 173.

7. Memmi, *Decolonization and the Decolonized*, 78.

8. Durmelat, *Fictions de l'intégration*, 60.

9. Gondola, "But I Ain't African, I'm American!," 207; Francis, "Embodied Fictions," 842; Keaton, "'Black (American) Paris,'" 96.

10. Dikeç, *Badlands of the Republic*.

11. In her study of African literature, Bennetta Jules-Rosette coins the term "Parisianism" to capture a new "cosmopolitan style of Franco-African writing" that idealizes individuality (*Black Paris*, 147). Similarly, in *Afrique sur Seine*, Odile Cazenave discusses "Afro-Parisian" writers in exile as a new generation who reject Africa and Africans and turn their gaze toward the individual self (4). For Charles Tshimanga, Didier Gondola, and Peter Bloom, Jules-Rosette along with Dominic Thomas have "persuasively demonstrated how Paris has ultimately become an African metropolis, invested by African writers who have infused the ambient literary tradition with an Afro-Parisianism and outward-looking aesthetics of universalism" (*Frenchness and the African Diaspora*, 9).

12. Waldron, "Sexual/Social (Re)Orientations," 191.

13. Tarr, *Reframing Difference*, 151.

14. Girard and Stoetzel, *Français et immigrés*, 15.

15. Stora et al., *Algériens en France*, 18.

16. Girard and Stoetzel, *Français et immigrés*, 60.

17. Girard and Stoetzel, *Français et immigrés*, 20.

18. Girard and Stoetzel, *Français et immigrés*, 20.

19. Girard and Stoetzel, *Français et immigrés*, 20.

20. Girard and Stoetzel, *Français et immigrés*, 20.

21. Girard and Stoetzel, *Français et immigrés*, 20.

22. MacMaster, *Colonial Migrants*, 4.

23. "Kabyle" refers to the indigenous populations of Northern Algeria. The etymology of "bicots" derives from military slang for small Arabs, "crouillat" is Arabic for "brother," "sidi" is Arabic for my lord, and "Noraf" is short for "Nord-Africains."

24. MacMaster, *Colonial Migrants*, 191.

25. Todd Shepard, "1970s France and L'Arabe-au-sexe-couteau: Rape, Sodomy, and Power," lecture for the Modern European Research Group, Yale University, October 2, 2013.

26. Céline, *Journey to the End of the Night*, 274.

27. In their article "How the Algerian War Shaped French Cities," Pierre Gilbert and Charlotte Vorms assert that police control over Algerians was a function of controlling the places where they lived and policing priorities influenced the way Algerian slum residents were rehoused (*Métropolitiques*, March 21, 2012).

28. See Gastaut, *L'immigration et l'opinion*; Deltombe, *L'Islam imaginaire*.

29. See Geisser, *La nouvelle islamophobie*; Henni-Moulai, *Petit précis de l'islamophobie ordinaire*; and Hajjat and Mohammed, *Islamophobie*.

30. See Slimane Zéghidour, "La peur des Français est exagérée," *Le Nouvel Observateur*, June 21, 1990, 46–51.

31. Packer, "The Other France."

32. Patrick Simon labels this absence of statistics "The Choice of Ignorance."

33. Balibar, *Race, Nation, Class*, 21.

34. Donadey, "Une Certaine Idée," 216; Kettane, *Droit de réponse*, 21–22; Hargreaves, "Une Culture Innommable?," 29.

35. Noiriel, *Le creuset*, 211.

36. Hargreaves, "Banlieue blues," 215.

37. Kleppinger, *Branding the "Beur" Author*, 5–12.

38. Geisser, *La nouvelle islamophobie*; Puar, *Terrorist Assemblages*; El-Tayeb, *Other Europeans*.

39. Fassin and Fassin, *De la question sociale à la question raciale*; Geisser, *La nouvelle islamophobie*; Keaton, *Muslim Girls and the Other France*; Silverstein, *Algeria in France*; Chapman and Frader, *Race in France*.

40. Shepard, *The Invention of Decolonization*, 4.

41. Shepard, *The Invention of Decolonization*, 4.

42. Ashcroft et al., *The Empire Writes Back*; Ball, *Imagining London*; McLeod, *Postcolonial London*; and Murdoch, *Creolizing the Metropole* demonstrate how black British writers have interrogated British colonialism, its self-representation, and legacies by composing a new imaginary of the capital.

43. D. Fassin, "Une mesure discriminatoire."

44. D. Fassin, "Une mesure discriminatoire."

45. D. Fassin, "Une mesure discriminatoire."

46. In "France's Permanent Emergency State," the *New York Times* reports that "some 3,600 warrantless searches and 400 house arrests have resulted in a mere six terrorism-related criminal investigations."

47. D. Fassin, "Une mesure discriminatoire."

48. Stoler, *Haunted by Empire*; Mendoza, *Metroimperial Intimacies*; Lowe, *The Intimacies of Four Continents*.

49. Bromley, *Intimacy and Sexuality in the Age of Shakespeare*, 5.

50. Stoler, *Haunted by Empire*, 13.

51. Sommer, *Foundational Fictions*.

52. Ricoux, *La démographie figurée de l'Algérie*.

53. Salhi, *Politics, Poetics and the Algerian Novel*, 55.

54. Lorcin, "Sex, Gender, and Race in the Colonial Novels," 115.

55. Lorcin, "Sex, Gender, and Race in the Colonial Novels," 117.

56. Lorcin, "Sex, Gender, and Race in the Colonial Novels," 117.

57. Lorcin, "Sex, Gender, and Race in the Colonial Novels," 120.

58. Lorcin, "Sex, Gender, and Race in the Colonial Novels," 117.

59. Cooper, *Colonialism in Question*, 113.

60. Mbembe, "On the Power of the False," 634.

61. Cooper, *Colonialism in Question*, 113.

62. Cooper, *Colonialism in Question*, 113.

63. Balibar, *Race, Nation, Class*, 21.

64. Balibar, *Race, Nation, Class*, 21.

65. Mignolo, *Darker Side of Western Modernity*.

66. Stora, *Algeria*, 163.

67. Boucher, *Les théories de l'intégration*, 26.

68. Boucher, *Les théories de l'intégration*, 42.

69. Weil, *La république*, 59.

70. Clancy-Smith, "Islam, Gender, and Identities," 154.

71. Spivak, "Can the Subaltern Speak?," 66–111.

72. See Kemp, *Voices and Veils*; Mahmood, "Feminism, Democracy, and Empire"; Scott, *The Politics of the Veil*.

73. Puar, *Terrorist Assemblages*; É. Fassin, "Homosexual City"; Mack, *Sexagon*.

74. Mehammed Mack describes "sexual modernity" as "an umbrella term, encompassing everything from the promotion of sexual diversity and gender equality, to a zero-tolerance policy regarding 'excessive' virilities (banlieue machos) and 'self-censoring' femininities (veiled women)" (*Sexagon*, 29).

75. See Fernando, *The Republic Unsettled*, 192; Conklin, *A Mission to Civilize*, 197; Wilder, *The French Imperial Nation-State*.

76. Perreau, *Queer Theory*, 116.

77. Chaumont, "Lettre ouverte au ministre de l'éducation nationale: L'école doit être le rampart contre l'homophobie dans les cités ghettos," *Le Monde*, November 11, 2009.

78. Mack, *Sexagon*, 31.

79. Guénif-Souilamas and Macé, *Les féministes et le garçon arabe*, 11.

80. Guénif-Souilamas and Macé, *Les féministes et le garçon arabe*, 11–12.

81. Fanon, *A Dying Colonialism*, 9.

82. Tévanian, *La République du mépris*.

83. House and MacMaster, *Paris 1961*, 1.

84. Citron, *La poésie de Paris*.

85. Castex, *Ecrire Paris*, 108.

86. Casanova, *The World Republic of Letters*, 29.

87. Casanova, *The World Republic of Letters*, 26.

88. Heise, *Urban Underworlds*, 101.

89. Heise, *Urban Underworlds*, 102.

90. Chevalier, *Laboring Classes and Dangerous Classes*.

91. Higonnet, *Paris: Capital of the World*, 305.

92. Hancock, "Capitale du plaisir," 64.

93. Hancock, "Capitale du plaisir," 69.

94. Rocamora, *Fashioning the City*, 144.

95. Higonnet, *Paris: Capital of the World*, 289.

96. Authors Edmond de Goncourt and Jean Lorrain respectively characterized the café-concerts as consisting of the "dance of an imbecile" or "a depressing, sexual meat rack"; Higonnet, *Paris: Capital of the World*, 302, 289.

97. Gopnik, *Americans in Paris*, xiii.

98. Benstock, *Women of the Left Bank*, 3.

99. Weiss, *Paris was a Woman*, 18,19.

100. Gopnik, *Americans in Paris*, xix.

101. Méral, *Paris in American Literature*, 209.

102. Wright, "I Chose Exile."

103. Stovall, *Paris Noir*; Fabre, *From Harlem to Paris*.

104. We find a similar portrayal of Paris in Toni Morrison's 1981 novel, *Tar Baby*, where Jadine Childs, a twenty-seven-year-old African American woman, engages in an interracial romance with a French man. Jadine reflects that the United States provided her with limited options: "marry a dope king or a doctor, model, or teach art at Jackson High. In Europe she thought there might be a fourth choice" (225).

105. Fanon, *Toward the African Revolution*, 19.

106. Fanon, *Toward the African Revolution*, 3.

107. Fanon, *Black Skin, White Masks*, 7.

108. As such, the capital "operated as an interchangeable metaphor for France itself" (D. Thomas, *Black France*, 42).

109. Dadié, *An African in Paris*, 3.

110. Naipaul, *The Enigma of Arrival*, 129.

111. Kincaid, "On Seeing England for the First Time," 365.

112. Naipaul, *The Enigma of Arrival*, 130.

113. Hall, "The Local and the Global," 24.

114. Selvon, *Lonely Londoners*, 29.

115. Selvon, *Lonely Londoners*, 74.

116. Stora and Amiri, *Algériens en France*, 29.

117. Chraïbi, *Les boucs*, 77, 60.

118. Goebel, *Anti-Imperial Metropolis*, 4.

119. Feraoun, *La terre et le sang*, 110–11.

120. The term "Francophone" has traditionally labeled writers of French language outside of France.

121. Casanova, *The World Republic of Letters*, 122.

122. Casanova, *The World Republic of Letters*, 124.

123. Stovall and Van den Abbeele, *French Civilization*, 3.

124. "Francophonie" not only designates all speakers of French across the world; it also refers to a politics of promotion and protection of the French language.

125. Sebkhi, *Une littérature naturelle*, 28.

126. Collectif Qui fait la France?, *Chroniques d'une société annoncée*, 7–13.

127. Collectif Qui fait la France?, *Chroniques d'une société annoncée*, 7–8.
128. Hargreaves and Murphy, "New Directions," 221.
129. Forsdick, "Beyond Francophone Postcolonial Studies," 1.
130. Hargreaves and Murphy, "New Directions in Postcolonial Studies," 221.
131. See Hargreaves and McKinney, *Post-colonial Cultures in France*; Forsdick and Murphy *Francophone Postcolonial Studies*; Murdoch and Donadey, *Postcolonial Theory*.
132. See Boubeker and Hajjat, *Histoire politique des immigrations (post)coloniales*; Blanchard and Bancel, *La fracture coloniale*; Guénif-Souilamas, *La république mise à nu*; MacMaster *Colonial Migrants and Racism*.
133. Saada, "More Than a Turn?," 34.
134. Saada, "More Than a Turn?," 35.
135. Saada, "More Than a Turn?," 37.
136. Forsdick, "Beyond Francophone Postcolonial Studies," 10.
137. McLeod, *The Routledge Companion to Postcolonial Studies*, 11.
138. See Rothberg, *Multidirectional Memory*; Gilroy, *Against Race*.

Chapter 1. Colonial Domesticity

1. Stora, *La gangrène*, 18.
2. Nourredine Saadi, quoted in Rosello, *France and the Maghreb*, 28.
3. Rosello, *France and the Maghreb*, 35.
4. Clancy-Smith and Gouda, "Introduction," in *Domesticating the Empire*, 9.
5. Vergès, *Monsters and Revolutionaries*; Rosello, *France and the Maghreb*; Clancy-Smith and Gouda, *Domesticating the Empire*.
6. Clancy-Smith and Gouda, *Domesticating the Empire*, 4.
7. Vergès, *Monsters and Revolutionaries*, 3.
8. Vergès, *Monsters and Revolutionaries*, 6.
9. Clancy-Smith and Gouda, *Domesticating the Empire*, 11, 15.
10. Camiscioli, *Reproducing the French Race*, 84.
11. Sayad, *The Suffering of the Immigrant*, 16–17.
12. Tillion, quoted in Haddour, *Colonial Myths*, 113.
13. Quoted in Aresu, "The Francophone Novel in North Africa," 106.
14. Aresu, "The Francophone Novel in North Africa," 105–7.
15. Orlando, *The New Algerian Novel*, 26.
16. Orlando, *The New Algerian Novel*, 26.
17. Chrestien, "Un Barbaresque écrit en Français," 12.
18. Figuéras, "Les événements d'Afrique du Nord," 12.
19. R. Kemp, "Les Boucs," 7.
20. Casanova, *The World Republic of Letters*, 122.
21. Monnoyer, "Plaisir de la lecture," 10.
22. C. Roy, "Mendiants, vagabonds, boucs, bonnes, misère," 10.
23. Guissard, "Des Proscrits parmi nous," 14; Prasteau, "Histoire d'un bouc émissaire," 11.
24. Rousseaux, "*Les Boucs* de Driss Chraïbi," 6.
25. Delayre, *Driss Chraïbi*; Gans-Guinoune, *Driss Chraïbi*.
26. Laffont and Bompiana, *Le nouveau dictionnaire des auteurs*.
27. Behdad, "Postcolonial Theory," 234.

28. In "Looking for Roots among the Mangroves," Jarrod Hayes explains that "bicot" is a pejorative French word referring to Maghrebis with no real English equivalent. See also Hayes, *Queer Roots for the Diaspora*, 289.

29. Rosenberg, *Policing Paris*, 134.

30. Lyons, *The Civilizing Mission in the Metropole*, 145.

31. Goebel, *Anti-Imperial Metropolis*, 41–42.

32. Fanon, *Wretched of the Earth*, 5.

33. Fanon, *Wretched of the Earth*, 5.

34. Etcherelli, *Elise ou la vraie vie (Elise or the Real Life)*, 210.

35. Ben Jelloun, *La plus haute des solitudes (The Highest of Solitudes)*, 12–13.

36. M. Thomas, *The French Empire*, 68.

37. Rager, *L'émigration en France des musulmans algériens*, 121.

38. Girard and Stoetzel, *Français et immigrés*, 96.

39. MacMaster, "The Role of European Women," 371.

40. Memmi, *The Colonizer and the Colonized*, 5.

41. Amer ou Kaci is related by blood to Marie, making this romance not really an encounter between different kinfolk.

42. Fanon, *Wretched of the Earth*, 5.

43. Camiscioli, *Reproducing the French Race*, 81–82.

44. Camiscioli, *Reproducing the French Race*, 116.

45. Camiscioli, *Reproducing the French Race*, 116.

46. Camiscioli, *Reproducing the French Race*, 114.

47. Camiscioli, *Reproducing the French Race*, 148.

48. Lyons, *The Civilizing Mission in the Metropole*, 5, 6.

49. Ben Jelloun, *La plus haute des solitudes*, 12.

50. MacMaster, *Colonial Migrants and Racism*, 191.

51. Corey, "Toward the Limits of Mystery," 32.

52. Blévis, "La citoyenneté française," 26.

53. Massad, *Desiring Arabs*, 16.

54. Fanon, *Dying Colonialism*, 149.

55. Fanon, *Dying Colonialism*, 149.

56. See, for example, Taos Amrouche's *Jacinthe noire*.

57. Armand-Jacques Leroy de Saint-Arnaud (1798–1854) was an army officer and later marshal of France under Napoleon III. He joined the Foreign Legion and in 1837 went to Algiers, where he rose rapidly in rank. In 1851 he was appointed minister of war in Algeria and commander of the province of Constantine.

58. Serrano, "Not Your Uncle," 174.

59. Cruz-Malavé and Manalansan, "Introduction," in *Queer Globalizations*, 2.

60. *Selected Documents of the Bandung Conference*, 2, 3.

61. Carlos P. Romulo, quoted in *Selected Documents of the Bandung Conference*, 12.

Chapter 2. Romance and Brotherhood

1. Wright, "Island of Hallucination," 190.

2. For Baldwin's full remark, see Campbell, *Exiled in Paris*, 103. Richard Gibson describes his experience in Paris during the Algerian war in "Richard Wright's 'Island of Hallucination' and the 'Gibson Affair.'" In his autobiography, *My Life of Absurdity*,

Himes states that he "didn't want to be on the street so late at night" in Paris during the Algerian war (185).

3. Miles Davis, quoted in Campbell, *Exiled in Paris*, 105–6.

4. African American women writers Gwendolyn Bennett and Jessie Redmon Fauset also spent time in Paris and debunked the myth of France and its capital as utopic or color-blind in their fiction. Fauset's *Comedy: American Style* (1934) and Bennett's short stories "Wedding Day" (1926) and "Tokens" (1927) are not part of this analysis because I limit my inquiry to representations of a Paris paradox. The texts that represent this paradox were written after 1947, when the Algerian demographic in Paris soared because of a new law on the status of Algeria that permitted natives to travel to the metropole without a passport. Male authors wrote about this Janus-faced Paris and hence the peculiar focus on men and masculinity in these narratives.

5. Stora, *Algeria*, 40.

6. Henderson, "In Another Country."

7. Fabre, *From Harlem to Paris*; Stovall, *Paris Noir*.

8. Stovall, *Paris Noir*, xv.

9. Campbell, *Exiled in Paris*; Maxwell, "Wright among the 'G-Men.'"

10. Edwards, *The Practice of Diaspora*, 5.

11. Gondola, "'But I Ain't African, I'm American!,'" 207; Francis, "Embodied Fictions," 842; Keaton, "'Black (American) Paris,'" 96; Bigsby, "The Divided Mind," 103.

12. See Baldwin, "James Baldwin, the Art of Fiction," 48–82.

13. Frazier, *Black Bourgeoisie*, 192.

14. Wright, quoted in Fabre, *From Harlem*, 177.

15. Wright, quoted in Fabre, *The World*, 146.

16. Wright, *The Long Dream*, 383.

17. Wright, *The Long Dream*, 74–77.

18. Gilroy, *The Black Atlantic*, 174.

19. Maxwell, "Wright among the 'G-men,'" 33.

20. This reference to the young white woman as "electrically" beautiful is reminiscent of the tragic fate of Bigger Thomas in Wright's novel *Native Son*. After accidentally killing the white daughter of his employer to avoid getting caught with her in her bedroom, he is ultimately sentenced to death.

21. In post–World War II Algerian novels by Mohammed Dib, Mouloud Feraoun, and Mouloud Mammeri, Algerian men become disillusioned with the promise of French democracy after migrating to Paris. Pushed into exile to settle debts or extricate their family from abject poverty, they come to the motherland full of hope, only to be confined to the overcrowded slums of Gennevilliers and Nanterre or the decrepit basements, dorms, and hotel rooms of La Goutte d'Or where they contract diseases, experience hunger, and endure racist hostility. Their stay in Paris accelerates their political awareness about their colonial exclusion and prompts their return home.

22. Ruquist, "Non, nous ne jouons pas la trompette," 288, 290.

23. Stovall, "The Fire This Time," 200.

24. Rowley, *Richard Wright*, 473; Keaton, "Black (American) Paris," 105.

25. Campbell, *Exiled in Paris*, 96.

26. Harrington, quoted in Rowley, *Richard Wright*, 488.

27. Fabre, *From Harlem to Paris*, 249.

28. Gibson, "Richard Wright's 'Island of Hallucination,'" 911.

29. Fabre, *The Unfinished Quest of Richard Wright*, 485, 486.

30. Fabre, *The Unfinished Quest of Richard Wright*, 515; Campbell, *Exiled in Paris*, 96.

31. Fabre, *Black American Writers*, 185.

32. Fabre, *The World of Richard Wright*, 183.

33. Fabre, *The Unfinished Quest of Richard Wright*, 488.

34. In "Alas, Poor Richard," Baldwin confided that Wright was "a road-block in my road. . . . He had been an idol; and idols are created to be destroyed" (*The Price of the Ticket*, 277).

35. Baldwin, *The Price of the Ticket*, 285.

36. Baldwin, *The Price of the Ticket*, 285.

37. Baldwin, *The Price of the Ticket*, 469.

38. Baldwin, *The Price of the Ticket*, 37.

39. Zaborowska, *James Baldwin's Turkish Decade*, 288.

40. Baldwin, *The Price of the Ticket*, 126.

41. Baldwin, "This Morning, This Evening, So Soon," 134.

42. Text citations in this section refer to James Baldwin, "This Morning, This Evening, So Soon," in *Going to Meet the Man*, 149, 158.

43. Baldwin, "This Morning, This Evening, So Soon," 173.

44. M. Ross, *Manning the Race*, 2.

45. Du Bois, *Dark Princess: A Romance*, 300.

46. Edwards, *The Practice of Diaspora*, 13–15.

47. Jacques Rabemananjara, quoted in Jules-Rosette, *Black Paris*, 47.

48. Baldwin, quoted in Jules-Rosette, *Black Paris*, 53.

49. Thomas Borstelmann notes that in 1960, editors of the *Crisis* would assert that "problems of race prejudice and discrimination are worldwide. And so is the rebellion against these twin evils" (*The Cold War and the Color Line*, 269).

50. Jackson, *The Indignant Generation*, 290.

51. Hodges, *Portrait of an Expatriate*, 17–18; Jackson, *The Indignant Generation*, 290.

52. Campbell, *Exiled in Paris*, 121.

53. See de Beauvoir and Halimi, *Djamila Boupacha*.

54. Smith does not engage with other aspects of the Algerian War, such as the discourse on assimilation or the use of violence dealt with in the Francophone writings of Kateb Yacine, Mohammed Dib, Frantz Fanon, or Mouloud Feraoun, or with the French anticolonial discourse of Henri Alleg or Jean-Paul Sartre.

55. Friedman, "The Unvarying Visage of Hatred," 53.

56. Gilroy, *Against Race*, 308; Sundquist, *Strangers in the Land*, 5–6; Rothberg, *Multidirectional Memory*, 230.

57. I am referring here specifically to Tyler Stovall's excellent article "The Fire This Time: Black American Expatriates and the Algerian War" and Ewa Barbara Luczak's perceptive book chapter "From Enchantment to Criticism of Colonial France: James Baldwin's 'This Morning, This Evening, So Soon' and William Gardner Smith's *The Stone Face*," in Luczak, *How Their Living Outside America Affected Five American Authors*, 27–70.

58. This fictional absence of Franco-Algerian romance is not corroborated by historical records. See MacMaster, "The Role of European Women."

59. Rothberg, *Multidirectional Memory*, 250.

60. Enloe, "Womenandchildren," 89.

Chapter 3. The New Harem

1. Unlike conventional male portrayals of the Orient, Raina Lewis and Mary Roberts demonstrate that Western women have at times identified with women in the harem. See Lewis, *Rethinking Orientalism*; Roberts, *Intimate Outsiders*.

2. Hayes, *Queer Nations*, 9.

3. Lorcin, *Historicizing Colonial Nostalgia*, 85.

4. Alloua, *The Colonial Harem*, 95; Mernissi, *Scheherazade Goes West*, 14; Aldrich, *Colonialism and Homosexuality*, 219.

5. Huggan, *The Postcolonial Exotic*, ix–x.

6. Huggan, *The Postcolonial Exotic*, xii.

7. Debord, *The Society of the Spectacle*, 20.

8. See Michel Laronde's discussion of *néo-exotisme* in *Autour du roman beur*, 213–19.

9. Charef, quoted in Hargreaves, *Immigration and Identity in Beur Fiction*.

10. Charef, quoted in Mahjoub, "An Interview with Mehdi Charef," 37–38.

11. Menanteau, *Les banlieues*, 54.

12. Menanteau, *Les banlieues*, 54–60.

13. Llaumett, *Les jeunes d'origine étrangère*, 44–45.

14. Menanteau, *Les banlieues*, 54–60.

15. Fourcault, "Au coeur des politiques publiques"; Llaumett, *Les jeunes d'origine étrangère*, 44–45.

16. Wihtol de Wenden, "North African Immigration and the French Political Imaginary," 206.

17. Weil, *La France et ses étrangers*, 207–9. This phenomenon became known as *la double peine* (double sentencing) because the offenders have already served time in France and are then sentenced to deportation with little chance of reentering the country legally because of their criminal record.

18. Bouamama, *Dix ans de marche des Beurs*, 52–53.

19. Laronde, "La 'mouvance beur,'" 690.

20. Ardjoum, "Entretien Avec Mehdi Charef."

21. Jazouli, *Les Années Banlieues*, 59.

22. Bouzid, a Franco-Arab participant in the 1983 national March for Equality and Against Racism, questions the lingering use of the expression "second generation," stating: "Why are Arabs the only immigrants who are assigned a number? We're not inmates . . . in this label, I see a desire to reduce us to the same status as our parents. But, that is precisely what I refuse" (Djeghloul, "L'irruption des Beurs dans la littérature française," 81).

23. Quoted in Silverstein, *Algeria in France*; see also Abou-Sada and Millet, *Générations issues de l'immigration*; Aïssou, *Les beurs, l'école, et la France*; Boulot and Boyzon-Fradet, *Les immigrés et l'école*; Gaspard and Servan-Schreiber, *La fin des immigrés*; and Jazouli, *L'action collective des jeunes Maghrébins de France*.

24. Silverstein, *Algeria in France*, 167.

25. For hybridity, see Afoullouss, "Three Generations of Francophone North African Writers in Exile"; Aitsiselmi, "Métissage linguistique dans le roman beur"; M. Delvaux, "L'ironie du sort"; and Hargreaves, *Immigration and Identity*. For integration, see Chossat, "Hospitality, Integration, and Daily Life"; Cohen, "Loubards"; Gajarawala, "Miseducation."

26. See M. Delveaux, "L'ironie du sort"; Ireland, "Les banlieues de l'identité"; Naudin, "Formation postmoderne des Beurs"; and Bacholle, *Un passé contraignant.*

27. Hargreaves, "Resistance and Identity"; Ireland, "Les banlieues de l'identité."

28. Jaccomard notes that beur literature centers on such a powerful symbolic of space that a subdivision emerged in its writing, known as banlieue literature ("Harem ou Galère," 105). Laronde devotes a chapter of his book on beur literature to the themes of imprisonment in beur fiction, which centers on the spatialized notion of the panopticon (*Autour du roman beur*).

29. Charles Bonn, quoted in Gafaïti, *Cultures Transnationales de France*, 15.

30. Hargreaves, "Resistance and Identity in Beur Narratives," 93.

31. M. Delvaux, "L'ironie du sort," 688.

32. Djeghoul, "L'irruption des Beurs," 80–81.

33. Fetzer, "Memory, Absence and the Consciousness," 333.

34. Ardjoum, "Entretien avec Mehdi Charef," 33.

35. Hargreaves, *Immigration and Identity in Beur Fiction*, 13; Mahjoub, "An Interview with Mehdi Charef," 37.

36. Hargreaves, *Immigration and Identity in Beur Fiction*, 33; Mahjoub, "An Interview with Mehdi Charef," 37.

37. Hargreaves, *Immigration and Identity in Beur Fiction*, 33.

38. J. Roy, "Ahmed sortit à cinq heures," 58.

39. Nourissier, "Mehdi Charef: Cinéma-vérité."

40. Nemmiche, "Le principe d'Archi Ahmed."

41. J. Roy, "Ahmed sortit à cinq heures."

42. J. Roy, "Ahmed sortit à cinq heures."

43. The *Grand Robert* dictionary of the French language defines both "bicots" and "bougnoules" as racist and injurious terms that refer, respectively, to North African natives and North African immigrant workers. The etymology of bicots refers to *arbicots* (1861), military slang for small Arabs, whereas that of bougnoule (1890) means "the one who does the chores."

44. Bonnafous, quoted in Noiriel, *Immigration*, 606.

45. *Grand Robert* dictionary, s.v. "ratonade."

46. Giudice, *Arabacides.*

47. Adamson, *Algeria: A Study in Competing Ideologies*, 190.

48. Hargreaves, *Multi-Ethnic France*; Derderian, *North Africans in Contemporary France.*

49. Wacquant, "Banlieues françaises."

50. Hargreaves, *Immigration*, 32; Laronde, "La 'mouvance beur,'" 686.

51. Keaton, *Muslim Girls and the Other France*, 100, 102.

52. Ross, *Fast Cars, Clean Bodies*, 164.

53. Fanon, *Wretched of the Earth*, 7.

54. In beur writer's Nini Soraya's novel, *Ils disent que je suis une beurette* (*They Say I Am a Beurette*, 1993), remedial classes are also described as a stigma, and as a result Samia mentions that she is going to "seventh grade but the seventh grade for suckers" (21).

55. Catani and Mohamed, *Le journal de Mohamed* (*Mohamed's Diary*, 1973).

56. Tadjer, *Les A.N.I. Du Tassili*; Sebbar and Huston, *Lettres parisiennes*; Kettane, *Le sourire de Brahim*; Begag, *Béni ou le paradis privé.*

57. See Dr. Anne Marie Obajtek-Kirkwood's excellent web page "Les écrivains

beurs des années quatre-vingts et leurs témoignages," February 2008, http://clicnet
.swarthmore.edu/leila_sebbar/recherche/anne_obajtek.htm.

58. Hall, "Cultural Identity and Diaspora," 222; Hall, "New Ethnicities," 163.

59. Jaccomard, "Harem ou Galère," 109–10.

60. Tarr, *Reframing Difference*, 31–36.

61. In the context of Western art, John Berger explains that "the convention of not painting the hair on a woman's body helps towards the same end. Hair is associated with sexual power, with passion. The woman's sexual passion needs to be minimized so that the spectator may feel that he has the monopoly on such passion" (Berger et al., *Ways of Seeing*, 55).

Chapter 4. Other Queers

1. Guénif-Souilamas, "*Straight* Migrants," 74.

2. Naït-Balk, *Un homo dans la cité*, 8.

3. Provencher, *Queer French*, 186.

4. Mack, *Sexagon*, 26.

5. Hayes, *Queer Nations*, 6.

6. É. Fassin, *Le Sexe Politique*.

7. *Le Monde Diplomatique*, January 2011.

8. Ticktin, *Casualties of Care*, 13.

9. Ticktin, *Casualties of Care*, 19.

10. Ticktin, *Casualties of Care*, 4.

11. Ticktin, *Casualties of Care*, 192.

12. Perreau, *Queer Theory*, 65.

13. É. Fassin, "Du pacs au mariage pour tous."

14. In the 1980s, too, a niche of pornographic films featured Arab men and were marketed as "ethnic." See Cervulle, Rees-Roberts, and Dyer, *Homo exoticus*.

15. Nick Rees-Roberts, for instance, salutes "the emergence of a critical engagement with the contemporary politics of migration in gay cinema, one which challenges the climate of increased national security and hostility towards so-called 'illegal' immigration" (*French Queer Cinema*, 41).

16. The term "intersectionality" was coined by Kimberlé Williams Crenshaw in 1989 to encourage the study of intersecting social identities related to multidimensional experiences of oppression and discrimination. These identities include but are not limited to gender, race, class, ability, sexual orientation, religion, age, caste, and nationality.

17. Halperin, *Saint Foucault*, 62.

18. Puar, *Terrorist Assemblages*.

19. É. Fassin, "Homosexual City"; Haritaworn, *Queer Lovers and Hateful Others*; Mack, *Sexagon*; Mepschen, *Homosexuality as a Modern Category*; Rosello and Dasgupta, *What's Queer about Europe?*

20. Eribon, *Insult and the Making of the Gay Self*.

21. Provencher, "Maghrebi French Sexual Citizens"; Mack, *Sexagon*; Waldron, "Sexual/Social (Re)Orientations."

22. Waldron, "Sexual/Social (Re)Orientations," 188–89.

23. Waldron, "Sexual/Social (Re)Orientations," 190.

24. Provencher and Pratt, "Recasting Sami Bouajila."

25. Provencher andPratt, "Recasting Sami Bouajila," 201.

26. Aldrich, *Colonialism and Homosexuality*; Boone, *The Homoerotics of Orientalism*; Massad, *Desiring Arabs*.

27. Sollors, *Beyond Ethnicity*, 6.

28. The *sénatus consulte* of 1865 is a colonial law that declared all Algerian natives to be French subjects, and it introduced the notion that they would be granted full citizenship as they assimilated the values of the French republic. Laure Blévis characterizes the citizenship granted by the French colonial administration (or naturalization) as "the legal translation of the rhetoric of the civilizing mission that promised the colonized population, equality, but a deferred equality, associated with a future when the objective of assimilation to French civilization will be attained" ("La citoyenneté française," 26). The naturalizations granted to natives were strikingly low: there were only six thousand during the colonial period (1865–1962) (Blévis, "La citoyenneté française," 26).

29. Tarr, *Reframing Difference*, 151.

30. Tarr, *Reframing Difference*, 15–16.

31. Hayes, *Queer Nations*, 4.

32. Durmelat, "Tasting Displacement," 115.

33. Durmelat, "Tasting Displacement," 116.

34. Aldrich, *Colonialism and Homosexuality*, 333.

35. Cervulle, Rees-Roberts, and Dyer, *Homo exoticus*, 17.

36. With Matthieu Kassovitz's landmark film on the banlieue that cast a black, white, and Arab trio, subsequent films followed suit with multiracial groups of men, such as *Le ciel, les oiseaux, ta mère*.

37. The 1996 film *Salut cousin!* (*Hi Cousin!*) by Algerian-born film director Merzak Allouache calls attention to this dynamic when Alilou, a young Parisian beur, is extradited to Algeria.

38. See Beaulieu, interview with Zakia and Ahmed Bouchaala. Algerian-born filmmaker Ahmed Bouchaala collaborated with Zakia Bouchaala (née Tahiri) on the script of his first long feature film, *Krim*, in which she also played the role of Krim's sister. *Krim* is the story of a Franco-Arab father who, released after sixteen years in jail for murdering his wife, struggles to adjust to his free life. Looking for his daughter, Yasmine, he returns to a banlieue of Lyon and eventually saves her from its nefarious influence.

39. Beaulieu, interview with Zakia and Ahmed Bouchaala.

40. Beaulieu, interview with Zakia and Ahmed Bouchaala.

41. Grasset, "Origine contrôlée prime à l'Alpe-d'Huez."

42. Baudin, "Origine contrôlée."

43. Mandelbaum, "Origine contrôlée."

44. Bleich, "Anti-racism without Races," 174. For a discussion of the right to difference as it relates to France's republican ideals, see Valérie Orlando's article "From Rap to Raï in the Mixing Bowl."

45. Durmelat and Swamy, *Screening Integration*.

46. Scott, *The Politics of the Veil*, 104.

47. Naficy, *An Accented Cinema*, 5.

48. Rees-Roberts, *French Queer Cinema*.

49. Butler, *Bodies That Matter*, 18.

50. Eng, *The Feeling of Kinship*, 4.

51. Provencher, "Maghrebi-French Sexual Citizens," 48.

52. Tarr, *Reframing Difference*, 212.

53. Tarr, *Reframing Difference*, 212.

54. Butler, *Bodies That Matter*, 109, 110.

55. Phelan, *Sexual Strangers*, 5.

56. Puar, *Terrorist Assemblages*, ix.

57. See chapter 3, note 43, for the etymology of "bougnoule."

58. Scott, *The Politics of the Veil*, 12.

59. Armbrecht, "Universal Particularities," 158.

60. É. Fassin, "Questions sexuelles."

61. Scott Herring notes that as a transitive verb, "queer" can also mean "to puzzle" or "to spoil, put out of order" (*Queering the Underworld*, 21). "Queer" can refer to "a project of disabling the psychic, social, and material functioning of sexual identifications—of self, group, and of everywhere in between" (*Queering the Underworld*, 22).

62. Garber, *Vested Interests*, 16.

63. For example, a French female minister, thirty-seven-year-old Cecile Dufflot, was wolf-whistled and jeered in parliament while delivering a speech. She was wearing a flowery summer dress in the National Assembly.

64. Brown, *Regulating Aversion*, 6–7.

65. Brown, *Regulating Aversion*, 7.

66. Mack, *Sexagon*, 5.

67. As Jack G. Shaheen claims, there's a global demand for "Reel Bad Arabs." Saïd Taghmaoui played Saïd in Kassovitz's film *Hatred*—a beur small-time thug in a Parisian housing project—and has since taken more lucrative terrorist roles in Hollywood, corroborating Djaïdani's view. He is Captain Saïd, a profoundly (if somewhat justified) anti-American Iraqi who captures and tortures Americans in *Three Kings* (1999). In *Traitor* (2008), he is Omar, a mid-ranking officer in a terrorist organization who blindly follows orders, killing French and American men and getting killed by US police. Taghmaoui again plays the terrorist in *Vantage Point* (2008), but this time he is the head behind a complex plot to kidnap the US president during his visit to Spain. His fate does not depart from the usual script of death by bullet. We find Taghmaoui in a similar role in a French TV movie *Djihad!* (2006). The drama recounts the story of three French Arabs who join a jihadi group in Baghdad, where they kidnap a French woman running a nongovernmental organization and a mid-level French diplomat. If for Djaïdani French mainstream cinema has been hijacked by stereotypical views about French Arab men, a global context and demand for these roles boosts and inflects this domestic trend. Catering to a Western audience, these films baffle the Arabic speaker by casting actors with French-accented Moroccan dialect (*darrija*) as Iraqi, or by lumping together actors whose Arabic betray their different national and regional origins though they are supposed to be from the same country.

68. Waldron, "Sexual/Social (Re)Orientations," 191.

69. Simon, "Muslims Social Inclusion and Exclusion."

Chapter 5. Embodying the City

1. Loeffler, "City as Skin," 115.

2. Ahmed, *The Cultural Politics of Emotion*.

3. Fanon, *Black Skin, White Masks*, 112. A moment in Bernard Dadié's *An African in Paris* echoes this train scene. Tanhoe, the African visitor in Paris, confides, "Yes, it's true, I scare people—especially women and children. They see me coming and immediately

try to escape; there's no getting beyond the initial expression—They must wonder what in the world possessed God to get the colors wrong and smear me with tar" (43).

4. Fanon, *Black Skin, White Masks*, 109.

5. Fanon, *Black Skin, White Masks*, 111.

6. Fanon, *Black Skin, White Masks*, 112.

7. Fanon, *Black Skin, White Masks*, 112.

8. Fanon, *Black Skin, White Masks*, 116.

9. Fanon, *Black Skin, White Masks*, 112.

10. Tuan, *Topophilia*, 11.

11. Bachelard, *Poetics of Space*, 7–8.

12. Gritti, *Déraciner les racismes*, 123–30.

13. Gritti, *Déraciner les racismes*, 116.

14. Maghrebi: Gastaut, *L'immigration et l'opinion en France*, 115; Muslims: Deltombe, *L'Islam imaginaire*, 261.

15. Fernando, *The Republic Unsettled*, 35.

16. Fernando, *The Republic Unsettled*, 185.

17. Beck, "Subpolitics," 39–40.

18. Baudrillard, *Symbolic Exchanges and Death*, 13.

19. According to Alison Young, "street art is no simple offshoot of graffiti; many of its practitioners drew inspiration from punk rock, 'zine' culture, skateboarding or protest movements (all of which emphasize a DIY, hand-made quality in their activities) instead of or as well as from hip hop graffiti" ("From Object to Encounter," 163).

20. Waclawek, *Graffiti and Street Art*, 30.

21. Zukin and Braslow, "The Life Cycle of New York's Creative Districts," 138.

22. Reynald and Elffers, "The Future of Newman's Defensible Space Theory"; Dovey, Wollan, and Woodcock, "Placing Graffiti," 23.

23. McLuhan, *Understanding Media*, 7.

24. Baudrillard, *Symbolic Exchanges and Death*.

25. Doran, "Alternative French, Alternative Identities," 7.

26. Cannon, "Paname City Rapping," 157.

27. Gross, McMurray, and Swedenburg, "Arab Noise and Ramadan Nights," 144.

28. Quoted in Silverstein and Tetreault, "Ultra Violence in France."

29. Henri Lefèbvre develops this notion of a right to the city, asserting that people are entitled to use urban spaces as spaces of encounter. Isn't the street, he asks, a "place of speech, a site of words, much more than things? . . . Where words can become 'wild,' daubed on walls that elude rules and institutions?" (*La révolution urbaine*, 19).

30. Milon and Whidden, "Tags and Murals in France," 89.

31. Baudrillard, *Symbolic Exchanges and Death*, 14.

32. Razane, "So Far So Close By."

33. Sebbar and Huston, *Lettres parisiennes*, 40; Laronde, *Autour du roman beur*, 15.

34. Sebbar and Huston, *Lettres parisiennes*, 29.

35. MacMaster, *Colonial Migrants*, 199.

36. House and MacMaster, *Paris 1961*, 135.

37. House and MacMaster, *Paris 1961*, 1.

38. Le Cour Grandmaison, "Sur la réhabilitation du passé colonial," 125.

39. Golsan, *The Papon Affair*.

40. Wieviorka, *The Era of the Witness*.

41. Nora, *Les lieux de mémoire*; Gasnier, "La France commémorante," 98; J. Young, "Ecrire le monument," 736; Blanchard, *Le paris arabe*, 11. Thierry Gasnier notes that France is a society that easily fabricates national consensus "with more than 1,571 national celebrations between 1986 and 1993" ("La France commémorante," 98).

42. Quoted in Chidester and Linenthal, "Introduction," in *American Sacred Space*, 8.

43. Renan, "What Is a Nation?"

44. Campos, "Youth, Graffiti," 35.

45. Donadey, "Retour sur mémoire," 190.

46. Bhabha, *The Location of Culture*, 86.

47. Donadey, "Retour sur mémoire," 195.

48. Jelin, *State Repression and the Labors of Memory*, 139.

49. Hirsch, *Family Frames*, 22.

50. House and MacMaster, *Paris 1961*, 319.

51. Jones, "Les fantômes d'une mémoire meurtrie," 92.

52. Ferrel advances a "spatial sociology of spots" to explain how the choice of locations is related to the choice of audience, the higher the circulation of people, the larger the audience (*Crimes of Style*, 48–62).

53. Eco, *Theory of Semiotics*, 150; Ferrel, *Crimes of Style*, 176; Baudrillard, *Symbolic Exchanges and Death*, 16.

54. Aburawa, "Veiled Threat."

55. Silverstein, *Algeria in France*, 146.

56. Silverstein, *Algeria in France*, 140.

57. Fernando, *The Republic Unsettled*, 87.

58. Gaspard and Khosrokhavar, *Le foulard et la république*.

59. Fernando, *The Republic Unsettled*, 45.

60. Amara, *Ni Putes Ni Soumises*, 69–75.

61. Mack, *Sexagon*, 43.

62. McRobbie, quoted in Stuelke, "Loving in the Iraq War Years."

63. Stuelke, "Loving in the Iraq War Years," 124.

64. These demonstrations by veiled girls are not new. Paul Silverstein noted, "In the wake of the 1989 exclusions, two Muslim cultural associations, the Voice of Islam and the Islamic Association in France, organized demonstrations in Paris to show their support for the girls in question, with more than one thousand headscarved women marching from the multiracial neighborhood of Barbès to the central Place de la République" (*Algeria in France*, 46).

65. Fernando, *The Republic Unsettled*, 55.

66. See Fernando, *The Republic Unsettled*.

67. Aburawa, "Veiled Threat."

68. Fernando, *The Republic Unsettled*, 31.

69. "JR, the Man Who Shot the Slums, Wins Humanitarian Award," *The Independent*, October 20, 2010.

70. *Déclic Urbain*, November 17, 2005.

71. *Déclic Urbain*, November 17, 2005.

72. The French word "cliché" in the title plays on a double entendre, as it signifies both a photograph and a stereotype.

73. A key reason for the destruction of schools is that the government will then have to rebuild them.

74. Dikeç, *Badlands of the Republic*.

75. JR interviewed in *The Independent*, March 11, 2006.

76. See Geisser, *La nouvelle islamophobie*; Mucchielli, *Le scandale des tournantes*.

77. Baudrillard, *Simulacra and Simulation*.

78. Cazenave and Célérier, *Contemporary Francophone African Writers*, 3.

79. Cazenave and Célérier. *Contemporary Francophone African Writers*, 11.

Coda

1. "Paris is today the capital of the world. Our entire country will rise up and show its best side," said François Hollande in a statement.

2. *Charlie Hebdo* is a weekly satirical publication known for its attacks on Islam and other religions as well as politicians. Agence France Presse reported 1.5 million demonstrators in Paris.

3. For discussion and opposition to the phrase "Je suis Charlie," see Olivier Cyran, "Charlie Hebdo, pas raciste? Si vous le dites," *Article 11*, December 5, 2013.

4. Far-right National Front leader Marine Le Pen said her party had been excluded from the Paris demonstration and would instead march in other events across France. Some observers have noted the homogeneity of the gatherings: mainly white, educated, and bourgeois (Lordon, "Charlie at Any Cost?").

5. Coulibaly used a bank loan of €6,000 to help finance his attack and lent money to the Kouachis.

6. Bertho, *Les enfants du chaos*, 22.

7. An article published on September 18, 2015, in the newspaper *Le Monde* was titled "Khaled Kelkal, premier djihadiste made in France."

8. The wave of terrorist attacks in Paris in 1986 was linked to foreign networks located in Lebanon and Palestine, whereas in 1995, the Armed Islamic Group, a guerrilla group fighting the Algerian army, claimed responsibility for the bomb explosion in a Paris subway station.

9. Higgins, "French Police Say Suspect in Attack Evolved from Petty Criminal to Terrorist."

10. Callimachi Jim Yardley, "From Amateur to Ruthless Jihadist in France."

11. Moore, "In France, Prisons Filled with Muslims."

12. Packer, "The Other France."

13. Meichtry, "Paris Attacker Amedy Coulibaly's Path to Terror."

14. *Le nouvel observateur*, March 30, 1984; *Politis*, October 26, 1989; *Le nouvel observateur*, December 3, 1987.

15. Césari, *Etre musulman en France*, 10–11.

16. Césari, *Etre musulman en France*, 11.

17. Davidson, *Only Muslim*, 12.

18. In March 2015 there was an announcement that the PEN Literary Gala (held in May 2015) would honor the magazine *Charlie Hebdo* with the PEN/Toni and James C. Goodale Freedom of Expression Courage Award. As a result, 204 PEN members wrote a petition to condemn this decision. In a collective letter, these authors note that "there is a critical difference between staunchly supporting expression that violates the acceptable, and enthusiastically rewarding such expression." They found unconvincing the

description that *Charlie Hebdo*'s cartoons were "equal opportunity offense," pointing out, "The inequities between the person holding the pen and the subject fixed on paper by that pen cannot, and must not, be ignored. To the section of the French population that is already marginalized, embattled, and victimized, a population that is shaped by the legacy of France's various colonial enterprises, and that contains a large percentage of devout Muslims, Charlie Hebdo's cartoons of the Prophet must be seen as being intended to cause further humiliation and suffering. Our concern is that, by bestowing the Toni and James C. Goodale Freedom of Expression Courage Award on Charlie Hebdo, PEN is not simply conveying support for freedom of expression, but also valorizing selectively offensive material: material that intensifies the anti-Islamic, anti-Maghreb, anti-Arab sentiments already prevalent in the Western world" (Volokh, "The PEN/ Charlie Hebdo Controversy").

19. There are over five million Muslims, and yet this population has little political representation.

20. Thomson, *Les Français Jihadistes*, 57.

21. Wallace-Wells, "What Makes a Jihadist?"

22. Wallace-Wells, "What Makes a Jihadist?"

23. The poll has been used by the French far right as evidence of the radicalization of French Muslims in France, even though several polling specialists have questioned the method's conclusion that one in seven French persons supports ISIS.

24. Gastaut, *L'immigration et l'opinion en France sous la Ve République*, 246. See the following articles: "Beurs: salut La Mecque" (*Politis*, June 9, 1989); "Banlieues: la tentation islamiste" (*Le nouvel observateur*, November 12, 1992); "Comment les islamistes recrutent en France" (*Le nouvel observateur*, September 29, 1994), "Comment les intégristes musulmans noyautent-ils les beurs?" (*L'Evénement du jeudi*, November 4, 1993).

25. Silverstein, *Algeria in France*, 1.

26. Dikeç, *Badlands of the Republic*, 25.

27. Dikeç, *Badlands of the Republic*.

28. Salas, *La volonté de punir*.

29. Amnesty International, *Public Outrage*, 5.

30. Amnesty International, *Public Outrage*, 6.

31. D. Fassin, "Une mesure discriminatoire."

32. Packer, "The Other France."

33. Deltombe, *L'Islam imaginaire*, 249.

34. Sociologist Laurent Mucchielli notes that the tournantes or gang rapes have received exceptional attention by the media following the popular and sensational movie *La squale* (2000) by French director Fabrice Genestal (nominated for a César for best first film in 2001). In his examination of the five main national newspapers (*Le Monde*, *Libération*, *L'Humanité*, *Le Figaro*, and *La Croix*), Mucchielli claims there is no reference to this phenomenon in the national media before 2000, and after 2003, the term again disappears, showing the media's attention was as intense as it was fleeting.

35. On October 4, 2002, Sohane Benziane, a seventeen-year-old French girl of Algerian descent, was burned alive in a basement of la cité Balzac, in the outskirts of Vitry-sur-Seine, by a nineteen-year-old who felt jilted. She became a symbol of Muslim men's violence against women in the banlieues across France.

36. Lassoued, "Le Français d'origine maghrébine face au prisme médiatique," 151.

37. Mahmood, "Feminism, Democracy, and Empire," 92.

38. Mahmood, "Feminism, Democracy, and Empire," 92–93; Bahramitash, "The War on Terror," 235.

39. Mahmood, "Feminism, Democracy, and Empire," 102.

40. Mahmood, "Feminism, Democracy, and Empire," 82.

Bibliography

Abou-Sada, Georges, and Hélène Millet. *Générations issues de l'immigration*. Paris: Arcantère, 1986.

Aburawa, Arwa. "Veiled Threat: The Guerilla Graffiti of Princess Hijab." *Bitchmedia*, November 16, 2009.

Adamson, Kay. *Algeria: A Study in Competing Ideologies*. New York: Cassell, 1998.

Afoullouss, Houssaine. "Three Generations of Francophone North African Writers in Exile: Driss Chraïbi, Tahar Ben Jelloun and Mehdi Charef." In *Exiles and Migrants: Crossing Thresholds in European Culture and Society*, 144–53. Brighton, UK: Sussex Academic, 1997.

Ahmed, Sara. *The Cultural Politics of Emotion*. New York: Routledge, 2013.

Aïssou, Abdel. *Les beurs, l'école, et la France*. Paris: L'Harmattan, 1987.

Aitsiselmi, Farid. "Métissage linguistique dans le roman beur." *Cahiers AFLS* (Association of French Language Studies) 5, no. 3 (1999): 11–22.

Aldrich, Robert. *Colonialism and Homosexuality*. New York: Routledge, 2003.

Alleg, Henri. *La question*. Paris: Minuit, 1958.

Alloua, Malek. *The Colonial Harem*. Minneapolis: University of Minnesota Press, 1986.

Allouache, Merzak, dir. *Chouchou*. Westmount, QC: Christal Films, 2003.

Amara, Fadela, and Sylvia Zappi. *Ni putes ni soumises*. Paris: Découverte, 2003.

Amnesty International. *Public Outrage: Police Officers above the Law in France*. London: Amnesty International Publications, 2009.

Amrouche, Taos. *Jacinthe noire: Roman*. Paris: Charlot, 1947.

Ardjoum, Samir. "Entretien Avec Mehdi Charef." *Fluctuat*, March 2002.

Armbrecht, Thomas. "Universal Particularities: Conceptions of Sexuality, Nationality, and Culture in France and the United States." In *Comparatively Queer: Interrogating Identities across Time and Cultures*, edited by William J. Spurlin, Jarrod Hayes, and Margaret R. Higonnet, 153–69. New York: Palgrave Macmillan, 2010.

Aresu, Bernard. "The Francophone Novel in North Africa." In *The Cambridge Companion to the African Novel*, edited by Abiola Irèle, 103–24. New York: Cambridge University Press, 2009.

Ashcroft, Bill, Gareth Griffiths, and Helen Tiffin. *The Empire Writes Back: Theory and Practice in Post-Colonial Literatures*. Boston: Houghton Mifflin, 2002.

Bachelard, Gaston. *The Poetics of Space*. Translated by Maria Jolas. Boston: Beacon Press, 1994.

Bacholle, Michèle. *Un passé contraignant: Double bind et transculturation*. Amsterdam: Rodopi, 2000.

Bahramitash, Roksana. "The War on Terror, Feminist Orientalism and Orientalist Feminism: Case Studies of Two North American Bestsellers." *Critique: Critical Middle Eastern Studies* 14, no. 2 (2005): 221–35.

Baldwin, James. "James Baldwin, the Art of Fiction No. 78." Interview by Jordan Elgrably. *Paris Review* 91 (Spring 1984): 48–82.

———. *Notes of a Native Son.* Boston: Beacon Press, 1955.

———. *The Price of the Ticket: Collected Nonfiction, 1948–1985.* New York: St. Martin's, 1985.

———. "This Morning, This Evening, So Soon." In *Going to Meet the Man*, 123–69. New York: Dial Press, 1995.

Balibar, Etienne. *Race, Nation, Class: Ambiguous Identities.* Edited by Etienne Balibar and Immanuel Wallerstein. New York: Verso, 1991.

Ball, John C. *Imagining London: Postcolonial Fiction and the Transnational Metropolis.* Toronto: University of Toronto Press, 2004.

Bancel, Nicolas, and Valérie Amiraux. *Ruptures postcoloniales: Les nouveaux visages de la société française.* Paris: Découverte, 2010.

Barthes, Roland. *Mythologies.* New York: Hill and Wang, 2012.

Baudin, Brigitte. "Origine contrôlée: Trio insolite." *Figaro*, January 24, 2001.

Baudrillard, Jean. *Simulacra and Simulation.* Ann Arbor: University of Michigan Press, 1994.

———. *Symbolic Exchanges and Death.* Translated by Iain Hamilton Grant. London: Sage, 1993.

Beaulieu, Cécile. Interview with Zakia and Ahmed Bouchaala. *Le Parisien*, February 2, 2001.

Beck, Ulrich. "Subpolitics: Ecology and the Disintegration of Institutional Power." In *World Risk Society*, 91–108. Cambridge: Polity, 1999.

Bedjaoui, Amal, dir. *Un fils.* Paris: Eurozoom, 2003.

Begag, Azouz. *Béni, ou, le paradis privé.* Paris: Seuil, 1989.

Bégéja, Liria, dir. *Change moi ma vie.* France: France Télévisions distribution, 2002.

Behdad, Ali. "Postcolonial Theory and the Predicament of 'Minor Literature.'" In *Minor Transnationalism*, edited by Françoise Lionnet and Shumei Shi, 223–36. Durham, NC: Duke University Press, 2005.

Ben Jelloun, Tahar. *Hospitalité française: racisme et immigration maghrébine.* Paris: Seuil, 1984.

———. *La plus haute des solitudes: misère sexuelle d'émigrés Nord-Africains.* Paris: Seuil, 1977.

Benstock, Shari. *Women of the Left Bank: Paris, 1900–1940.* Austin: University of Texas Press, 1986.

Berger, John, Sven Blomberg, Chris Fox, Michael Dibb, and Richard Hollis. *Ways of Seeing.* London: BBC, Penguin Books, 1973.

Berlant, Lauren. "Intimacy: A Special Issue." *Critical Inquiry* 24, no. 2 (Winter 1998): 281–88.

Bertho, Alain. *Les enfants du chaos: Essai sur le temps des martyrs.* Paris: Découverte, 2016.

Bhabha, Homi. *The Location of Culture.* New York: Routledge, 1994.

Bigsby, Christopher. "The Divided Mind of James Baldwin." In *Critical Essays on James Baldwin*, edited by Fred L. Stanley and Nancy V. Burt, 94–111. Boston: Hall, 1988.

Blanchard, Pascal. *Le paris arabe: deux siècles de présence des orientaux et des maghrébins.* Paris: Découverte, 2003.

Blanchard, Pascal, and Nicolas Bancel. *La fracture coloniale: La société française au prisme de l'héritage colonial.* Paris: Découverte, 2005.

Bleich, Erik. "Anti-racism without Races: Politics and Policy in a 'Color-Blind' State." In *Race in France: Interdisciplinary Perspectives on the Politics of Difference,* edited by Herrick Chapman and Laura L. Frader, 162–88. New York: Berghahn Books, 2004.

Blévis, Laure. "La citoyenneté française au miroir de la colonization." *Genèses* 53 (2003): 25–47.

Boone, Joseph A. *The Homoerotics of Orientalism.* New York: Columbia University Press, 2014.

Borstelmann, Thomas. *The Cold War and the Color Line: American Race Relations in the Global Arena.* Cambridge, MA: Harvard University Press, 2001.

Bouamama, Saïd. *Dix ans de marche des Beurs: Chronique d'un mouvement avorté.* Paris: Desclée de Brouwer, 1994.

Boubeker, Ahmed, and Abdellali Hajjat. *Histoire politique des immigrations (post)coloniales: France, 1920–2008.* Paris: Amsterdam, 2008.

Bouchaala, Ahmed, dir. *Krim.* Paris: Welcome, 1996.

Bouchaala, Ahmed, and Zakia Bouchaala, dirs. *Origine contrôlée.* Paris: Universal pictures vidéo France SA, 2002.

Boucher, Manuel. *Les théories de l'intégration entre universalisme et différencialisme: Des débats sociologiques et politiques en France, analyse de textes contemporains.* Paris: L'Harmattan, 2000.

Boulot, Serge, and Danielle Boyzon-Fradet. *Les immigrés et l'école: Une course d'obstacle.* Paris: CIEMI/L'Harmattan, 1988.

Bourcier, Marie-Hélène. *Queer zones: Politique des identités sexuelles et des savoirs.* Paris: Amsterdam, 2011.

Bromley, James M. *Intimacy and Sexuality in the Age of Shakespeare.* Cambridge: Cambridge University Press, 2011.

Brown, Wendy. *Regulating Aversion: Tolerance in the Age of Identity and Empire.* Princeton, NJ: Princeton University Press, 2006.

Butler, Judith. *Bodies That Matter: On the Discursive Limits of "Sex."* New York: Routledge, 1993.

———. *Precarious Life: The Powers of Mourning and Violence.* New York: Verso, 2006.

Callimachi, Rukmini, and Jim Yardley. "From Amateur to Ruthless Jihadist in France." *New York Times,* January 17, 2005.

Camiscioli, Elisa. *Reproducing the French Race: Immigration, Intimacy and Embodiment in the Early Twentieth Century.* Durham, NC: Duke University Press, 2009.

Campbell, James. *Exiled in Paris: Richard Wright, James Baldwin, Samuel Beckett, and Others on the Left Bank.* New York: Scribner, 1995.

Campos, Ricardo. "Youth, Graffiti, and the Aesthetization of Transgression." *Social Analysis* 59, no. 3 (Autumn 2015): 17–40.

Cannon, Steve. "Paname City Rapping: B-Boys in the Banlieues and Beyond." In *Postcolonial Cultures in France,* edited by Alec Hargreaves and Mark McKinney, 150–66. New York: Routledge, 1997.

Casanova, Pascale. *The World Republic of Letters.* Translated by Malcolm DeBevoise. Cambridge, MA: Harvard University Press, 2004.

Castex, Pierre-Georges. *Ecrire Paris.* Paris: Seesam, 1990.

Catani, Maurizio Catani, and Mohamed. *Journal de Mohamed: Un algérien en France parmi huit cent mille autres.* Paris: Stock, 1973.

Cazenave, Odile M. *Afrique sur Seine: A New Generation of African Writers in Paris*. Lanham, MD: Lexington Books, 2005.

Cazenave, Odile M., and Patricia Célérier. *Contemporary Francophone African Writers and the Burden of Commitment*. Charlottesville: University of Virginia Press, 2011.

Céline, Louis-Ferdinand. *Journey to the End of the Night*. Translated by Ralph Manheim. New York: New Directions, 2006.

Cervulle, Maxime, Nick Rees-Roberts, and Richard Dyer. *Homo exoticus: Race, classe et critique queer*. Paris: A. Colin, 2010.

Césari, Jocelyne. *Etre musulman en France: Associations, militants et mosquées*. Paris: Karthala, 1994.

Chapman, Herrick, and Laura L. Frader. *Race in France: Interdisciplinary Perspectives on the Politics of Difference*. New York: Berghahn Books, 2004.

Charef, Mehdi, dir. *Le thé au harem d'archimède*. Paris: KG édition, 2000.

———. *Tea in the Harem*, translated by Ed Emery. London: Serpent's Tail, 1989.

———. *Thé au harem d'archi Ahmed*. Paris: Mercure de France, 1983.

Chaumont, Franck. *Homo-ghetto*. Paris: Le cherche midi, 2009.

———. "Lettre ouverte au ministre de l'éducation nationale: L'école doit être le rampart contre l'homophobie dans les cité ghettos." *Le Monde*, November 11, 2009.

Chevalier, Louis. *Laboring Classes and Dangerous Classes in Paris during the First Half of the Nineteenth Century*. New York: H. Fertig, 1973.

Chidester, David, and Edward Linenthal, eds. *American Sacred Space*. Bloomington: Indiana University Press, 1995.

Chossat, Michèle A. "Hospitality, Integration, and Daily Life: Le Thé Au Harem D'archi Ahmed and Le Gone Du Chaaba." *West Virginia University Philological Papers* 50 (2003): 61–66.

Chraïbi, Driss. *The Butts*. Washington, DC: Three Continents Press, 1983.

———. *Le monde à côté*. Paris: Denoël, 2003.

———. *Les boucs*. Paris: Denoël 1955.

———. *Vu, lu, entendu*. Folio. Paris: Denoël, 2007.

Chraïbi, Driss, and Kadiri Abdeslam. *Une vie sans concessions*. Lèchelle, France: Zellige, 2009.

Chrestien, Michel. "Un Barbaresque écrit en Français." *La Semaine internationale*, November 15, 1956.

Citron, Pierre. *La poésie de Paris dans la littérature française de Rousseau à Baudelaire*. Paris: Minuit, 1961.

Clancy-Smith, Julia. "Islam, Gender, and Identities." In *Domesticating the Empire: Race, Gender, and Family Life in French and Dutch Colonialism*, edited by Julia A. Clancy-Smith and Frances Gouda, 154–74. Charlottesville: University Press of Virginia, 1998.

Clancy-Smith, Julia, and Frances Gouda, eds. *Domesticating the Empire: Race, Gender, and Family Life in French and Dutch Colonialism*. Charlottesville: University Press of Virginia, 1998.

Cohen, Kfir. "Loubards: 1980s French-Algerian Activism and the Conceptual Limits of Beur Scholarship." *French Cultural Studies* 24, no. 1 (2013): 116–28.

Collectif Qui fait la France? *Chroniques d'une société annoncée: nouvelles*. Paris: Stock, 2007.

Conklin, Alice L. *A Mission to Civilize: The Republican Idea of Empire in France and West Africa, 1895–1930*. Stanford, CA: Stanford University Press, 1997.

Cooper, Frederick. *Colonialism in Question: Theory, Knowledge, History.* Berkeley: University of California Press, 2005.

Coquio, Catherine. *Retours du colonial? Disculpation et réhabilitation de l'histoire coloniale française.* Nantes: Atalante, 2008.

Corey, Susan. "Toward the Limits of Mystery: The Grotesque in Toni Morrison's *Beloved.*" In *The Aesthetics of Toni Morrison: Speaking the Unspeakable,* edited by Marc C. Conner, 31–48. Jackson: University Press of Mississippi, 2000.

Cruz-Malavé, Arnaldo, and Martin F. Manalansan IV. *Queer Globalizations: Citizenship and the Afterlife of Colonialism.* New York: New York University Press, 2002.

Cyran, Olivier. "Charlie Hebdo, pas raciste? Si vous le dites." *Article 11,* December 5, 2013.

Dadié, Bernard B. *An African in Paris.* Urbana: University of Illinois Press, 1994.

Daeninckx, Didier. *Meurtres pour mémoire.* Paris: Gallimard, 1984.

Davidson, Naomi. *Only Muslim: Embodying Islam in Twentieth-Century France.* Ithaca, NY: Cornell University Press, 2012.

de Beauvoir, Simone, and Gisèle Halimi. *Djamila Boupacha.* Paris: Gallimard, 1962.

Debord, Guy. *The Society of the Spectacle.* Translated by Donald Nicholson-Smith. New York: Zone Books, 1995.

Delayre, Stéphanie. *Driss Chraïbi, Une écriture de traverse.* Pessac: Presses universitaires de Bordeaux, 2006.

Deltombe, Thomas. *L'Islam imaginaire: La construction médiatique de l'islamophobie en France, 1975–2005.* Paris: Découverte, 2013.

Delvau, Alfred. *Les plaisirs de Paris: Guide pratique illustré.* Paris: Achille Faure, 1867.

Delvaux, Martine. "L'ironie du sort: le tiers espace de la littérature beure." *French Review* 68, no. 4 (1995): 681–93.

Derderian, Richard L. *North Africans in Contemporary France: Becoming Visible.* New York: Palgrave Macmillan, 2004.

Dib, Mohammed. *La grande maison.* Paris: Seuil, 1962.

Dikeç, Mustafa. "Immigrants, *Banlieues,* and Dangerous Things: Ideology as an Aesthetic Affair." *Antipode* 45, no. 1 (2012): 23–42.

———. *Badlands of the Republic: Space, Politics and Urban Policy.* Malden, MA: Blackwell, 2007.

Djaïdani, Rachid. *Viscéral.* Paris: Seuil, 2007.

Djeghloul, Abdelkader. "L'irruption des Beurs dans la littérature française." *Arabies* (1989): 80–87.

Donadey, Anne. "Retour sur mémoire: La Seine était rouge de Leïla Sebbar." In *Leïla Sebbar,* edited by Michel Laronde, 187–98. Paris: L'Harmattan, 2003.

———. "'Une Certaine Idée de la France': The Algeria Syndrome and Struggles over 'French' Identity." In *Identity Papers: Contested Nationhood in Twentieth-Century France,* edited by Steven Ungar and Tom Conley, 215–32. Minneapolis: University of Minnesota Press, 1996.

Doran, Meredith. "Alternative French, Alternative Identities: Situating Language in la Banlieue." *Contemporary French and Francophone Studies* 11, no. 4 (October 2007): 497–508.

Dovey, Kim, Simon Wollan, and Ian Woodcock. "Placing Graffiti: Creating and Contesting Character in Inner-City Melbourne." *Journal of Urban Design* 17, no. 1 (February 2012): 21–41.

Du Bois, W. E. B. *Dark Princess: A Romance*. Oxford: Oxford University Press, 2007.

Ducastel, Olivier, and Jacques Martineau, dirs. *Drôle de Félix*. Amsterdam: Cinemien Homescreen, 2001.

Dugas, Guy. "Une mémoire en train de se constituer: Interview avec Driss Chraïbi." In *Driss Chraïbi: Dossier*, edited by Jeanne Fouet, 153–75. Paris: Coordination Internationale des Chercheurs sur les Littératures Maghrébines, CICLIM, 2004.

Durmelat, Sylvie. *Fictions de l'intégration: Du mot beur à la politique de la mémoire*. Paris: L'Harmattan, 2008.

———. "Tasting Displacement: Couscous and Culinary Citizenship in Maghrebi-French Diasporic Cinema." *Food and Foodways* 23 (2015): 104–26.

Durmelat, Sylvie, and Vinay Swamy. *Screening Integration: Recasting Maghrebi Immigration in Contemporary France*. Lincoln: University of Nebraska Press, 2011.

Eco, Umberto. *A Theory of Semiotics*. Bloomington: Indiana University Press, 1979.

Edwards, Brent Hayes. *The Practice of Diaspora: Literature, Translation, and the Rise of Black Internationalism*. Cambridge, MA: Harvard University Press, 2003.

Einaudi, Jean-Luc. *La bataille de Paris: 17 Octobre 1961*. Paris: Seuil, 1991.

El-Tayeb, Fatima. *European Others: Queering Ethnicity in Postnational Europe*. Minneapolis: University of Minnesota Press, 2011.

Eng, David L. *The Feeling of Kinship: Queer Liberalism and the Racialization of Intimacy*. Durham, NC: Duke University Press, 2010.

Enloe, Cynthia H. "Womenandchildren: Propaganda Tools of Patriarchy." In *Mobilizing Democracy: Changing the U.S. Role in the Middle East*, edited by Greg Bates, 89–95. Monroe, ME: Common Courage Press, 1991.

Eribon, Didier. *Insult and the Making of the Gay Self*. Durham, NC: Duke University Press, 2004.

Etcherelli, Claire. *Elise ou la vraie vie: Roman*. Paris: Denoël, 1967.

Fabre, Michel. *From Harlem to Paris: Black American Writers in France, 1840–1980*. Urbana and Chicago: University of Illinois Press, 1993.

———. *The Unfinished Quest of Richard Wright*. Urbana and Chicago: University of Illinois Press, 1993.

———. *The World of Richard Wright*. Jackson: University Press of Mississippi, 2007.

Fanon, Frantz. *Black Skin, White Masks*. New York: Grove Press, 1967.

———. *A Dying Colonialism*. New York: Grove Press, 1967.

———. *Toward the African Revolution: Political Essays*. New York: Monthly Review Press, 1967.

———. *The Wretched of the Earth*. Translated by Richard Philcox. New York: Grove Press, 1963.

Fassin, Didier. "Une mesure discriminatoire qui accentue les fractures française." *Le Monde*, January 29, 2016.

Fassin, Didier, and Éric Fassin, eds. *De la question sociale à la question raciale: Représenter la société française*. Paris: Découverte, 2009.

Fassin, Éric. "Du pacs au 'mariage pour tous': Enjeux sociaux et politiques." Rencontre avec Eric Fassin. Société Louise Michel, Paris, January 16, 2013.

———. "Homosexual City, Homophobic Banlieue?" *Métropolitiques* 9, March 2011.

———. *Le sexe politique: Genre et sexualité au miroir transatlantique*. Paris: Ecole des hautes études en sciences sociales, 2009.

———. "Questions sexuelles, questions raciales: Parallèles, tensions et articulations."

In *De la question sociale à la question raciale: Représenter la société française*, edited by Didier Fassin and Éric Fassin, 230–48. Paris: Découverte, 2009.

Feraoun, Mouloud. *Land and Blood*. Translated by Patricia Geesey. Charlottesville: University of Virginia Press, 2012.

———. *La terre et le sang*. Paris: Seuil, 1953.

———. *Le fils du pauvre*. Paris: Seuil, 1954.

———. *The Poor Man's Son: Menrad, Kabyle Schoolteacher*. Translated by Lucy R. McNair. Charlottesville: University of Virginia Press, 2005.

Fernando, Mayanthi L. *The Republic Unsettled: Muslim French and the Contradictions of Secularism*. Durham, NC: Duke University Press, 2014.

Ferrel, Jeff. *Crimes of Style: Urban Graffiti and the Politics of Criminality*. Boston: Northeastern University Press, 1996.

Fetzer, Glenn W. "Memory, Absence and the Consciousness of Self in the Novels of Mehdi Charef." *CLA Journal* 38, no. 3 (1995): 331–41.

Figuéras, André. "Les événements d'Afrique du Nord." *Combat*, September 2, 1955.

Flaubert, Gustave. *Madame Bovary*. Translated by Francis Steegmuller. New York: Random House, 1957.

Forsdick, Charles. "Beyond Francophone Postcolonial Studies: Exploring the Ends of Comparison." *Modern Languages Open*, May 8, 2015. https://www.modernlanguages open.org/articles/10.3828/mlo.v0i0.56/.

Forsdick, Charles, and David Murphy. *Francophone Postcolonial Studies: A Critical Introduction*. London: Arnold, 2003.

Fourcault, Annie. "Au Coeur des politiques publiques: La construction des grands ensembles." Podcast, June 11, 2009. http://www.histoire-immigration.fr/agenda /2010-09/au-coeur-des-politiques-publiques-la-construction-des-grands-ensembles.

Francis, Terri. "Embodied Fictions, Melancholy Migrations: Josephine Baker's Cinematic Celebrity." *Modern Fiction Studies* 51, no. 4 (2005): 824–45.

Frazier, Franklin, E. *Black Bourgeoisie*. Glencoe, IL: Free Press, 1957.

Friedman, Joseph. "The Unvarying Visage of Hatred." *New York Times Book Review*, November 17, 1963, 53.

Gafaïti, Hafid. *Cultures transnationales de France: Des "Beurs" aux*. Paris: L'Harmattan, 2001.

Gajarawala, Toral Jatin. "Miseducation: Dalit and Beur Writers on the Antiromance of Pedagogy." *Comparative Literature Studies* 47, no. 3 (2010): 346–68.

Gans-Guinoune, Anne-Marie. *Driss Chraïbi, de l'impuissance de l'enfance à la revanche par l'écriture*. Paris: L'Harmattan, 2005.

Garber, Marjorie B. *Vested Interests: Cross-Dressing and Cultural Anxiety*. New York: Routledge, 1992.

Gasnier, Thierry. "La France commémorante." *Le débat* 78 (January–February 1994): 89–98.

Gaspard, Françoise, and Farhad Khosrokhavar. *Le foulard et la république*. Paris: Découverte, 1995.

Gaspard, Françoise, and Claude Servan-Schreiber. *La fin des immigrés*. Paris: Seuil, 1984.

Gastaut, Yvan. *L'immigration et l'opinion en France sous la Ve République*. Paris: Seuil, 2000.

Geisser, Vincent. *La nouvelle islamophobie*. Paris: Découverte, 2003.

Gibson, Richard. "Richard Wright's 'Island of Hallucination' and the 'Gibson Affair.'" *Modern Fiction Studies* 51, no. 4 (2005): 896–920.

Gilroy, Paul. *Against Race: Imagining Political Culture beyond the Color Line*. Cambridge, MA: Belknap Press of Harvard University Press, 2000.

———. *The Black Atlantic: Modernity and Double Consciousness*. Cambridge, MA: Harvard University Press, 1993.

Girard, Alain, and Jean Stoetzel. *Français et immigrés*. Paris: Presses universitaires de France, 1953.

Giudice, Fausto. *Arabicides: Une chronique française, 1970–1991*. Paris: Découverte, 1992.

Goebel, Michael. *Anti-Imperial Metropolis: Interwar Paris and the Seeds of Third World Nationalism*. New York: Cambridge University Press, 2015.

Golsan, Richard. *The Papon Affair: Memory and Justice on Trial*. New York: Routledge, 2000.

Gondola, Didier. "'But I Ain't African, I'm American!': Black American Exiles and the Construction of Racial Identities in Twentieth-Century France." In *Blackening Europe: The African American Presence*, edited by Heike Raphael-Hernandez, 201–15. New York: Routledge, 2004.

Gopnik, Adam. *Americans in Paris: A Literary Anthology*. New York: Library of America, 2004.

Grasset, Alain. "Origine contrôlée prime à l'Alpe-d'Huez." *Le Parisien Libéré*, January 14, 2001.

Gritti, Jules. *Déraciner les racismes*. Paris: SOS-Racisme Éditions, 1982.

Gross, Joan, David McMurray, and Ted Swedenburg. "Arab Noise and Ramadan Nights: *Rai*, Rap, and Franco-Maghrebi Identities." In *Displacement, Diaspora, and Geographies of Identity*, edited by Smadar Lavie and Ted Swedenburg, 119–56. Durham, NC: Duke University Press, 1996.

Guène, Faïza. *Kiffe Kiffe Tomorrow*. Translated by Sarah Ardizzone. Orlando: Harcourt, 2006.

Guénif-Souilamas, Nacira. *La république mise à nu par son immigration*. Paris: Fabrique, 2006.

———. "*Straight* Migrants Queering European Man." In *What's Queer about Europe? Productive Encounters and Re-Enchanting Paradigms*, edited by Mireille Rosello and Sudeep Dasgupta, 69–78. New York: Fordham University Press, 2014.

Guénif-Souillamas, Nacira, and Éric Macé. *Les féministes et le garçon arabe*. La Tour-d'Aigues: l'Aube, 2004.

Guissard, Lucien. "Des proscrits parmi nous." *La Croix*, Paris, October 3, 1955.

Haddour, Azzedine. *Colonial Myths: History and Narrative*. Manchester: Manchester University Press, 2000.

Hajjat, Abdellali, and Marwan Mohammed. *Islamophobie: Comment les élites françaises fabriquent le problème Musulman*. Paris: Découverte, 2013.

Hall, Stuart. "Cultural Identity and Diaspora." In *Identity: Community, Culture, Difference*, edited by Jonathan Rutherford, 222–37. London: Lawrence & Wishart, 1990.

———. "The Local and the Global: Globalization and Ethnicity." In *Dangerous Liaisons: Gender, Nation, and Postcolonial Perspectives*, edited by Anne McClintock, Aamir Mufti, and Ella Shohat, 173–87. Minneapolis: University of Minnesota Press, 1997.

———. "New Ethnicities." In *Black British Cultural Studies: A Reader*, edited by Houston A. Baker, Manthia Diawara, and Ruth H. Lindeborg, 163–72. Chicago: University of Chicago Press, 1996.

Halperin, David M. *Saint Foucault: Towards a Gay Hagiography*. New York: Oxford University Press, 1995.

Hancock, Claire. "Capitale du plaisir: The Remaking of Imperial Paris." In *Imperial Cities: Landscape, Display, and Identity*, edited by Felix Driver and Gilbert David, 64–77. Manchester: Manchester University Press, 1999.

Hargreaves, Alec G. "Banlieue Blues." In *The Cambridge Companion to the Literature of Paris*, edited by Anna-Louise Milne, 212–27. New York: Cambridge University Press, 2013.

———. *Multi-Ethnic France: Immigration, Politics, Culture and Society*. 2nd ed. New York: Routledge, 2007.

———. *Immigration and Identity in Beur Fiction: Voices from the North African Immigrant Community in France*. New York: Berg, 1997.

———. *Immigration, "Race" and Ethnicity in Contemporary France*. New York: Routledge, 1995.

———. "Resistance and Identity in Beur Narratives." *Modern Fiction Studies* 35, no. 1 (1989): 93.

———. "Une Culture Innommable?" In *Cultures transnationales de France: Des "Beurs" aux. . . . ?*, edited by Hafid Gafaïti, 27–36. Paris: L'Harmattan, 2001.

Hargreaves, Alec G., and Mark McKinney. *Post-colonial Cultures in France*. London: Routledge, 1997.

Hargreaves, Alec G., and David Murphy. "New Directions in Postcolonial Studies." *Journal of Postcolonial Writing* 44, no. 3 (2008): 221–25.

Haritaworn, Jinthana. *Queer Lovers and Hateful Others: Regenerating Violent Times and Places*. Chicago: University of Chicago Press, 2015.

Hayes, Jarrod. "Looking for Roots among the Mangroves: 'Errance enracinées' and Migratory Identities." *Centennial Review* 42, no. 3 (Fall 1998): 459–74.

———. *Queer Nations: Marginal Sexualities in the Maghreb*. Chicago: University of Chicago Press, 2000.

———. *Queer Roots for the Diaspora: Ghosts in the Family Tree*. Ann Arbor: Michigan University Press, 2016.

Heise, Thomas. *Urban Underworlds: A Geography of Twentieth-Century American Literature and Culture*. New Brunswick, NJ: Rutgers University Press, 2011.

Henderson, Mae. "In Another Country: Afro-American Expatriate Novelists in France, 1946–1974." Dissertation, Yale University, 1983.

Henni-Moulai, Nadia. *Petit précis de l'islamophobie ordinaire*. Paris: Points sur les i, 2012.

Herring, Scott. *Queering the Underworld: Slumming, Literature, and the Undoing of Lesbian and Gay History*. Chicago: University of Chicago Press, 2007.

Higgins, Andrew. "French Police Say Suspect in Attack Evolved from Petty Criminal to Terrorist." *New York Times*, December 23, 2016.

Higonnet, Patrice. *Paris: Capital of the World*. Cambridge, MA: Belknap Press of Harvard University Press, 2002.

Himes, Chester. *My Life of Absurdity: The Later Years; The Autobiography of Chester Himes*. New York: Paragon House, 1990.

Hirsch, Marianne. *Family Frames: Photography, Narrative, and Postmemory*. Cambridge, MA: Harvard University Press, 1997.

Hodges, LeRoy S. *Portrait of an Expatriate: William Gardner Smith, Writer*. Westport, CT: Greenwood Press, 1985.

House, Jim, and Neil MacMaster. *Paris 1961: Algerians, State Terror, and Memory*. Oxford: Oxford University Press, 2006.

Huggan, Graham. *The Postcolonial Exotic: Marketing the Margins*. London: Routledge, 2001.

Ireland, Susan. "Les banlieues de l'identité: Urban Geography and Immigrant Identities." *French Literature in / and the City* 24 (1997): 171–88.

Jaccomard, Hélène. "Harem ou Galère: Le déterminisme géographique dans deux écrits beurs." *Australian Journal of French Studies* 37, no. 1 (2000): 105–15.

Jackson, Lawrence P. *The Indignant Generation: A Narrative History of African American Writers and Critics, 1934–1960*. Princeton, NJ: Princeton University Press, 2011.

Jazouli, Adil. *L'action collective des jeunes Maghrébins de France*. Paris: CIEM/L'Harmattan.

———. *Les Années Banlieues*. Paris: Seuil, 1992.

Jelin, Elizabeth. *State Repression and the Labors of Memory*. Translated by Judy Rein and Marcial Godoy-Anativia. Minneapolis: University of Minnesota Press, 2003.

Jones, Kathryn N. "'Les fantômes d'une mémoire meurtrie': Representing and Remembering la Bataille de Paris in Novels by Nacer Kettane, Mehdi Lallaoui and Tassadit Imache." *Romance Studies* 24, no. 2 (2006): 91–104.

Jules-Rosette, Bennetta. *Black Paris: The African Writers' Landscape*. Urbana: University of Illinois Press, 2000.

Kaplan, Amy. *The Anarchy of Empire in the Making of U.S. Culture*. Cambridge, MA: Harvard University Press, 2002.

Kassovitz, Mathieu, dir. *La haine*. Paris: Tartan Video, 1996.

Keaton, Trica. "'Black (American) Paris' and the French Outer-Cities: The Race Question and Questioning Solidarity." In *Black Europe and the African Diaspora*, edited by Darlene Clark Hine, Trica Keaton, and Stephen Small, 95–118. Urbana: University of Illinois Press, 2009.

———. *Muslim Girls and the Other France: Race, Identity Politics, and Social Exclusion*. Bloomington: Indiana University Press, 2006.

Kemp, Anna. *Voices and Veils: Feminism and Islam in French Women's Writing and Activism*. London: Legenda, 2010.

Kemp, Robert. "Les Boucs." *Le Soir*, September 28, 1955.

Kleppinger, Kathryn A. *Branding the "Beur" Author: Minority Writing and the Media in France, 1983–2013*. Liverpool: Liverpool University Press, 2015.

Kessas, Ferrudja. *Beur's Story*. Paris: L'Harmattan, 1990.

Kettane, Nacer. *Droit de réponse à la démocratie française*. Paris: Découverte, 1986.

———. *Le sourire de Brahim*. Paris: Denoël 1985.

Kincaid, Jamaica. "On Seeing England for the First Time." *Harper's*, August 1991, 13–16.

Kristeva, Julia. *Intimate Revolt: The Powers and Limits of Psychoanalysis*. Translated by J. Herman. New York: Columbia University Press, 2002.

Laffont, Robert, and Valentino Bompiani. *Le nouveau dictionnaire des auteurs de tous les temps et de tous les pays*. Paris: R. Laffont, 1994.

Lamar, Jake. *Ghosts of Saint Michel*. New York: St. Martin's Minotaur, 2006.

Lamming, George. *The Emigrants*. London: Allison & Busby, 1980.

Lange, Rémi, dir. *Tarik el hob*. New York: Water Bearer Films, 2004.

Laronde, Michel. *Autour du roman beur: Immigration et identité*. Paris: L'Harmattan, 1993.

———. "La 'mouvance beur': Émergence médiatique." *French Review* 161, no. 5 (1988): 684–92.

Lassoued, Hassiba. "Le Français d'origine maghrébine face au prisme médiatique." *Présence Francophone* 65 (2005): 150–67.

Le Cour Grandmaison, Olivier. "Sur la réhabilitation du passé colonial de la France." In *La fracture coloniale: La société française au prisme de l'héritage colonial*, edited by Pascal Blanchard, Nicolas Bancel, and Sandrine Lemaire, 121–28. Paris: Découverte, 2005.

Lefèbvre, Henri. *La révolution urbaine.* Paris: Gallimard, 1979.

Lewis, Reina. *Rethinking Orientalism: Women, Travel, and the Ottoman Harem.* New Brunswick, NJ: Rutgers University Press, 2004.

Llaumett, Maria. *Les jeunes d'origine étrangère: De la marginalisation à la participation.* Paris: L'Harmattan, 1984.

Llorens, David. "The Fellah, the Chosen Ones, the Guardian." In *Black Fire: An Anthology of Afro-American Writing*, edited by Amiri Baraka and Larry Neal, 169–77. Baltimore: Black Classic Press, 2007.

Loeffler, Silvia. "City as Skin: Urban Imaginaries of Flesh and Fantasy." *Architectural Design* 83, no. 6 (2013): 114–19.

Lorcin, Patricia M. E. *Historicizing Colonial Nostalgia: European Women's Narratives of Algeria and Kenya, 1900–Present.* New York: Palgrave Macmillan, 2012.

————. "Sex, Gender, and Race in the Colonial Novels of Elissa Rhaïs and Lucienne Favre." In *The Color of Liberty: Histories of Race in France*, edited by Sue Peabody and Tyler Stovall, 108–30. Durham, NC: Duke University Press, 2003.

Lordon, Frédéric. "Charlie at Any Cost?" *Verso*, January 20, 2015.

Lowe, Lisa. *The Intimacies of Four Continents.* Durham, NC: Duke University Press, 2015.

Luczak, Ewa Barbara. *How Their Living Outside America Affected Five American Authors: Toward a Theory of Expatriate Literature.* Lewiston, NY: Edwin Mellen Press, 2010.

Lyons, Amelia H. *The Civilizing Mission in the Metropole: Algerian Families and the French Welfare State during Decolonization.* Stanford, CA: Stanford University Press, 2013.

Mack, Mehammed A. *Sexagon: Diversity, Sexuality, and Belonging in Contemporary France.* New York: Fordham University Press, 2017.

MacMaster, Neil. "The Role of European Women and the Question of Mixed Couples in the Algerian Nationalist Movement in France, circa 1918–1962." *French Historical Studies* 34, no. 2 (2011): 357–86.

————. *Colonial Migrants and Racism: Algerians in France, 1900–62.* Houndmills, UK: Macmillan, 1997.

Mahjoub, Jamal. "An Interview with Mehdi Charef." *Wasafiri*, March 2000.

Mahmood, Saba. "Feminism, Democracy, and Empire: Islam and the War of Terror." In *Women's Studies on the Edge*, edited by Joan Scott, 81–114. Durham, NC: Duke University Press, 2008.

Mandelbaum, Jacques. "Origine contrôlée." *Le Monde*, January 24, 2001.

Mammeri, Mouloud. *The Sleep of the Just.* Boston: Beacon Press, 1958.

Massad, Joseph A. *Desiring Arabs.* Chicago: University of Chicago Press, 2007.

Maxwell, William J. "Wright among the 'G-Men': How the FBI Framed Paris Noir." In *Richard Wright: New Readings in the 21st Century*, edited by Alice Mikal Craven and William Dow, 27–38. New York: Palgrave Macmillan, 2011.

Mbembe, Achille. "On the Power of the False." *Public Culture* 14, no. 3 (2002): 629–41.

McLeod, John. *Postcolonial London: Rewriting the Metropolis.* London: Routledge, 2004.

————. *The Routledge Companion to Postcolonial Studies.* London: Routledge, 2007.

McLuhan, Marshall. *Understanding Media: The Extensions of Man.* Cambridge, MA: MIT Press, 1994.

Meichtry, Stacy. "Paris Attacker Amedy Coulibaly's Path to Terror." *Washington Post*, January 14, 2015.

Memmi, Albert. *The Colonizer and the Colonized*. Translated by Howard Greenfield. Boston: Beacon Press, 1991.

————. *Decolonization and the Decolonized*. Translated by Robert Bononno. Minneapolis: University of Minnesota Press, 2006.

Menanteau, Jean. *Les banlieues*. Paris: Marabout, 1994.

Mendoza, Victor R. *Metroimperial Intimacies: Fantasy, Racial-Sexual Governance, and the Philippines in U.S. Imperialism, 1899–1913*. Durham, NC: Duke University Press, 2015.

Mepschen, P. *Homosexuality as a Modern Category*. Amsterdam: UVA, International School of Humanities and Social Sciences, 2000.

Méral, Jean. *Paris in American Literature*. Chapel Hill: University of North Carolina Press, 1989.

Mernissi, Fatima. *Scheherazade Goes West: Different Cultures, Different Harems*. New York: Washington Square Press, 2001.

Mignolo, Walter. *The Darker Side of Western Modernity: Global Futures, Decolonial Options*. Durham, NC: Duke University Press, 2011.

Milon, Alain, and Seth Whidden. "Tags and Murals in France: A City's Face or Natural Landscape." In *Black, Blanc, Beur: Rap Music and Hip Hop Culture in the Francophone World*, edited by Alain-Phillipe Durand, 87–98. Lanham, MD: Scarecrow, 2002.

Monnoyer, Maurice. "Plaisir de la lecture." *L'effort algérien*, Alger, October 13, 1955.

Moore, Molly. "In France, Prisons Filled with Muslims." *Washington Post*, April 29, 2008.

Morrison, Toni. *Tar Baby*. New York: Vintage, 1981.

Mucchielli, Laurent. *Le scandale des tournantes: Dérives médiatiques, contre-enquête sociologique*. Paris: Découverte, 2005.

Muñoz, José E. *Disidentifications: Queers of Color and the Performance of Politics*. Minneapolis: University of Minnesota Press, 1999.

Murdoch, Adlai. *Creolizing the Metropole: Migrant Caribbean Identities in Literature and Film*. Bloomington: Indiana University Press, 2012.

Murdoch, Adlai, and Anne Donadey. *Postcolonial Theory and Francophone Literary Studies*. Gainesville: University Press of Florida, 2005.

Naficy, Hamid. *An Accented Cinema: Exilic and Diasporic Filmmaking*. Princeton, NJ: Princeton University Press, 2001.

Naipaul, V. S. *The Enigma of Arrival: A Novel*. New York: Knopf, 1987.

Naït-Balk, Brahim. *Un homo dans la cité*. Paris: Calmann-Lévy, 2009.

Naudin, Marie. "Formation postmoderne des Beurs chez Mehdi Charef, Leïla Sebbar, et Azouz Begag." *Francographies* 4 (1995): 97–103.

Nemmiche, Mohamed. "Le principe d'Archi Ahmed." *Libération*, March 11, 1983.

Noiray, Jacques. *Littératures francophones: Le Maghreb*. Paris: Belin, 1996.

Noiriel, Gérard. *Immigration, antisémitisme et racisme en France, XIXe–XXe Siècle: Discours publics, humiliations privées*. Paris: Fayard, 2007.

————. *Le creuset français: Histoire de l'immigration, XIXe–XXe Siècles*. Paris: Seuil, 1988.

Nora, Pierre. *Les lieux de mémoire*. Paris: Gallimard, 1984.

Nourissier, François. "Mehdi Charef: Cinéma-vérité." *Figaro*, March 5, 1983, 18.

O'Dell, J. H. "A Special Variety of Colonialism." *Freedomways* 7, no. 1 (1967): 7–15.

Orlando, Valérie. "From Rap to Raï in the Mixing Bowl: Beur Hip-Hop Culture and Banlieue Cinema in Urban France." *Journal of Popular Culture* 36, no. 3 (2003): 395–415.

————. *The New Algerian Novel: The Poetics of a Modern Nation, 1950–1979*. Charlottesville: University of Virginia Press, 2017.

Packer, George. "The Other France: Are the Suburbs of Paris Incubators of Terrorism." *New Yorker*, August 31, 2015.

Paris guide, 1867, par les principaux écrivains et artistes de la France. Paris: Librairie internationale, 1867.

Perreau, Bruno. *Queer Theory: The French Response*. Stanford, CA: Stanford University Press, 2016.

Phelan, Shane. *Sexual Strangers: Gays, Lesbians, and Dilemmas of Citizenship*. Philadelphia: Temple University Press, 2001.

Pinçonnat, Crystel. "Le Paris Maghrébin: Une capitale invisible?" In *Paris, cartographies littéraires*, edited by Crystel Pinçonnat and Chantal Liaroutzos, 275–303. Paris: Manuscrit, 2007.

Prasteau, Jean. "Histoire d'un bouc émissaire." *Figaro*, February 20, 1937.

Provencher, Denis. "Maghrebi French Sexual Citizens." *Cineaste* (Winter 2007): 47–51.

————. *Queer French: Globalization, Language, and Sexual Citizenship in France*. New York: Routledge, 2007.

Provencher, Denis, and Murray Pratt. "Recasting Sami Bouajila: An Ambiguous Model of Integration, Belonging, and Citizenship." In *Screening Integration: Recasting Maghrebi Immigration in Contemporary France*, edited by Sylvie Durmelat and Vinay Swamy, 194–210. Lincoln: University of Nebraska Press, 2011.

Puar, Jasbir K. *Terrorist Assemblages: Homonationalism in Queer Times*. Durham, NC: Duke University Press, 2007.

Rager, Jean J. *L'émigration en France des musulmans d'algérie*. Alger, 1956.

Razane, Mohamed. "So Far So Close By." Translated by Laura Reeck. *Brooklyn Rail*, July 2011. http://intranslation.brooklynrail.org/french/so-far-so-close-by.

Rees-Roberts, Nick. *French Queer Cinema*. Edinburgh: Edinburgh University Press, 2008.

Renan, Ernest. "What Is a Nation?" In *The Nationalism Reader*, edited by Omar Dahbour and Micheline R. Isbay, 143–55. Atlantic Highlands, NJ: Humanities, 1995.

Reynald, Danielle, and Henk Elffers. "The Future of Newman's Defensible Space Theory and the Routine Activities of Place." *European Journal of Criminology* 6, no. 1 (2009): 25–46.

Ricoux, René. *La démographie figurée de l'algérie: Étude statistique des populations européennes qui habitent L'Algérie*. Paris: Masson, 1880.

Roberts, Mary. *Intimate Outsiders: The Harem in Ottoman and Orientalist Art and Travel Literature*. Durham, NC: Duke University Press, 2007.

Rocamora, Agnès. *Fashioning the City: Paris, Fashion and the Media*. London: I. B. Tauris, 2009.

Rosello, Mireille. *France and the Maghreb: Performative Encounters*. Gainesville: University Press of Florida, 2005.

Rosello, Mireille, and Sudeep Dasgupta. *What's Queer about Europe? Productive Encounters and Re-Enchanting Paradigms*. New York: Fordham University Press, 2014.

Rosenberg, Clifford D. *Policing Paris: The Origins of Modern Immigration Control between the Wars*. Ithaca, NY: Cornell University Press, 2006.

Ross, Kristin. *Fast Cars, Clean Bodies: Decolonization and the Reordering of French Culture*. Cambridge, MA: MIT Press, 1995.

Ross, Marlon. *Manning the Race: Reforming Black Men in the Jim Crow Era.* New York: New York University Press, 2004.

Rothberg, Michael. *Multidirectional Memory: Remembering the Holocaust in the Age of Decolonization.* Stanford, CA: Stanford University Press, 2009.

Rousseaux, André. *"Les Boucs* de Driss Chraïbi." *Figaro littéraire*, September 24, 1955.

Rowley, Hazel. *Richard Wright: The Life and Times.* Chicago: University of Chicago Press, 2008.

Roy, Claude. "Mendiants, vagabonds, boucs, bonnes, misère." *Libération*, October 5, 1955.

Roy, Jules. "Ahmed sortit à cinq heures." *Le Nouvel Observateur*, April 22, 1983, 88–89.

Ruquist, Rebecca. "Non, nous ne jouons pas la trompette: Richard Wright in Paris." *Contemporary French and Francophone Studies* 8, no. 3 (2004): 285–303.

Saada, Emmanuelle. "More Than a Turn? The 'Colonial' in French Studies." *French Politics, Culture & Society* 32, no. 2 (2014): 34–39.

Said, Edward W. *Orientalism.* New York: Vintage Books, 1979.

Salas, Denis. *La volonté de punir: Essai sur le populisme penal.* Paris: Hachette, 2005.

Salhi, Zahia Smail. *Politics, Poetics and the Algerian Novel.* Lewiston, NY: E. Mellen Press, 1999.

Sayad, Abdelmalek. *The Suffering of the Immigrant.* Malden, MA: Polity, 2004.

Scott, Joan W. *The Politics of the Veil.* Princeton, NJ: Princeton University Press, 2007.

Sebbar, Leïla. *The Seine Was Red.* Translated by Mildred Mortimer. Bloomington: Indiana University Press, 2008.

Sebbar, Leïla, and Nancy Huston. *Lettres parisiennes: Autopsie de l'exil.* Paris: Barrault, 1986.

Sebkhi, Habiba. *Une littérature naturelle: Le cas de la littérature beur.* Paris: L'Harmattan, 1982.

Selected Documents of the Bandung Conference: Texts of Selected Speeches and Final Communique of the Asian-African Conference, Bandung, Indonesia, April 18–24, 1955. New York: Distributed by the Institute of Pacific Relations, 1955.

Selvon, Samuel. *The Lonely Londoners.* London: Penguin, 2006.

Serrano, Richard. "Not Your Uncle: Text, Sex, and the Globalized Moroccan Author." In *World Writing: Poetics, Ethics, Globalization*, edited by Mary Gallagher, 167–89. Toronto: Toronto University Press, 2008.

Shaheen, Jack G., *Reel Bad Arabs: How Hollywood Vilifies a People.* New York: Olive Branch Press, 2001.

Shepard, Todd. *The Invention of Decolonization: The Algerian War and the Remaking of France.* Ithaca, NY: Cornell University Press, 2006.

Silverstein, Paul. *Algeria in France: Transpolitics, Race, Nation.* Bloomington: Indiana University Press, 2004.

Silverstein, Paul, and Chantal Tetreault. "Ultra Violence in France." *Middle East Report Online*, November 2005. http://www.merip.org/mero/interventions/urban-violence-france.

Simon, Patrick. "The Choice of Ignorance: The Debate on Ethnic and Racial Statistics in France." *French Politics, Culture & Society* 26, no. 1 (2008): 7–31.

———. "Muslims Social Inclusion and Exclusion." Presentation, Council for European Studies Conference, Paris, July 8, 2015.

Sinapi, Jean-Pierre, dir. *Vivre me tue.* Paris: One Plus One, 2004.

Smith, William G. *The Stone Face: A Novel.* New York: Farrar, Straus, 1963.

Smouts, Marie-Claude. *La situation postcoloniale: Les postcolonial studies dans le débat français.* Paris: Fondation nationale des sciences politiques, 2007.

Sollors, Werner. *Beyond Ethnicity: Consent and Descent in American Culture.* New York: Oxford University Press, 1986.

Sommer, Doris. *Foundational Fictions: The National Romances of Latin America.* Berkeley: University of California Press, 1991.

Soraya, Nini. *Ils disent que je suis une Beurette.* Paris: Fixot, 1993.

Spivak, Gayatri. "Can the Subaltern Speak?" In *Colonial Discourse and Post-Colonial Theory,* edited by Patrick Williams and Laura Chrisman, 66–111. New York: Columbia University Press, 1994.

Stoler, Ann L. *Haunted by Empire: Geographies of Intimacy in North American History.* Durham, NC: Duke University Press, 2006.

Stora, Benjamin. *Algeria, 1830–2000: A Short History.* Ithaca, NY: Cornell University Press, 2004.

———. *La gangrène et l'oubli: La mémoire de la guerre d'Algérie.* Paris: Découverte & Syros, 1998.

Stora, Benjamin, and Linda Amiri. *Algériens en France: 1954–1962.* Paris: Autrement/Cité nationale de l'histoire de l'immigration, 2012.

Stovall, Tyler E. "The Fire This Time: Black American Expatriates and the Algerian War." *Yale French Studies* 98 (2000): 182–200.

———. *Paris Noir: African Americans in the City of Light.* Boston: Houghton Mifflin, 1996.

Stovall, Tyler E., and Georges Van den Abbeele. *French Civilization and Its Discontents: Nationalism, Colonialism, Race.* Lanham, MD: Lexington Books, 2003.

Stuelke, Patricia. "Loving in the Iraq War Years." *College Literature: A Journal of Critical Literary Studies* 43, no. 1 (2016): 121–44.

Sundquist, Eric J. *Strangers in the Land: Blacks, Jews, Post-Holocaust America.* Cambridge, MA: Harvard University Press, 2005.

Tadjer, Akli. *Les A.N.I. du "Tassili."* Paris: Seuil, 1984.

Tarr, Carrie. *Reframing Difference: Beur and Banlieue Filmmaking in France.* Manchester: Manchester University Press, 2005.

Tévanian, Pierre. *La république du mépris: les métamorphoses du racisme dans la France des années Sarkozy.* Paris: Découverte, 2007.

Thomas, Dominic. *Black France: Colonialism, Immigration, and Transnationalism.* Bloomington: Indiana University Press, 2007.

Thomas, Martin. *The French Empire between the Wars: Imperialism, Politics and Society.* Manchester: Manchester University Press, 2005.

Thomson, David. *Les Français jihadistes.* Paris: Arènes, 2014.

Ticktin, Miriam I. *Casualties of Care: Immigration and the Politics of Humanitarianism in France.* Berkeley: University of California Press, 2011.

Tillion, Germaine. *L'Algérie en 1957.* Paris: Minuit, 1957.

Tshimanga, Charles, Didier Gondola, and Peter J. Bloom, eds. *Frenchness and the African Diaspora: Identity and Uprising in Contemporary France.* Bloomington: Indiana University Press, 2009.

Tuan, Yi-Fu. *Topophilia: A Study of Environmental Perceptions, Attitudes, and Values.* Englewood Cliffs, NJ: Prentice Hall, 1974.

Vergès, Françoise. *Monsters and Revolutionaries: Colonial Family Romance and Métissage.* Durham, NC: Duke University Press, 1999.

Volokh, Eugene. "The PEN/ Charlie Hebdo Controversy." *Washington Post*, May 4, 2015.

Von Eschen, P. M. *Race against Empire: Black Americans and Anticolonialism, 1937–1957.* Ithaca, NY: Cornell University Press, 1997.

Waclawek, Anna. *Graffiti and Street Art.* London: Thames and Hudson, 2011.

Wacquant, Loïc. "Banlieues françaises et ghetto noir américain: De l'amalgame à la comparaison." *French Politics and Society* 10, no. 4 (1992): 81–103.

Waldron, Darren. "Sexual/Social (Re)Orientations: Cross-Dressing, Queerness, and the Maghrebi/*Beur* Male in Liria Bégéja's *Change-moi ma vie* and Amal Bedjaoui's *Un fils.*" In *Screening Integration: Recasting Maghrebi Immigration in Contemporary France*, edited by Sylvie Durmelat, 178–93. Lincoln: University of Nebraska Press, 2011.

Wallace-Wells, Benjamin. "What Makes a Jihadist?" *New Yorker*, May 18, 2016.

Weil, Patrick. *La France et ses étrangers: L'aventure d'une politique de l'immigration, 1938–1991.* Paris: Calmann-Lévy, 1991.

———. *La république et sa diversité: Immigration, intégration, discrimination.* Paris: Seuil, 2005.

Weiss, Andrea. *Paris Was a Woman: Portraits from the Left Bank.* San Francisco: Harper San Francisco, 1995.

Wieviorka, Annette. *The Era of the Witness.* Ithaca, NY: Cornell University Press, 2006.

Wihtol de Wenden, Catherine. "North African Immigration and the French Political Imaginary." *Race, Discourse, and Power in France*, edited by Maxim Silverman, 98–110. Brookfield, VT: Gower, 1991.

Wilder, Gary. *The French Imperial Nation-State: Negritude and Colonial Humanism between the Two World Wars.* Chicago: University of Chicago Press, 2005.

Wright, Richard. "I Chose Exile." Unpublished article, Beinecke Rare Book and Manuscript Library, Yale University, 1952.

———. "Island of Hallucination." N.d. Ts. Box 34, Folder 472. James Weldon Johnson Collection, Beinecke Rare Book and Manuscript Library, Yale University.

———. *The Long Dream.* Boston: Northeastern University Press, 2000.

Young, Alison. "From Object to Encounter: Aesthetic Politics and Visual Criminology." *Theoretical Criminology* 18, no. 2 (2014): 159–75.

Young, James. "Ecrire le monument: Site, mémoire, critique." *Annales ESC* 3 (1993): 729–43.

Zaborowska, Magdalena J. *James Baldwin's Turkish Decade: Erotics of Exile.* Durham, NC: Duke University Press, 2009.

Zappi, Sylvia. "Manuel Valls, l'apartheid et les banlieues." *Le Monde*, January 26, 2015.

Zukin, Sharon, and Laura Braslow. "The Life Cycle of New York's Creative Districts: Reflections on the Unanticipated Consequences of Unplanned Cultural Zones." *City, Culture and Society* 2, no. 1 (2011): 131–40.

Index

Page numbers in italics indicate figures.

Abbas, Mahmoud, 176
abject subjects, 19, 34–35, 47, 147, 153. *See also*
topophobia
Aburawa, Arwa, 165, 168
The Adventures of Félix/ Drôle de Félix (dirs. Ducastel
and Martineau, 2000), *33–34*, 120, *121*,
133–34, 137
African American expatriate authors: about,
32–33, 64–68, 192–93n2, 193n4; brotherhood, 66–67; Francophilia as complicit
with racism, 6, 7, 25, 65–66, 74; interracial
romance and, 6, 25, 32, 33, 54, 64, 66–67,
190n104; Left Bank cafés and lodgings
and, 6, 32, 67; liberation narrative and, 6,
64, 66, 67, 78–79, 80; lynching and subjugation in US as frame for, 64, 69, 76–77;
manhood and, 32, 64, 67; masculinity
and, 20, 33, 66, 67, 76; racial equality and,
6, 20, 25, 33, 64, 66–67, 76; second-class
citizenship for, 7, 25, 64; segregation in
US, 32, 64–65; space/imagined space in
Paris and, 5, 6, 32, 65, 66, 67; surveillance
by US of, 64, 65, 72, 73; universalism and,
6, 67, 187n11. *See also* Paris noir literature
Africans and African authors, 6, 27, 28, 40,
187n11
Agar (Memmi), 15–16, 48
agency, 59, 163, 166
Ahmed, Sara, 148
AIDS Coalition to Unleash Power (ACT UP
Paris), 119
"Alas Poor Richard" (Baldwin), 75, 194n34
Aldrich, Robert, 128

Algeria: authors in, 15–16, 27–28, 38–39,
193n21; citizenship for Algerians in, 12, 80,
198n28; Franco-Algerian relations in, 15,
37; gendered/sexualized rescue narrative
for Muslim women in, 18, 19; interracial
marriage in, 37, 48; Kabyle/Kabylia, 9,
37, 48–49, 103, 138, 188n23; manhood for
Algerians in, 61, 82; migration to France
from, 7, 8, 12, 37, 42–43; myth of Paris
in, 26; nationalism and, 15, 28, 48, 158,
161; poverty in, 27, 193n21; sexualization
of Arabs in, 91; state of emergency in, 58,
65; transvestites and, 131. *See also* Algerians
in Paris; Algerian War of Independence;
Arabs
Algerians in Paris: Algerian descendants, 5, 12,
13–14; assimilation of, 15, 56; exclusion of
nonwhites and, 193n21; Franco-Algerian
romance and, 86, 194n58; integration for,
8; interracial intimacy and, 48; intimacy
and, 45, 48; lived realities of, 13–14, 37–38,
105; population statistics, 12; as returnees
to Algeria, 31–32, 37, 193n21; second-class
citizenship for, 49; as settlers, 32, 41, 46;
sexualization of Arab men and, 9; stereotypes and, 8–9, 11–12, 45, 149, 188n23;
surveillance of, 43, 56; white French
woman's colonial role and, 50, 53. *See also*
Algeria; Arabs
Algerian War of Independence: *The Butts*
(Chraïbi) and, 73, 75, 81, 86, 88, 194n54;
censorship during, 7, 58, 65, 68, 72–74, 75,
160; Cold War policies and, 62; colonial

119-20, 122, 130-31; riots and, 155, 171; securitization and, 175, 185; space/imagined space and, 118
misogyny, 6, 118, 133, 136, 143, 144
Miss Mona (dir. Charef, 1987), 120, 124-26
Mistinguette, 22
Mitterrand, François, 12, 36, 95, 131
Mitterrand, Frédéric, 128
modernity values: about, 7, 26; assimilation and, 17, 18, 19, 20, 55-57; cultural difference and, 17; exceptionalism/French values and, 10, 13, 30, 159, 175, 179; exclusion of nonwhites from, 41, 49, 167; films with Arab male queer subjects, 120; integration and, 17-18; intimacy and, 16-17; Islamophobia and, 179; in postcolonial Paris, 16-17; power dynamics and, 122; tolerance and, 17
Morel, Gaël, 128
Moroccans: as authors, 5, 18, 37, 39, 45; homosexuality and, 60-61, 128
Morrison, Toni, 190n104
Mucchielli, Laurent, 203n34
multiculturalism, 131, 140, 149, 151. *See also* cultural difference
multiracial population in banlieues: about, 4, 6, 7, 12; films and, 124, 129-30, 151, 153; *Tea in the Harem* (Charef) and, 90, 95-96, 99-100
Muñoz, José Esteban, 121
Muslims: assimilation of, 56, 118; citizenship and, 17-18, 122, 183, 198n28; gendered/sexualized rescue narrative and, 18, 19, 137-38, 165-66, 175, 182-85, 203nn34-35; integration and, 17; Islamic radicalization and, 10, 19-20, 131, 144, 177, 180-81, 182-83, 184, 203n23; Islamophobia and, 10, 11, 178-79, 184, 202-3n18; lived realities of, 3-4, 7, 18, 184; media and, 7, 178-79, 202n2, 202-3n18; Muslim descendants and, 4, 10, 177, 178; myth of Paris for, 3-4; police activities against, 13, 181; political disenfranchisement and, 18, 47, 67, 179, 203n19; population statistics, 4, 203n19; prison system and, 11, 177, 182; queer writers and, 18; riots of 2005 in Grigny, 178; stereotypes and, 5, 149, 184; terms of

use for, 8, 11. *See also* sartorial practices of Muslims
Muslims Against Advertising, 165
My City Is Going to Crack/Ma6-T va crack-e (dir. Richet, 1997), 124
My Family's Honor/L'Honneur de ma famille (dir. Bouchareb, 1997), 122-23
myth of Paris: about, 3-4, 21-25; African American authors and, 25, 190n104; in Algeria, 26; British travelers and, 24; equality and, 3, 6, 10; freedom of speech and, 6, 7; gendered freedom and, 24-25, 69, 118; in literature, 7, 21, 22, 23; Muslim experience and, 3-4; pleasures/culture of pleasure and, 24, 167, 190n96; race versus, 10; US visitors and, 24-25; West Indians and, 25-26. *See also* color-blindness myth; modernity values; universalism

Nadeau, Maurice, 39
Naficy, Hamid, 132
Naipaul, V. S., 26-27
Naït-Balk, Brahim, 18, 116-17
nationalism: African, 27; Algeria/Algerian nationalists, 15, 28, 48, 158, 161; black, 80; borders and, 16, 33, 48, 50, 87, 93, 95, 96, 169; *The Butts* (Chraïbi) and, 39, 41, 56, 61; consensus and, 159-60, 163, 201n41; as crisis, 163; decolonization and, 41, 162; in French literature, 28; homonationalism, 121; identity and, 22, 56, 96-97; of infant subjects, 54; interracial unions and, 15, 48; queer sexualities and, 61; tricolor flag of France and, 140
national security (securitization). *See* securitization (national security)
Native Son (Wright), 193n20
Nemmiche, Mohamed, 98
neo-Orientalism, 18, 183. *See also* Orientalism
Netanyahu, Benjamin, 176
1952 Generation, 38-39
Ni Putes Ni Soumises (NPNS, Neither Whores Nor Submissive), 151, 166, 183-84
nonwhites: about, 8, 20; homosexuality and, 7, 11-12, 21; masculinity and, 20-21; media's stereotypes of, 7, 8-9, 32, 52-53, 92, 108, 149, 153, 185, 188n23; patriarchal power

AFRICA AND THE DIASPORA
History, Politics, Culture

SERIES EDITORS

Thomas Spear
Neil Kodesh
Tejumola Olaniyan
Michael G. Schatzberg
James H. Sweet